Behind Lace Curtains
A Memoir

Behind Lace Curtains
A Memoir

Dorothy Burston Brown

Behind Lace Curtains, A Memoir

Copyright © 2023 Dorothy Burston Brown

ISBN: 978-1-61170-322-1

All rights reserved. No part of this publication may be reproduced or utilized in any form or by any means, electronic or mechanical, including photocopying, recording, or by any information or retrieval system, without written permission from the publisher. For further information, you may write to the publisher.

Cover images and all interior images are from the author's personal archive unless otherwise noted.

First Printing, 2024
Printed and bound in the USA and UK on acid-free paper.

Published by:
Robertson Publishing™
www.RobertsonPublishing.com

I am beauty;
    Born of years of *Blues People*.
    I am the only child,
    I am, was, and continue to be much loved.
    My name means "a gift from god."
        I am black.
                      Dorothy Burston Brown

Blues People: Negro Music in White America is a seminal study of Afro-American music (and culture generally) by Amiri Baraka, who published it as LeRoi Jones in 1963.

                (*https://en.m.wikipedia.org/wiki/Blues_People*)

Contents

Chapter		Page
1	Conditions	1
2	Reservations	3
3	Through Lace Curtains	13
4	Company Coming	19
5	June German	29
6	Negotiation	41
7	Now Starring	45
8	Green Tobacco	51
9	Tee	55
10	Talks with Tee	67
11	Partiality	75
12	Happy Birthday	81
13	Follow Your Hunch	85
14	Secrets	89
15	New York	93
16	Man of the House	99
17	Making Ends Meet	109
18	Street's End	115
19	Behind Lace Curtains	123
20	Next	129
21	Stumbling Blocks	139
22	Realizations	153
23	Leaving Home	161
24	Rules, Rules, Rules	171
25	Betterment	183
26	I Confront Life	195
27	Changes	203
28	Adulthood	211
29	Coping	223

Chapter		Page
30	Where Do We Go From Here	243
31	Learning My Way	251
32	Lucky Number	269
33	Second Time Around	277
34	Consequences	289
35	Adjustments	305
36	A Reckoning	315
37	No More Discussion	323
38	The Denouement	331
	Acknowledgements	339

Conditions

Four decades ago, I severed my ties with the South—that enigma of manners, virtue and religion. I vowed to never return but family always brought me back for brief visits and immersed me in its mire. At its core, the South is a powerful place, embellished with people of a different ilk, people who speak in devious ways. Growing up, I had no choice in the matter. I had to listen. Listen as they spewed me with their venom, but in oh, such a polite fashion.

My staunch position held until September 2006 when I was summoned home to Rocky Mount, North Carolina. The occasion, my fiftieth high school reunion, would be celebrated in July of the following year. To my surprise, the chance to see old classmates tickled my fancy. What harm could a few days do? I was stronger, all grown up. Months later, I was still muddling it over when my husband Bill announced, "Honey Bunch, I've got you all set up for your reunion with a plane ticket and a hotel!"

I don't know those people anymore. I cringed at the stain segregation still left on the South. *And what about those casual but hurtful remarks? Would I be caught off guard?*

I recalled the "whites only" park just blocks away from my family's home. Across the dirt road was the farmers' curb market. As my grandmother, who I called Mama, and I left it one Saturday morning, she said, "Dot, you can go on them swings in that park . . . if you want to."

I thought she was teasing but she took me across the road to "their park." We stopped in front of the giant, black, metal swing set. I stared at it. "Go on, swing. I pay taxes on it, too."

I checked both ways for white people like I did for cars before crossing the street. The coast was clear, so I ran to the closest swing, grasped as much of the fat metal chains my six-year-old hands could hold. Then backed up a long way and jumped onto the black leather seat, like the big kids did at the colored school yard where only one swing was left. "Heist yourself up, Dot. Pump your legs." Soon I was as high as my grandmother's shoulder. "You show'em, baby."

My mother Tee, given name Christine, dedicated herself to making me unique. She said, "Dorothy Leigh, say it like this, in correct English." I became the too-dark Southern colored girl who spoke like a Northerner. Now my sweet husband was returning me to all I sought to escape. In a way, going home imitated what family and friends from my childhood had done. Although they, too, had escaped, each year they returned from up North. Their reason? June German, our annual dusk to dawn dance which featured the best music of the day. They continued to come even after the dancing stopped.

Eight weeks prior to my anticipated departure, Bill dropped dead. My trip so lovingly planned by him, was his last gift to me. I desperately needed to go there. There was no other place where people knew the naked me. I needed to swelter in that sizzling, summer heat. I needed the South's callous, caustic cleansing. I longed for its sweet, dripping endearments. I craved that cunningly Southern injection—to release me from my numbness.

Reservations

It was dusk when I landed at Raleigh-Durham airport, easily an hour's drive from my hometown. As I exited the terminal, the pungent stench of pine trees permeated the warm air, my allergies threatened. There was no time to pamper them. My mission was to pick up my rental car and find my "minutes away from the airport" motel. Darkness was approaching and dark in the South is pitch black. My reserved motel was nowhere in sight. Doggedly, I retraced my drive on a two mile stretch of highway. I was ready to yield to defeat when my elusive motel winked at me from behind an office building. Amongst the other muttering, frustrated travelers in the motel's office, I gave the desk clerk my name. "Where you from?"

"California."

"Knowed you weren't from around here. I kinda figured you were from New York, some place up North. Hmmm . . . California . . . .."

I wanted to snatch the key out of his hand, but remembered I was in the land of gentility and accepted it graciously. By then, all I wanted was a shower. Outside my assigned building, a convenient parking space appeared. After pulling in and shutting off the ignition, I noticed the downstairs rooms were separated from the parking lot by a mere walkway. My safety-driven husband's admonishments surfaced, "Dorothy, never take a first-floor room which opens directly onto the parking lot." Just as I started back to the office, it dawned on me—I never had to tell him.

Minutes later, laden with luggage and other stuff, I stepped out of the car into the growing darkness, and shuddered. A rabbit must have run over my grave. My old superstitions were cued up. I chided myself, *"Dorothy, you stayed by yourself last night in the motel near the San Francisco airport."* True, but I didn't sleep a wink. It was hard being alone. Even when Bill was alive, he never planned to accompany me to my reunion. Actually, he was a bit of a nag. "Dorothy, check out your surroundings. And don't look lost."

I shrugged it off and went in search of my room. A few steps later, a beer drinking couple stepped jovially in my way. Once they cleared my path, I pulled my suitcase up onto the walkway. Ahead of me stood two white men in the vicinity of my room. One of them was smoking. I slowly advanced towards them. With only steps away, 121, my room appeared. There would be no contact with the men. I juggled my stuff and managed to insert the key.

The lock remained engaged. The second try yielded the same result. "Could either of you nice gentlemen help me with my door?"

"My pleasure," the non-smoker said. I all but screamed, "no." What had I instigated? I stood there like a lamb to the slaughter. He drew closer, "Evening, ma'am, may I have your key?" While surrendering it to him, a plan surfaced. The second he opens the door, charge inside. Maybe trip him in the process. He inserted the key. Again, it was rejected. He examined it. "This is for room 221."

Unfortunately, the ground would not open up and swallow me. I did the next best thing: "That desk clerk . . ." I caught myself. "Thank you so much."

"Here let us help you with your things."

"Oh, no, I wouldn't hear of it."

In an effort to turn around, my camera bag banged my left leg and my right hand cramped up. Regardless, I lugged all my belongings back to the starting point, next to my parked rental car. From there, the slow tugging and planting of stuff up the steep, narrow, waist high staircase began. My weary body rode the handrail for leverage and support. It was so excruciating, I chanted *Let there be a vodka martini waiting in 221.*

The next morning, I removed the chair wedged under the doorknob and went to my free breakfast. Aside from nourishment, it guaranteed an easy freeway access. I was bound for Charleston, South Carolina to see Dorothy, an old college friend. The visit provided time, unfettered by the familiarity of Rocky Mount, to readjust to the South's slow pace. I could tune into its rhythmic, sometimes irritating idiom and acclimatize my body to the steaming heat. Best of all, I'd kill three whole days.

On that bright, sunny Thursday I entered the sterile, empty freeway and accepted its terms—no stops in little towns and no chats with people. Freeways, dictatorial by nature, frown on whims and side trips. A few hours later, my resolve was tested at Myrtle Beach, the getaway place of my parents' courting days. It was only three exits ahead. At the mere mention of it, they had always exchanged glances, drifted together, and danced. I wanted to see their paradise, their Eden. I was willing to risk everything for one sand castle on Myrtle Beach.

Before signaling my exit, I noted Myrtle Beach was a very long way from my hometown. The places my parents vetoed when I was a teenager were nothing by comparison. I was so incensed—I missed the exit. Shucks. Myrtle Beach mattered only to me. Sam, my father, died decades earlier. My mother, Tee, was still alive, but her memory was gone.

I continued to Charleston and arrived in the midst of rush hour. I couldn't find Dorothy's address in the maze of new houses, townhouses, and shops. Finally, I gave up and called her. She found me lurking on a bank's front porch.

Dorothy rescued me from the loneliness which clung to me like lint. She knew me from my young adult life. I could recapture that spirit, begin anew. With gratitude, I followed her large, luxurious automobile to her neighborhood where a house number was imperative. Once inside, I discovered a new bond. "Dorothy, you and I have the same French Bergère chair. Don't you just love it?"

"I could hardly wait for them to deliver it." She said and gave me a tour of her two-story home. We ended up in her bedroom. "I've prepared my best for you."

I protested in kind, "Oh don't go to any special trouble for me." I could hardly wait to climb up into that comforter puffed up bed. By then I was in dire need of a good night's sleep, but that delight had to wait; we went out for seafood.

During my oyster dinner, Dorothy said, "Tomorrow morning, you can wander around the nearby shopping area while I make a brief stop in my office. Then we'll take a little tour of Charleston."

Sure enough, the next day after lunch, we drove on cobblestone streets with pastel painted houses. Charleston bore a different flavor than my hometown. A certain elusive charm enveloped it. I couldn't put my finger on it. We turned a corner, Dorothy slowed down to a crawl and shared, "Here is the private elementary school I attended." It wasn't a particularly impressive building, but I was taken aback at the very idea of a private school. In our era, Rocky Mount's colored children attended public schools; private schools were non-existent.

A few blocks later, street vendors appeared. "Dorothy, do you mind if we stop here? I'd like to look at those baskets."

"You'll get a better bargain on the island on Saturday when we go over there to see a play." Both of us had acted in college. Theatre had been her major, my minor. As for the vendors' wares, I offered up no argument, just kicked myself for not taking my rental car. Dorothy continued her role of tour guide with a chuckle, "I'm not going to show you the old slave market." Since I was denied the basket experience, I didn't share the fact that my own state's slave market was a mere 100 miles from my hometown.

That evening, a few of her sorority sisters came by to meet me. Technically, they were mine, too. Dorothy and I had pledged at the end of our freshman year in college. Aside from the sorority and the matching French chairs, Dorothy revealed another connection. "Through everything, I'm lucky. I survived cancer." So had I. Here we were, the two of us, with our lives separated by distance (three thousand miles) and time, and our existences were parallel. Dorothy had been married twice; me, too. The only major difference—she had only one child, I had two.

The following morning our island trip was washed away by torrential rain, strident thunder, and serrated lightning. There would be no play performance or baskets. We spent the day at home. The next day, Sunday, greeted us with sunshine. By 7 a.m. I was enroute to Rocky Mount. Happy Hill, my old neighborhood, was holding its second annual picnic that afternoon. Weeks earlier, my high school sweetheart, Billy, had assured me, "You'll have fun, fun, fun." Too bad he wouldn't be there; he always made me laugh.

I arrived around noon and headed for my old neighborhood. In less than two miles, the railroad trestle which spanned the Tar River was parallel to me. It all appeared unchanged from my childhood. I felt a strong urge to explore the river's banks, to return to the very spot where Mama had fished.

"Dorothy Leigh, come on baby. You and me's going fishing. I dug the worms last night. Just need to grab my pail for our catch and get my poles." I found a stick and took off behind Mama. It was a long walk.

When we reached the city lake, I said, "Mama, let's fish here. It's closer. We don't have to slide down that hill to the water."

"They ain't got no good fish in that hole, baby. White folks don't know what's good to eat."

We continued on to the muddy river. Near the bend in the road, Mama shifted her poles and things to one hand. "Come on now, hold onto my hand. Don't want you getting hit by no car. No sidewalk along here and it's real narrow."

"We oughta take the trestle, Mama. No train is on it. Want to, Mama?"

"Reckon, I don't. There're some big gaps in the crossties over the river. What we gonna do if one of us falls all the way down to the water? No, we gonna stick to this here road. Safer."

I took her hand. I liked the way she rocked from side to side like a song, even when a thunderstorm was coming and she tried to run. On the other side, we went down the path, all the way down to the trees by the bank. Mama baited her hooks, threw out her lines, and shoved the poles into a hole in the ground. After loading up her lip with snuff, she said, "You can play. But don't get too far away."

Within earshot of her, I played a long time in the tall wild grasses. When she yelled, "Dorothy Leigh . . ." I hurried back. I bet Mama caught an eel for me to play with. Or maybe it's time for a snack from her pockets, sardines or potted meat with saltines. We drank water from a pint jar. The ice always melted quickly. Too bad we didn't own a Thermos bottle like Aunt Burrell, Mama's sister.

Rocky Mount was still not an easy place in which to kill time on a Sunday. I was too late for church and probably too early for the shopping mall. My alternative was lunch. I hadn't eaten since Charleston. The fast-food places off the freeway held little to no appeal. Nothing would do but some delicious North Carolina barbeque. I was ready to wrap my lips around that sweet, vinegary, peppered, chopped pork topped with tangy coleslaw snuggled into a warm bun. The barbeque place was across town. I set my sights on it.

Less than a block away, the city lake appeared. I jerked the car to the right and pulled into a parking space. A small group of black and white joggers, either together or separately, caught my eye. Probably racial enlightenment extended to the lake, too. I yearned for Mama. That old pail of hers would have overflowed with butterfish, croakers, catfish, and not a single eel. I got out of the car and strode towards the water but Mama's words halted my progress, "Ain't no good fish in that hole." I turned back to the car. Shortly, Sunset Street appeared. Some blocks ahead, it crossed Howell, my old street.

Howell had one end for colored people and the other for whites. Ours was dirt; theirs was pavement, including the sidewalks. I used to think the city ran out of tar and concrete when it came to us. Just before reaching Main Street and its railroad tracks, I came across a small, brick office. The sign read "Dr. Kornegay, Psychologist." It had to refer to that same family of doctors my parents used to work for.

In the 1940s, Sam worked at the Kornegay's hospital and Tee ironed for them some Saturday mornings. She and I always went to their back door. Once, I said, "Tee, let's go in the front door. It's closer."

"We can't."

"Why?"

"It just is." If I asked more questions, I'd get into trouble. Still, it seemed silly going all around cock robin to the back driveway, past the dog kennel, by the fish pond, up ten steps to the service porch, and through the French door into the kitchen. Even though it wore me out, seeing Miss Etta—the colored maid—first made it all worthwhile. As soon as we opened the door, she started up. "That heifer expects too much work for too little pay. I fixed her yistidy. Looked her dead in the face and said, you mess with me, I'll be like a goose in high corn. Short here and long gone." I laughed.

Tee said, "You right, Miss Etta. You have to straighten them out all the time." I really liked Miss Etta. She knew how to handle that white lady. Too bad. I'd never get to use her advice; Sam and Tee wouldn't let me be a maid. All they talked about was, "When you get to college . . .."

We couldn't stay in the kitchen long. Tee ironed in the dining room. We went through the butler's pantry to reach it. There stood the board, the iron, and the basket of sprinkled laundry on the floor. Across the room I saw that front door as plain as day on the other side of the living room. I wanted to point that out to Tee, but I couldn't sass her like that. Still, it wouldn't have been one bit of trouble for Mrs. Kornegay to open that front door for us. As soon as the iron heated up, Tee started on the starched long-sleeve, white shirts for the white lady's husband. He delivered me. She ironed some things for the lady, too. I stretched out on the sunlit rug in front of the board, real close to Tee.

From there I began looking at magazines—*LIFE, LOOK,* and *THE SATURDAY EVENING POST.* Mrs. Kornegay always put them there for me. As I turned the pages, mist rising from the sprinkled laundry, lightly landed on me, the gray, ugly war pictures, the kind face of Miss Eleanor or on her husband, President Roosevelt. The only sound in the room came from the creaky ironing board. After a while, Mrs. Kornegay's black, short-heeled, lace-up shoes clicked on the hardwood floor across the room. Without looking, I knew exactly when she reached the sideboard. I could count to five before I heard the tinkling of glass. That meant her pretty blue candy dish was in her chubby hands. "Dorothy Leigh."

She said my name real proper-like. Mama said that was because she was a German lady from Canada. I had to get up and go to her. She was too old and fat from singing opera to bend down to me. In her dish were pretty candies wrapped in red, yellow, or blue papers. She only let me pick two candies. I'd take a long time deciding.

After Tee ironed some more, Miss Etta called us to eat lunch in the kitchen. I could hardly wait. Mrs. Kornegay ate by herself in her big, old dining room. She missed all of Miss Etta's stories.

I continued on Sunset Street. I really wanted to find some down-home barbeque. It would have been nice to partake of it with a relative or two but they were all dead or had moved away. Only one cousin, Warren, on my daddy's side was left. When I was growing up, I was so crazy about him. Aunt Burrell would tease me, "Gonna marry little boy named Warren. That pretty little brown-eyed boy."

The last time I saw him, he was downright flamboyant, energized by a new flashiness. I could have sworn a halo of self-assuredness surrounded him. He was a preacher, like his grandfather, only better. Warren had a city church, a country church, and a religious bookstore off Main Street. When I saw him, he looked real handsome dressed in all white with his dark chocolate, round face, and brown eyes, just like me.

I stopped thinking about him. Besides, he was probably in a pulpit somewhere working. He couldn't join me for barbeque until after he shook each church sister's hand or pumped the arms of his deacons. For all I knew, there may have been eating on the church grounds, too. I left Warren for another day.

It was strange being back in my hometown. I'd never seen the streets so empty. Not a soul was out and about. I laughed. Maybe my fellow classmates and I had been lured back under false pretenses. Maybe the neighborhood picnic was a ruse, too. Right about then, the street I wanted, Leggett Road, turned up. As I drove by the old Negro ballpark, I noticed a new park full of green grass across from it, named for Dr. Martin Luther King. I'd eat my barbeque right there.

The café was so close; the smell of barbeque sure enough tickled my nose. Shortly I pulled onto its unpaved parking lot. I got out, stretched my legs, and ambled up to it. Boarded up windows and doors greeted me. Hunger hit me with a wallop.

Turning back to my car, I decided to eat at the picnic. It looked like an hour or so wait. However, if measured in black folks' time, I needed to double it.

My drive back to Happy Hill, via West Thomas Street, was intentionally slow. Still there was time to kill when I reached it. I decided to drop by my grandparents' old Victorian house. Their street appeared in no time. The old hill of my youth turned out to be barely a slope. In rapid succession, our church's parsonage and my Aunt Burrell's old house flew by. Papa, as I called my grandfather, and Mama's house with its choice location on the corner of Howell and Star sat almost diagonally across from Aunt Burrell's. I reflected on how smooth my old street's surface seemed. Pavement. Finally, when it no longer mattered, I could walk out my front door and roller skate.

I gazed across the street at our old Victorian. Time had erased its haughtiness. Had devoured its gingerbread charm.

My father, Sam

My mother, Tee (given name, Christine)

Me, Dorothy

Aunt Burrell, one of Mama's sister

Papa and Mama's old Victorian on the corner of Howell and Star

Through Lace Curtains

In the early 1940s, I was still little next to the tall windows in Mama's house. They reached all the way to the ceiling. Tee, Sam, and I lived with Mama. Papa, my grandfather, died just before I turned four years old. My parents' room was near the front door. It was my favorite place to be. Every morning before going to her job, my mother pulled up her dark-green shades, gave me a kiss, and said, "Dorothy Leigh, while I'm gone, do not play in my room." I always nodded my head yes. Mama used to work too but after Papa died, she stayed home with me. Tee said, "Mama gets a pension."

When Mama got busy, I played in Tee's room. One time, I put on her lipstick. That evening when Tee opened the front door, I ran and kissed Mama a whole bunch. Tee still saw the lipstick. Another time, I was swinging between the yellow armchair and her big trunk when I fell. I almost bit off my tongue. All that blood scared me and Mama. She rushed around screaming, "What are we gonna do? They don't treat colored people no more at that hospital where your daddy works."

All I did was cry and bleed. Aunt Burrell ran over from across the street, calling Mama by her real name. "Smithie, just hush up. Scaring this baby to death. Go call Tee."

Mama just stood there. "I don't want to ask Mattie to let me use her telephone."

"It's an emergency, she'll let you."

Mama left. Aunt Burrell took me to the icebox on the back porch and chipped off a piece of ice. "Let's go in the kitchen and wrap this in a towel. I want you to hold it on your tongue."

I did; my tongue felt better.

Pretty soon, my daddy drove up in somebody's car because we didn't own one. He put me up front with him. I sat real close. We went to the old doctor's house. When we got there, Tee ran out. I started crying all over again. Then I got the hiccups.

Sam carried me inside. The doctor said, "James, put Dorothy Leigh on the table in the living room." *Why was he calling my daddy, James?* " Sam put me down on top of a puzzle. Some of the pieces stuck to my hands. "Dorothy Leigh, stick out your tongue." He looked at it. "There's nothing for me to do. We'll wait for it to heal."

Mrs. Kornegay said, "Here Dorothy Leigh, two candies for being so brave."

Even after all of that, I still sneaked into Tee's bedroom another day, but I didn't touch nothing. Not the drawers in the wardrobe. Not the hats behind the little door on it. I only touched the lace curtains. Grown people didn't want kids doing that; they were too hard to clean.

I watched Mama clean ours. First, she washed them. Then dipped them in hot, wet Argo starch. I tasted dry starch one time. It wasn't sweet or sour. It was just nothing but hard. I didn't like it at all. Next, she put the drippy curtains into a bucket and toted them to the backyard. The curtain stretcher was set up out there in the sunshine. It was a big open thing with yardsticks on all its four sides. It was dangerous because teeny, sharp nails stuck out all over it. Mama pushed lace curtain pieces onto those nails. A lot of times she pricked her fingers. She had to suck them real hard to stop the bleeding. The curtains stayed outside to dry. After supper, she pulled them off the stretcher carefully and hanged them back at the windows. Her fingers were really sore. But she didn't cry. That's how come grown people don't want kids touching lace curtains.

But they were in my way, I really needed to get close to the window. Before, I couldn't pull them apart. Now I could. I pushed them wide open and put my nose on the window. It was cold but I saw everything on Howell Street but not on Star Street. I had to be in the living room, or dining room, or kitchen to do that.

Our porch rockers didn't get in my way. I saw through the skinny space across the street—between Miss Lucille's duplex and Miss Ida Lee's shotgun house. Mama called it a shortcut. It was a rickety board across the ditch. Miss Lucille knew all about me. Papa hired her to take care of me.

He said, "Christine don't know nothing about taking care of no baby." Nobody took the short cut while I looked.

So I backed up. My hair got caught in the curtains. That's when I heard a car coming. I wanted to see who it was. I yanked my hair loose and squished back up to the window. There it was . . . a black, humpback car. Only two people got to ride in it. It stopped in front of the duplex. A real light skinned colored man got out. He had a small black bag. I knew him. He was here again. I had to hurry.

I tried to run. I couldn't find the opening between the curtains. I fought with all my might, got all scratched up. Finally, I poked my fingers through the curtain holes and pulled. The curtains opened real wide. I was free. "Mama! Mama!" I ran into her bedroom right next to Tee's. No Mama. I ran into the bathroom hallway. No Mama. I hurried across the back porch and tripped into the kitchen. I was out of breath. "Mama, the doctor who killed Papa is across the street at Miss Lucille's."

The first time the war really hit me was in 1942 when I was four and a half. One night Mama and Tee were wallpapering the dining room. Suddenly the lights went out. I said, "I'm scared."

"Don't worry, Dorothy Leigh. Probably a fuse just blew. You stay right where you are. Mama, you stay here with her. I'll go outside and check the fuse box."

Mama said, "Hush, baby. Tee, pick up one of those new fuses in the kitchen drawer. Save yourself a trip. Meanwhile, I'll raise one of these shades, let in the light from the street." Her bare feet padded across the wooden floors to the side window of the room. She yelled, "Tee, forget about that fuse. It's pitch-black outside, too. Bring me some matches instead. I'll light some of these candles we been using for decoration."

"Okay, Mama. Reckon we finally getting them blackouts people over on the coast been talking about?"

"You probably right. I sure hope them Germans ain't moving inland, closer to us. They've been creating all kinds of mess offshore."

I started crying. "I don't like the blackout."

Before that night, I paid no attention to the war. But afterwards, I watched the newsreels when we went to the movie theater. I saw those

Germans Mama talked about. I said, "Tee, the Germans are already here. Mrs. Kornegay is one of 'em."

"She's different from the ones in Germany. We are fighting World War II."

"Are they going to make more? How many?"

She just shrugged her shoulders. "Wars happen for different reasons. They claim it's about freedom."

One day, World War II walked up Mama's walkway, climbed up her steps, and landed on her front porch. It didn't look like the movie newsreels. I got mixed up because the mailman brought it—a letter for my daddy.

Tee took it and burst into tears—so I cried, too.

Just then someone banged on our screen door. Tee hurried to answer it. There stood Ida Lee, our neighbor from across the street. Tears ran down her face, too. She held the hand of her son, Dollbaby. Aunt Burrell called him that "'Cause he's as pretty as a doll." He was trying to break away but his mother held on tightly and waved a letter.

"Oh, oh, no, your husband got one from Uncle Sam, too?" Tee unhooked the screen door and let her inside. They held onto each other like a magnet and a nail. Dollbaby ran and played on our porch banister.

Who was Uncle Sam? Was Ida Lee our relative? Why did he write letters that made people cry?

When Sam came home, Tee gave him the letter and cried some more. Soon everybody on our end of Howell Street knew Dollbaby's daddy and my daddy were going overseas to fight the Germans.

The day they left, Tee and Ida Lee cried. I thought Sam would be home in time for supper but he wasn't. Many, many days went by. We heard nothing from him or about him. During the daytime, I forgot about it. At night, I was scared for him.

Then one day, he showed up—on our front porch. I thought I was dreaming.

"Come here, baby."

I ran and jumped in his arms. "Where is your uniform and your hat?"

Before he answered, Tee came from inside. They hugged for a long time. Then came Mama. All four of us hugged and hugged until Tee said, "What about Ida Lee's husband?"

Sam said, "He must have qualified."

In a few days, Ida Lee came over. "A letter just came from Uncle Sam—my husband's in the army."

Everybody felt sorry for her and Dollbaby.

Aunt Burrell said, "Look on the bright side, Ida Lee will get an allotment."

Whatever that meant. My family took Ida Lee and Dollbaby under our wings. Other neighbors did, too. Her next-door neighbor, a part-time preacher who wore a bow tie and a white suit couldn't do enough for Ida Lee every day, but nobody thought that was very kind of him.

Tee's father & my grandfather, Papa

Tee's mother & my grandmother, Mama

Neighbor, Ida Lee and son, Dollbaby

*Hospital where I was born,
and my daddy worked*

Company Coming

"Company coming!" Those two words set my teeth on edge. It didn't matter who they were . . . gospel singers doing a show, preachers saving souls, or relatives and friends staying in touch. I hated company. It was Mama's fault. Before they arrived, she said, "Dorothy Leigh, you have to smile and say 'How do you do.'." I never smiled.

No matter who came to visit, Mama could sleep the company and I wasn't put out. She fed them, too. Every summer in our neighborhood, white farmers hawked peaches, butter beans, purple hull peas, and stuff. Their voices were music to Mama's ears. She lowered her right shoulder and rocked on out to greet them like long lost relatives. Soon, bushels of vegetables and pecks of fruit lined our back porch. In a few minutes, I couldn't squeeze through to play in the backyard. The kitchen buzzed like a beehive. Wood crackled in the cook stove. Mason jars tingled against each other. Rushing cold water filled large pots. Mama lifted them onto the cook stove. Soon scalding hot water sterilized the jars. Above all that commotion, Mama sang "Blest Be the Ties That Bind."

I hid in the corner of the little hallway outside our bathroom and watched from across the screened in back porch. I saw Mama lift that scary pressure cooker onto the stove. I never went near it. Its rocking valve scared me. Mama said, "I have to keep an eye on that; it could blow up." Pretty soon, she yelled, "Dorothy Leigh, time to snap string beans and shell butter-beans." I hated that job so much I threw a lot of them away when she wasn't looking. Still, she canned tons of jars. When winter came, she opened those preserves and vegetables, baked homemade salty ham biscuits, and fried chicken to go with them.

We raised the chickens in our backyard between the fig tree and the corrugated tin garage Papa built for the car he was going to buy, but he died. Sometimes Mama said, "Dot, go out to the chicken yard. Grab me one of them pullets." When I did, a mean, old red combed, white rooster always charged at me so I grabbed the first pullet I saw. She wrung its neck. "Pretty soon, you can do this."

Our company could eat all they wanted; I was a poor eater. Mama and Tee called Britches, the nine-year-old boy across the street, to talk me into eating a skinny chicken wing. He was Papa's idea. After Papa died, nobody saw fit to stop calling him. I was glad, I liked him a whole bunch.

Greeting guests was hard. I preferred the men. Those fat perfumed ladies with the bosoms that looked like bunnies lived there didn't listen to my "How do you do." They pulled me up so close, I liked to 've suffocated. Afterwards, they gave me a funny looking white doll or a new lace handkerchief. The men were easier. I just walked over, put out my right hand, and said, "How do you do." Smiles didn't matter to them. For my daddy's friends, I sang "You Are My Sunshine." Then I waited while they opened their wallets or reached into their pockets which took forever. Finally, I got a silver dollar or green paper money. One time there was a ten on it. Mama shouted, "Praise the Lord!"

Out of all the men who came, Uncle Rhone, my mother's brother, was my favorite. I never had to say "How do you do." to him. As soon as he saw me, he tossed me up in the air. Then he dug his chin into my back. It tickled me so much that I forgot about money. On one of his visits, he went to see some friends. He didn't say when he'd be back. Later, when the doorbell rang, Mama said, "Tee ain't here, you can answer that, baby. Don't tell her about it though."

First, I peeked through the curtains on the door to see who was there. Uncle Rhone stared down at me. A fancy woman held his arm. I opened the door just wide enough for my face, then held on to the doorknob, and propped one foot behind the door. I yelled, "Mama, its Rhone. He's got that Puddin' with him. You told him, 'Don't bring that Puddin' to my house ever again.'"

Right away, pots banged around in the kitchen. Uncle Rhone was going to get it. The swinging door into the dining room flew open and Mama rocked out. I could hardly wait. I pressed my foot harder against the door and put both hands on the knob. Just before she reached us, Mama said, "Dorothy Leigh, go and play, baby."

"Yes, ma'am." I shook my finger at Uncle Rhone. I slowly started to leave. He was in big trouble.

Mama spoke in her best airs, "It's so nice to see you again, Puddin'."

One day a gray car with two colored men in suits parked in front of Mama's house. They got out and walked up to our front porch. "Afternoon, Mrs. Best. Thought we'd stop by, try to interest you in a business proposition."

Mama nodded.

The tall one took over, "Mrs. Best, beenst that you have such a lovely home and all, we were wondering if you'd provide accommodations for the best singer in the world, Sister Rosetta Tharpe."

Mama got all proper, "Why I'd be honored to provide accommodations for a singer of her caliber." While they talked about Mama's pay, I ran off to spread the news of Sister Rosetta Tharpe's visit. That evening, Mama said, "Tee, you know with colored people not having a hotel in town, special guests need a quality place to stay. Two business gentlemen stopped by this very afternoon to see if I could provide accommodations for none other than Sister Rosetta Tharpe, the gospel singer."

"Oh, Mama! They picked you for Sister Rosetta Tharpe? That's great! Who knows who they'll bring the next time."

"Now, Tee, calm down a minute. You know she deserves the very best room in the house."

"I know, Mama, I know."

"I'll pay you and Sam good money to give up your bedroom for two nights for Sister Rosetta."

"Of course, Mama. Of course. It's your house. Papa said so. Besides, Sister Rosetta Tharpe will be our most important company ever. I'm gonna go and play her 78 record right now."

Every day, I asked, "Is Sister Rosetta coming?" Tee always said no. Finally, one afternoon she said, "Dorothy Leigh, go play on the front porch. We're trying to get everything ready for Sister Rosetta."

"Is she coming today?"

"Only if you get out of our hair."

After waiting on the front porch a long time, I was about to give up. Just then a long, shiny, black car, like the funeral car we rode in when Papa died, pulled up. It couldn't be Sister Rosetta Tharpe; her sponsors drove an old gray car. As I watched, the front door opened, out stepped the tall sponsor. A fancy lady sat in the back seat. "Hot diggety dog! She's here! She's here!" Mama and Tee came a-running. "Don't you worry, Mama, when I say, 'How do you do.', I'll smile real pretty."

Tee pulled me over and pressed my face into her stomach. I couldn't breathe or see anything. By the time I got some air, Sister Rosetta Tharpe, her sponsors, and her suitcases were almost to the front porch. She was beautiful from head to toe. Shiny glitter covered the shoulders of her purple suit. A sassy little fish tail was at the bottom of her jacket. (Tee had a fish tail one, too, but hers was black). Sister Rosetta wore a sparkly hat with a veil. She was rich—earrings and bracelets jangled. Her lipstick was like ripe strawberries. Her cheeks were as pink as roses. She knew how to draw lines over her eyes real good. And she smelled better than Mama's flowers. "Hello," she said in a voice like a kitten.

She took a liking to us right away; she smiled real hard at Tee. Mama excused herself and rushed back to the kitchen. I stepped up to do my part. Tee pushed me aside and ushered Sister Rosetta into her and my daddy's front bedroom like the singer owned it. I waited around to be introduced, but nobody paid me any attention. Since I wasn't allowed in the bedroom, I went outside to the front porch windows to peek through the lace curtains. Down came the shades. There was nothing left for me except to wait outside the bedroom door. They laughed and carried on like best friends. I made myself comfortable on the floor. When Tee popped out of the room, she almost stepped on me and didn't even say excuse me.

Instead, she hurried to the kitchen. In no time, she was back carrying southern hospitality—a tray filled with a pretty little plate of small sandwiches (no crusts), a tall pitcher of lemonade, and two glasses. "Please, Tee, let me go in with you."

"No children allowed."

I couldn't get in and Sister Rosetta never came out. Not even to practice on Tee's piano. The next night was her first show. Her sponsors arrived in that same black car. We gathered to watch her leave. She had on a red dress with a long white furry cape and a lot of makeup. Her pearl earrings and necklace were as white as my Crayola crayon. A pretty white flower perched on one side of her head. She swooped down to the car. Before getting in, she turned and blew us a kiss. I didn't care about that; we needed to get ready. I hoped Mama had boiled enough water for three baths. We had free tickets for her show.

At least, we didn't have to walk all the way across town to the community center. Aunt Burrell was taking us. Nobody in the family trusted her driving anymore. She had an accident, ran over a policeman and his motorcycle. They got stuck under the front of her car. She laughed, "He shouldn't have stopped so sudden like."

Aunt Burrell got us there in time for Sister Rosetta's show. Watching her on stage, I could hardly believe she had accommodations at our house. I wanted to tell the people behind me, but I had to be good—I was sitting between Tee and Mama.

The next night, Tee was in the room helping Sister Rosetta dress for her last show. I waited outside the door to see her outfit. Suddenly, Tee screamed, "Stop! Don't you dare kiss me like that."

I jumped up to get Mama. Tee burst from the room and ran towards the kitchen. I was on her heels but stopped and headed back to her room. At the door, Sister Rosetta blocked my way. Then she cackled and slammed the door in my face.

Her dress was black.

I don't know why, but religion worked real hard in the summertime. It had Sunday service and church every night but Saturday. Maybe that was because grownups were always saying, "It's hot as hell." Or maybe it had a lot to do with June German.

Anyway, to beat the devil, religion held vacation bible school for children and revival for the grown-ups. Each one had two weeks to do it. Vacation bible school was fun and filled with art. Each day, after a bible story or two, we practiced "glory to Jesus" songs and recited bible verses for the closing night show. Sometimes the teachers tried to scare us, "Be good so you don't go to Hell when you die."

The big kids told me, "Don't worry, only old people die."

The best part of bible school was playtime. That's when we rushed outside and lined up at the open kitchen window of the church's annex. Members of the Ladies' Auxiliary stood there with ladles at a big wash tub filled to the brim with grape Kool-Aid. A large block of ice bobbed up and down in that purple goodness. A few yellow lemon slices floated on top. If I was lucky, one of the ladies might add one to my cup of Kool-Aid. That sour taste in the grape drink was so delicious, one big kid said, "Bible school Kool-Aid can bring a lot of sinners to Jesus."

One summer day, Mama said, "Burrell, revivals ain't one bit of fun."

My aunt said, "You want a show? I hear tell 'Daddy Grace' is coming to town."

Mama said, "I'd give anything to see them bring him in on his throne. Hear he wears lots of rings and stuff. Women faint when they see him."

One night the next week, Aunt Burrell took me and Mama to a real skinny, long, wooden church across town. There was no Jesus or his cross outside . . . just some faded words and a picture of a loaf of bread on one wall. It looked like Brown's Grocery Store on Star Street. It was on a corner, too. Mama always said. "Corners are important. They cost more. Usually, you get a lot more land; makes people think you're rich."

When we got to the door, it was so crowded, we couldn't get inside. Aunt Burrell told the usher, "My sister's old and feeble. She can't stand for too long."

He said, "Sister, follow me." We did. Mama pretended to hobble all the way down the skinny aisle to the front row. Up front, the church looked exactly like Brown's store except the pulpit was where the meat counter belonged. They must have forgot to pay their 'lectric bill 'cause candles burned everywhere. All the ladies were dressed in white. The candlelight made everything look soft and pretty.

I said, "Aunt Burrell, we should wear white to greet Daddy Grace."

"Dot, it ain't necessary to get all fancy. Nobody gonna be studyin' us. They gonna be watching Daddy Grace."

Mama said, "Dot, honey, they trying to impress him. This being his first visit and all."

I relaxed and waited for their "Daddy" to show up.

"He's late." Aunt Burrell tried to whisper but her voice carried.

It was boring until somebody started a song. Mama joined in. Aunt Burrell said, "Smithie, stop pretending you know that song."

After two songs, two men walked up front and rolled out a long, red rug all the way back to the door. Things really picked up, the songs had a lot of spirit, and pretty ladies caught the holy ghost.

At that moment, Aunt Burrell said, "Look, they bringing him in." Sure enough, four big men held Daddy Grace up high in a white, furry, high-backed chair. He was almost to the ceiling. His rings, necklaces, and crown sparkled so brightly, I had to close my eyes. When I looked again, he was waving kinda funny to everybody. He was something to see in that white suit with a cape. People cried out, "Daddy Grace!"

We stayed to the end 'cause we couldn't get out. Besides, Mama was having a ball. Aunt Burrell couldn't make her stop laughing. After a long time, Daddy Grace ended his story and they passed around the collection plate. Aunt Burrell put in money; Mama didn't. Nobody announced how much they took in. After that, it was time for "Daddy Grace" to leave. His men brought his chair, got him settled, raised him up, and carried him out through the screaming people.

Once we were back in the car, I said, "Aunt Burrell, is he cripple?"

"No. He just prefers to ride on the backs of others."

Things got dull after the "Daddy Grace" show. Too bad he didn't come to town every day. But Mama found something interesting for me and her to do—visit the Pentecostal Sanctified and Holiness Church on Middle Street. Before we even opened their door, music poured out. Mama said, "I can feel the spirit." Inside, we sat down on a wooden bench; not a slippery pew like in our church. There was a board across the back and another to sit on. The church sisters and brothers shouted and carried on the whole time. Some of them clanged tambourines. Others pulled golden trombones. Mama said, "Dot, look at that old man tickle those piano keys."

"Mama, I think they'll do anything to keep from sitting on these seats."

"I reckon you right, baby." And she clapped her hands to hide her laughing.

Everybody sang; not just the choir, like in our church. Actually, there was no choir. The songs were new to me but easy to learn. I joined in on "Old Sheep You Know the Way, Young Lamb Got to Learn the Road."

Me and Mama paid close attention. At the end, one of the church members spoke to us. "We saw you enjoying the service. One of the sisters mentioned you offer accommodations for visiting ministers and singers."

Mama got all proper, "Why, yes I do."

"Wonderful. We need accommodations for Reverend Gilcrist, our visiting preacher." She and Mama worked things out. *Our church never asked for accommodations for Reverend Underwood at Mama's.* I remember one time when Reverend Underwood stopped by, he said, "Sister Best, it's time you brought your florist skills back to God's holy house."

Mama said, "It's time alright. Time y'all started paying me for my skills. Same as you do that white florist downtown."

He pulled hard on his suspenders. "The Lord wants all of us working in his vineyard. His are not earthly rewards. Your name will be on Saint Peter's roll when your time comes."

Mama spit a long stream of snuff juice.

I really hoped she wouldn't honor the Pentecostal Church's request for accommodations. A preacher could speak directly to the Lord 'nem. Living with Mama, he'd have a lot to tell. But Reverend Gilcrist came for two weeks and asked to come back the next summer. I guess so he could sit on our front porch every afternoon and laugh with Mama.

Mama and Aunt Sister Hattie

Britches

Tee's brother, Rhone

June German

My favorite company didn't preach no revival sermons in the heat of the summer nights, didn't sing any gospel songs. They didn't need to hear me say, "How do you do." My kind of company only cared about June German. When they arrived, Tee wanted me to disappear, "Go and play with Betty Ruth or something." I didn't, I stayed right there in that big old Victorian house underfoot.

June German. The air just changed all around me. Neighbors sang their hellos. It was the biggest thing that ever happened in Rocky Mount. In spite of everything, it was just another white folks' hand me down, like their old clothes or furniture. But it was their best give away ever.

Actually, there were two dances—like the drinking fountains, the toilets, the neighborhoods, the public schools. We went second; but we didn't hold white folks accountable for going first as usual. After all, it was their Cotillion Club's idea. Shucks, June German was the closest thing to "separate but equal" there was in Rocky Mount; maybe in the whole South.

The rich white one was held on Saturday night in a tobacco warehouse, amidst flowing blue and white crepe paper. Although the tobacco scent lingered like a strong perfume, it was not a problem. Practically everybody smoked or lived with someone who did. To make the dance even better, they hired bands like Kay Kaiser, the local boy who made it in the music world, Little Jack Little, or Tommy Dorsey. As if that wasn't enough, Cotillion members held intermission parties in their homes for their out-of-town guests; no local people were allowed to participate in any thing. Poor whites couldn't even serve them a drink.

The colored one was more democratic, open to anybody who could buy a ticket. That didn't set well with some colored people, "It isn't exclusive." Tee didn't feel that way about it. "My friend's daddy was a smart business man. He wasn't going to let all that pretty blue and white decoration go to waste after the white folks were done with it on Saturday night. No sirree, Burrell. Mr. Westry arranged to keep everything in the same place for a colored June German on Monday night."

"Too bad, he didn't ask for Sunday, crepe paper tends to droop after hanging like that."

Tee said. "You know that wasn't going to happen. Dancing on the Sabbath?"

Aunt Burrell laughed. "I bet he had to throw in cleanup for both dances."

Tee laughed, too. "I bet you right. Rich white folks don't give nothing away without trying to squeeze out something extra."

"You know what amazes me, Tee? Who would have guessed it would turn into something big like this. There's posters everywhere—on telephone poles, in barber shops and beauty parlors, in café windows, you name it."

"Burrell, some people just know how to make money. June German is the time to do it. Even Sam and me rake in some sheckles at parties the week before the dance. And on that Saturday night at the Robbin's intermission party. Sam mixes drinks while I serve the cute party sandwiches, deviled eggs, ham biscuits, and the like."

"Tee, I want to know how your friend's daddy manages to bring in bands like Count Basie, Billy Eckstein, Ella Fitzgerald, Cab Calloway, Nat King Cole? Suppose he had some white backing?"

"I wouldn't rule it out, Burrell."

I loved Nat King Cole. I listened to his 78 records on my parents' radio/record player or I sneaked the record to Uncle Rhone's old room and played it on the Victrola. I was careful not to scratch the record when I put the needle into the first groove. If I was in my parent's room I sank into their yellow chair and let Nat King Cole sing over and over. His words were so clear, I understood everything. And he could really carry a tune. I thought he was handsome with his very dark face and hair every bit as slick and black and shiny as Billy Eckstein's or The Ink Spots. He dressed real sharp, too, just like my daddy. He always wore a suit, shirt, and a tie with a tie pin and cuff links. Nat paid for his but some of my daddy's suits came from the young white doctor.

Too bad nobody asked Mama to provide accommodations for Nat King Cole. The family would have been proud of me when I greeted him. Instead, our June German company was usually Uncle Rhone and his "maybe" wife, Louella. Mama said, "Nobody showed me no marriage license."

Not everybody loved June German; colored and white preachers hated it. The white ones got their opinions in the newspaper. On the Sunday before the dance, Reverend Underwood condemned June German from his pulpit like it was a mad dog. He made it so real, I could see it—all green and scaly with scraps of red and purple cloth clinging to its body, foaming at the mouth, and biting dance couple after dance couple. When it got indigestion and begged for baking soda, Reverend Underwood wouldn't give it any. Sitting there in church next to Tee, I guess I made some demon noises. She said, "Be quiet."

Just then Reverend Underwood said, "The doors of the church are open." Nobody came forward to join. Collection was taken and a prayer was offered up for the June German sinners' souls. Tee bowed her head. She and Sam would be jitterbugging the very next night.

One year, Cousin Laura, one of the many school teachers on Papa's side of the family, and her husband, Billy, a porter on the Atlantic Coastline Railroad, decided to come. Tee said, "Cousin Billy belongs to the Brotherhood of Sleeping Car Porters. He makes good money. Sometimes we get to say 'hello' to him when the train passes through on its way to Florida. He is real nice. Cousin Laura likes to remind us they are well-to-do in Richmond, Virginia."

The summer before I turned six, Tee and I spent three days in Richmond visiting with my daddy's mother, Grandmother Bessie. I loved it at her house. There were cousins everywhere. Three of them and their mother lived with her and three more lived across the street. I didn't miss Sam and Mama at all.

On the fourth day, it was time to go and stay at Cousin Laura's house. Uncle Alphonso, the spitting image of my daddy, took us on the bus and we got off at a park. He picked the right path through the park to her house. When we came out, her house was across the street. It looked just like the witch's cottage in the fairy tale. I pretended to be brave and pushed open the little white gate to her yard. After only three steps, I stopped. I couldn't make up my mind about what to do first—swing in her white porch swing or knock on her door. While I was trying to choose, Tee rang the doorbell. She appeared right away, like she had been peeking through her lace curtains. She only opened the door a crack. Tee said, "Hi, Cousin Laura, we made it."

"Hello, Christine." She waited a minute before letting us inside then began to boss around Uncle Alphonso. "Bring their suitcase to the guest room."

It was good she was impolite; my uncle didn't have time to lollygag, he had a job to go to. I tagged along to see our accommodations. Tee tried to stop me; I pretended not to hear her. I couldn't believe my eyes. It was the most beautiful room I'd ever seen . . . all pink and green with pretty yellow flowers in the wallpaper and a pretty pink bed for Tee and me. I wanted to touch things but everybody was watching. We were lucky to be visiting Cousin Laura.

Before bedtime, I wanted to leave; Cousin Laura was spying on me all the time. "Dorothy Leigh, don't put your feet on the rounds of the kitchen chair." She scared me in the guest room. "Little fingers shouldn't walk up and down the wallpaper." While brushing my teeth, "Dorothy Leigh, squeeze the toothpaste from the bottom of the tube." And it wasn't even her toothpaste.

The next day Uncle Alphonso saved me and took us shopping. With him I laughed out loud, danced around, skipped. He was always happy but that day he was excited, too. "My wife, Babe, is making extra money doing inventory." I didn't know what inventory was, but if it made my uncle happy it made me happy, too. We went to a big store called Thalheimer's. After a fun day, we took the bus back and walked on the path through the park again but the house was missing. We laughed. I hoped it was lost forever, but Tee found it. For two more days, Cousin Laura taught me manners and Tee bought me ice cream.

On our last day, I waited outside for Uncle Alphonso. As he got closer, he looked sad, like he was missing us already. Turned out, I was half right. The other part had to do with Babe. I learned what inventory meant—Babe ran away with her boss.

Manners was why I worried about Cousin Laura coming for June German. I said, "Mama, is she right all the time?"

"Laura thinks she is but she ain't. You can put that in your pipe and smoke it."

"When we visited her, she bothered me all the time about my manners. I started to tell her you love my manners but I was too scared to talk to her."

"Well, I . . . that heifer."

"Mama, when are we going to practice 'How do you do."

"Never."

Sometimes, June German company came from Mama's side of the family: another sister, Leatha, her husband, and their two grown sons, Jiggs and J.D. They drove their big green Oldsmobile from Norfolk, Virginia. They used to live near us. Now the men had real good jobs, made a ton of money, and everybody dressed real nice. With so many relatives in town at the same time, parties just shot up like wild flowers. It would start at Mama's, move across the street to Aunt Burrell's, and end up in Little Raleigh at Aunt Sister Hattie's. She was older than Mama and religious. Mama always set her off by saying, "Lord, Hat, you certainly have a lot to atone to your savior for. Don't you? My, my, my."

"Smithie, you watch yourself. Don't go messing with me."

Mama shook with laughter.

One time, Aunt Sister Hattie was fed up with her. "At least when I'm responsible for someone else's care. I'm responsible all the time." Mama got real quiet. I stopped jumping rope. Mama pulled her lace handkerchief from her top dress pocket and played with it. Aunt Sister Hattie fanned herself real hard with a Stokes' Funeral Parlor fan. I swung my jump rope slowly over my head and watched them stare at each other. *What was wrong?* It didn't take me long. *I had it.*

Aunt Sister Hattie always made a difference between her daughters, Willie Mae and Marie. She liked Willie Mae the most. Probably, Mama told her about it. Made Aunt Sister Hattie mad. She was the mother of her church and claimed to be real close to the Lord. The Lord 'nem frowned on making differences. Mama always talked about Aunt Sister Hattie. She said, "Hat ought to be shamed of herself. Acting like that at June German time. She can't tell Marie to stay away; she's grown and married. So, Hat says, 'How you gonna explain dancing and carrying on like that all night—when they call you up to the front of the church?'"

Cousin Marie was not like her sister, Willie Mae, who was something else. If the Lord or his people said anything to her about June German, she would bless them out. Not one bit of goodness in her. I didn't really like her. One time she messed with me, like I was her age or something. "How you doing, Chocolate Snap?"

I looked at her yellow skin and said, "I'm fine, Vanilla Wafer."

Unlike me, Aunt Sister Hattie was always as happy as pie to see Willie Mae. Even the time when she showed up for June German with a car load of her women's club members and their husbands. Mama said, "Hat just made sure those 'heathens' were comfortable."

To tell the truth, Cousin Marie reminded me of Cinderella; did all the work. Like that Sunday before June German when two carloads of us showed up from our neighborhood. She laid out a Thanksgiving feast and it was summer. Everybody started in eating baked chicken with sausage stuffing, baked ham with those funny wooden sticks and yellow pineapple slices, smothered brown pork chops with onions, white fluffy rice, potato salad with sweet relish, deviled eggs trimmed with tiny strips of red on top, collard greens with smoked ham hocks, fresh sliced tomatoes and cucumbers in vinegar, freshly grated coconut on white cake with white frosting, lemon pie with brown-tipped meringue on top, sweet potato pie, and homemade peach ice cream. There was a whole lot of lip smacking and sighing. Not from me. I didn't eat other people's cooking—just Tee's, Mama's, and Sam's, that's it. Everybody said, "Just the way Dot is, sticks close to home."

That was odd in a way 'cause I liked Cousin Marie. She was my mother's favorite. If it weren't for her, my parents wouldn't have met. There would have been no me. She saw my daddy first. She said, "Tee there's a cute delivery boy at Hinson's grocery store and he wears the prettiest white buck shoes I've ever seen."

Tee said, "I'll come over to your house and you can take me to the store to see him." By the time she saw him, she said, "His shoes are dirty now but you're right, he is cute."

The day after Cousin Marie's feast was June German Monday. It was quiet until evening came. I couldn't sit still, ran in and out of rooms. June German was in my bones. Finally, I sat down at the foot of my parent's bed, right in front of Tee's big round dresser mirror. She and Uncle Rhone's "maybe" wife, Louella, stood there looking at their outfits: Tee wearing her black two-piece dress with the fish tail, magenta (my favorite Crayola color) on the top part of her jacket, and finished off with black shoes; Louella wearing a skinny, shiny, black dress, no sleeves, and red high heel shoes with the toes out. I couldn't take my eyes off her shoes until I saw Tee slide on her ear bobs and reach for her makeup. Lately, she hid her makeup from me—I hoped she'd forget to put it away.

Tee sat down at the mirror, opened her white jar of Pond's Vanishing Crème, and rubbed a little on her face. Her skin looked smooth; the oily shine was gone. Closing the jar, she picked up her black eyebrow pencil next and made one curving eyebrow over each eye. At first, she stared wide-eyed at herself in the big round mirror, then slant-eyed. Now with darker eyebrows, she was ready for rouge. Hers came in a tiny, blue, silver trimmed Evening in Paris rouge case. It was no bigger than a silver dollar, only fatter. Inside the case was a tiny puff which I loved. Tee lightly patted on rouge. It looked so good, Louella said, "Tee, may I borrow it?"

"Sure, but your makeup looks perfect already."

"A girl can't be too sure." And she reached back and put that pretty little puff on my cheeks. Right then and there, I warmed up to "Aunt" Louella; wife or no wife. Let Mama worry about that. Next thing I noticed, I was alone in the mirror. Tee and my new aunt had left the room. I caught up to them in the living room. They were both wearing lipstick; Tee's wasn't as red as my aunt's. My daddy and Uncle Rhone stood up. Everybody kissed me goodnight and left.

I was hightailing it back to Tee's dresser and the makeup but stopped in my tracks. Mama, Aunt Leatha, Uncle Quincy and their son, J.D., were coming into the living room from the front porch. Everyone, except Mama, was dressed for June German. She was taking care of me.

Aunt Leatha said, "Where is Jiggs?"

Mama yelled, "Jiggs, you better hurry. You 'bout to be left behind."

Jiggs appeared at the French doors between the dining room and the living room, "Ta da." My mouth dropped open. Aunt Leatha wailed and moaned like at a funeral. Uncle Quincy turned and walked outside. The rest of us stared.

Jiggs posed like a movie star in a shiny, royal-blue dress covered with beautiful, twinkling rhinestones. He looked pretty, for a boy. His black, high heels were fancy cutouts. Rhinestone earrings sparkled like his bracelet and his silver evening bag. His makeup was better than Aunt Louella's. I could see it all the way across the room and started to tell him so, then I remembered I should be seen and not heard. I sealed my lips and waited, but nobody in that room complimented Jiggs on anything. Finally, he switched his hips to the front door and left.

Aunt Leatha wailed again. Mama said, "Aw, honey, that's just Jiggs' way. Course, he should have asked your permission about your dress." She laughed so hard, I thought she would pass out.

Shortly, me and Mama were alone on the front porch. As people walked by, Mama said, "Won't see them again until tomorrow morning." It sounded so exciting. I started daydreaming about me going to June German one day. Suddenly, Mama stared at me. I said, "What?"

"Dot, it's high time we got to see what all this excitement is about." Without another word, she went inside, turned off the lights, and closed the front door. She started down the front steps. I still stood on the porch. She turned back to me, "You gonna let me go off to the big dance without you?"

I flew down the steps and grabbed her hand. We walked on over to Mangrum's warehouse for my first June German. Good thing Aunt Louella put rouge on me. I looked pretty. We could hear the band before we got to the warehouse. As we drew closer to one of the tobacco loading doors, the opening was covered half way with chicken wire—much easier to see through than lace curtains.

Everything was beautiful. All blue, white, and glittery like Jiggs' dress. I could never have imagined any of it. The dance floor was busy. There were dresses in all the colors in my crayon box and high heeled shoes, some with the toes out. Men wore shiny black or brown shoes, dark suits with starched white shirts, and striped or one-color ties. I even saw some bow ties. On the dance floor, swinging partners, close up partners, and separated apart jitterbugging partners were having a ball. Colored and white people seated in the stands watched the dancers, swayed to the music. Oh, it was all too, too wonderful. If this was the "demon", I'd follow him anywhere.

    I squeezed Mama's fingers. June German was as good as Christmas. Then I heard the music. At first, I wasn't sure but I knew the words and they were loud and clear, "Straighten Up and Fly Right." I couldn't believe my ears. It sounded just like our 78 record . . . back at Mama's house. I strained and twisted my body to see all the way to the bandstand.

    Oh, my goodness. There he was—Nat King Cole!

[1]*Nat King Cole – 1947*

My family's church

[1]*General Artists Corporation (management), "Photo of Nat King Cole in 1947," photograph, 1947,* commons.wikimedia.org, *https://commons.wikimedia.org/wiki/File:Nat_King_Cole_1947.jpg#file (accessed April 17, 2023)*

My dad's mother, Bessie

Younger Mama and Aunt Sister Hattie

Mama & Aunt Sister Hattie in back Marie with husband & me in front

Willie Mae

Aunt Leatha

Jiggs

Photographs below by Walter Bryant:

Billy Eckstein

Cab Calloway

Ella Fitzgerald

Wild Bill Davis

and more highlights...

Negotiation

Mama always rose early, especially in the springtime. There were petunias to deadhead, black earth to rake, a large Victorian porch to sweep, and everything to admire. Me and Mama slept together. She believed in ghosts and was real scared of dead people, including Papa. Right after he died, we slept foot to head with Tee and Sam—until they kicked us out. We went back to Mama's room and her bed. To help us out, she burned a small, round, kerosene stove. It made pretty patterns on the ceiling all night. "Dorothy Leigh, the ghosts won't come now; they don't like lights."

One morning, she said, "Last night your grandfather came to the head of the bed and looked right down on you." *How did Papa's ghost get out of that deep hole they put him in at the cemetery?*

Even when his ghost visited, we still got up early to watch Mama's garden come alive. One particular morning, a red-faced, skinny, white man in overalls showed up, interrupted our routine. He was too early and too poorly dressed to be an insurance man. When one of them showed up for the premium, Mama always sent me to the front door to tell them, "My grandmother isn't home."

No. He wasn't no agent. We watched him drive his black four-door car around our corner. The minute he parked in front of our house, Mama stopped her morning business to see just who he thought he was. She never was timid. I remember the time Santa Claus didn't throw candy canes to me at the end of the parade. Boy, was she mad at him. "You mess with me, you white son of a bitch, I'll tell Dorothy Leigh exactly who you really is!" She forgot to put on airs when she was mad.

That morning when the strange white man came, Mama propped her head on her rake and watched him get out of his car. Smoke blew over the top of it, probably from a cigarette. My daddy smoked, too. He reached the back of his car and started to climb up to our dirt sidewalk. In about six giant steps he would be on our cement walkway, a straight shot to our front porch.

Mama cleared her throat and stopped him dead in his tracks. I knew he wanted to get back in his old car. I grinned and waited for it to happen but he didn't turn tail and run. I scooted out of the rocking chair, walked towards the steps. I glanced at Mama's serious face. She shifted her rake and gripped it in both hands. I checked on the white man. He touched the brim of his hat to Mama, "Good morning."

In her best airs, Mama said, "Morning," as she held onto the rake. I stayed on the porch and watched. Mama was way taller than him. An old crinkled straw hat with a point at the front made him look mean. I bet he was so mean he dared that hat to move any place but where he put it. I watched his every move, every twitch. He tried a little smile and stepped on our walkway. That wasn't fooling nobody. Mama wasn't accepting him. Me neither. Just then he added an extra roll to his already rolled up blue shirtsleeves. It wasn't even that hot. He got brave and started talking. Good thing, too, 'cause we didn't have no telephone to call the police. Even if we did, they wouldn't show up. They never cared about colored neighborhoods. "I'm Robert Coggins, tobacco farmer."

Mama didn't say nothing, just kept her distance and her hold on her rake. I stayed right there on the porch, ready to run inside and get Tee.

"I'm a-looking for hands. Tobacco should be ready by Monday. Only four days away. That's how come I'm in town so early in the morning."

I had no idea what he was talking about. I looked at Mama to see what she thought. Her right hand had let go of the rake. It hung at her side. What did that mean?

"Oh, I see," she said.

I didn't see nothin'. What was he doing in our yard? We didn't owe him. He wasn't selling vegetables or fruits from a truck. Besides it was too early in the season for fresh green string beans and butterbeans. Watermelons and peaches and the like were a long way away. I knew 'cause ice cold watermelon was my favorite. It wasn't even hot enough to go barefoot. And anybody could see he wasn't the iceman; he came on Thursdays.

While I was thinking, Mama and Mr. Coggins came closer together. There was still a gap between them but not much. I started creeping off the porch towards Mama. As I inched along, I pulled a leaf off a nearby bush, pretended to smell a petunia. All the time, I got closer and listened.

"Just how many hands do you need?"

"Six. That's about all I can squeeze into my car. I'll need two of them to be loopers."

I didn't understand a thing.

"I'll have to bring my granddaughter. She can sit on my lap, of course. How much you paying?"

He looked down at the ground, kinda smoothed out some of Mama's rake marks. "Four dollars a day for hands and four fifty for loopers."

"And just how long is your day?"

That was Mama—quick; couldn't get away with that stuff with her.

He reached into his overall pocket, pulled out a cigarette, and coughed a couple of times before he lit it. After he got it going, he coughed again. I watched him suck in the smoke. He held it so long, he got redder than he was. Sam never did that. Finally, Mr. Coggins let it out while he talked. "The way I figure, I pick everybody up at five a.m. We get to my place a little before six . . ."

"Do you provide lunch?"

"No. No lunch."

Everything got quiet again. I wanted to go to that white man's place. I wanted to ride in his old car.

"Beenst that you ain't providing lunch, I reckon you oughta pay more," Mama said and raked real close to his feet.

He jumped back.

I liked this part the best. Who was gonna give in first? I crossed my fingers for Mama to win. She kept up her raking, even where he hadn't messed up.

Finally, he said, "Hell, I don't really need to be on the road that early. Say I pick up at six, 'stead of five. Plenty of day . . ."

"Fine. That'll get us back on the road at five in the evening." And she planted her rake and leaned on it.

Since there was no referee like on the Gillette Blue Blade fights with Joe Louis on the radio, I wasn't sure who won. I looked from one to the other.

He smiled. "My word is my bond . . . ."

I felt sorry for Mama. She usually won. Mostly though, I worried about Mr. Coggins with all that coughing, he might be getting TB.

Mama said, "Smithie. My name is Smithie."

"Good day to you, Smithie. I'll see y'all Monday morning, bright and early."

Mama followed him to the end of the walkway. I tagged along. When he started down the slope, she yelled, "That hour lunch break should be just long enough for a good nap."

He cut his eyes back at Mama and almost slid down to the street, "Damn."

Now Starring

Me and Tee went to the movies a lot; any day we wanted, except Sundays. God or the Lord, I never knew which to call the Savior, frowned on that. Our neighbors did, too. Mama said, "Religion hates fun things."

One day at my friend's house, her grandmother who was mostly blind, grabbed her heart and said, "Lord, Betty Ruth, your grandfather would turn over in his grave if he knew you were playing jacks. The Lord don't want you doing that."

She turned to me, "Take your jacks and that little red rubber ball and go home."

To me, jacks wasn't as sinful as playing the numbers which Mama and Aunt Burrell did every day the good Lord sent . . . except Sundays. The first thing they asked me each morning was, "What did you dream last night, baby?"

When I told them, Aunt Burrell would whip out that old, soiled, dream book which explained dreams. They didn't care about what they meant; they just wanted the three dream numbers next to it. My dream numbers went straight to their list. They loved that book more than they loved the Bible which neither of them owned. Then they smiled at me like I was special.

Aunt Burrell wrote their number lists on little bits of paper, in pencil. I ran them to the numbers lady on Star Street. I had to beat the pick-up man. Aunt Burrell said, "Dot, scraps is good. Not much for you to chew up and swallow, if the police stop you."

A numbers player was lucky to have a kid. The law hardly ever stopped us. If Mama won, hit the number, she gave me some change. If Aunt Burrell hit, I had to remind her she owed me.

Thanks to my grandmother and her sister, I was a criminal before I turned six.

If Betty Ruth's grandmother knew about all that, she'd move her to a new street to protect her from evil. I kept my lips sealed.

On movie nights, Tee and me ate supper real fast, without my daddy, and hurried to the theater. We always walked; never rode the bus. The fare paid for our popcorn. We went straight down West Thomas Street to Church and turned right. I really liked that street. I got to see different car license tags from up North. I could have stayed there on Church Street forever but I was with Tee. Mama didn't mind if I dawdled; she did it, too.

Tee and I walked down to Western Avenue but even before we turned left, the Center Theater's marquee pulled us to it. Another theater over on Main Street, the Cameo, had a marquee, too, but they didn't want any coloreds in there. We were kinda lucky the Center Theater's owner liked money and showed movies we wanted to see . . . *Imitation of Life* starring Lana Turner, *Leave Her to Heaven* with Gene Tierney playing the meanest woman ever.

True, it wasn't easy for us there. We had to climb a long flight of stairs to a tiny box office—a closet with only the bottom half of a door. The top part was open so the colored lady could sell us tickets, popcorn, candy, and drinks. With all our stuff, we climbed the second flight of stairs where the colored ticket taker stood. It was like going to heaven.

It was okay but I would've swapped my best marbles to buy tickets from the "under the marquee lady in the cute little box." Sometimes, I doubted she was real. She bore a close resemblance to the fake witch in the fortune telling machine outside Efird's department store on Main Street. There, I put a coin in the slot and my little fortune card slid out. Tee'd read it to me. I liked knowing my future and stuff like that.

One time someone was working roots, conjuring up spells, right there in our neighborhood. They did it to Zelda, a young girl who wasn't married. Whoever put the spell on her was mean. Maybe she was jealous of how pretty Zelda was or maybe she just didn't like her. Poor Zelda started having real bad headaches. No amount of Stanback in Pepsi Cola would make them go away. Then a miracle happened—her sister found some of Zelda's hair under their front porch steps. Nobody knew how it got there. But like the snapping of a finger, Zelda was cured.

People in my town did things like that, disliked somebody for no reason. Nobody in my family knew how to conjure but they knew what it could do. Mama said, "One night, Hat and Marie bundled up Burrell and took her out to the country to see a root doctor to get her cured."

And Mama just laughed like she would burst open. "Turned out, Burrell had been messing round with some men. Hat made her go to the real doctor by herself."

There was one movie theater where we could buy tickets under a pretty marquee, the Booker T. Theater. Colored people owned it and a colored young lady sold the tickets. We walked into their pretty lobby where popcorn jumped out of that machine and we bought whatever we wanted. At a nearby door, a young man took our tickets and we entered the dark theater with the big movie screen straight ahead. Best part of all was the colored audience. They acted right along with the movie, even yelled to the actors, "Watch out!"

So much fun. Before the movie ended, I was doing it, too. At the Center Theater, white people watched and kept quiet. We were always on our best behavior there; except a few boys threw trash and stuff to the lower balcony where some of them sat.

The Booker T. was across the railroad tracks that ran down the middle of Main Street, opposite a tobacco warehouse, near the end of a long block. Colored people and their businesses—Johnson's Barber Shop, Star Cab Company where Cool Breeze, our neighbor worked, a pool hall, two doctors' offices and two dental offices, Bryant's Photography Studio, and two drugstores on the two corners, took up the whole block. I loved the drug stores' white floor tiles and their cute wire ice cream parlor chairs and tables.

Everything looked so clean and pretty, it was special enough just being there but Tee made it even better. She bought me a tall dish of butter pecan ice cream with a long silver spoon. "This will make the time pass faster while our colored pharmacist fills our prescription. It sure beats standing and waiting over at Rexall's Drugstore. Can't even have a bite to eat at their lunch counter."

The whole section of town across the railroad tracks was called "acrosstown." Many more colored businesses were scattered about. Acrosstown wasn't like Happy Hill where we lived all scrunched up beside white people. It was just as prejudiced, but I saw a world that looked more like me. At the Booker T., Lena Horne, Ethel Waters, Bojangles starred in the movies. Everybody else was colored, too. They weren't just maids, butlers, or cooks; they were lawyers, doctors, teachers, everything.

I liked Tarzan movies, too; but not the endings. I fixed that. I made up my own game about him and played it all summer after dark. It always started with a chase through the shadows, around trees and bushes. Sometimes Mama yelled, "Watch out for my hot, smoking rag pot. It chases away the mosquitoes. They don't care for smoke."

Sometimes in the middle of running, a lightning bug caught my eye. Its glowing yellow part made the best ring if I pulled it off before it blinked or went dark. I put it on my finger real fast; it never glowed for very long. Sometimes when I put a bunch of lightning bugs in a jar, they would die.

In my game, the slowest runner had to be Tarzan. He was always in trouble. He got captured by us, the natives. We danced in a circle around poor Tarzan and chanted, "Men of fire have come to kill Tarzan."

We killed him every night.

I knew all about movies and movie stars. That's why on our very first day at Mr. Coggins' farm, I knew Tee was a star. He could tell she was special, too. She stood out from the rest of Mama's work crew—Aunt Sister Hattie, Aunt Burrell, Cousin Marie, and my teenage cousin, Olivia. Mr. Coggins could have picked any of them. Well, maybe not any of them. Cousin Marie, even though she was pretty and had long thick hair, was kinda heavy.

Tee, the cute one, got to drive Mr. Coggins' horse, Red. He pulled the tobacco truck from the field to the barn. It was the best job of all. I was so proud of Tee. She had never been in charge of a horse before. When Mr. Coggins asked her to do it, she didn't hesitate.

She was brave. To tell the truth, I was scared for her, especially when Guy, his teenage son, showed her how. He stood on his toes, at the very edge of the back of the truck, a wooden wheeled thing with burlap sides.

His barefoot heels were in the air. He held some skinny, long, leather straps which were tied to Red. Guy jerked those straps and yelled at him.

Mama said, "He runs that horse and tobacco truck like a bat out of hell."

I cringed when Tee took his spot. She was smart but I doubted she could do it. As she rolled away towards the tobacco field, I crossed my fingers. I was glad Guy walked beside Red.

Mama 'nem watched Tee disappear in the fat green leaves of the tobacco. I stared so hard; I didn't notice a white, red-haired girl about my size was close to me. Turned out, Mr. Coggins was her daddy. Her name was Hazel. We took to each other right away. We needed someone to play with. Color didn't matter to us.

We were getting to know each other—quietly staring, picking up a stick, finding some pretty rocks. Meanwhile her daddy explained

Tee's new job. She had to keep the tobacco truck in between two rows of tobacco. It had to be convenient for the primers who pulled the bottom tobacco leaves from the stalk to put them into the truck. Hazel's daddy said, "Tee has to be firm with Red. Let him know who's boss."

I worried about her; those straps looked too skinny for a horse.

[2]*Center Theater
Rocky Mount, NC
circa 1951*

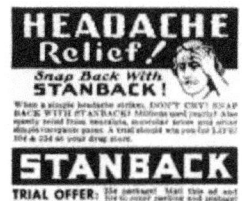

Headache products from the forties

[2]*Granola, "Center Theater," photograph,* cinematreasures.org, *http://cinematreasures.orgtheaters11713photos141416, (accessed July 26, 2023)*

Green Tobacco

I was proud of Tee driving Red, but I was jealous, too. She did it without me. We could have taken turns standing on the end of that aging tobacco truck. I couldn't pout long; Hazel was next to me. She had lots of freckles. We didn't talk, just kicked dirt all the way over to the edge of the tobacco field. The tobacco grew like the beanstalk Jack climbed. I touched a leaf—it was wet and sticky.

"Tobacco is real gummy," she said and disappeared into the tobacco field. She thought I would follow her but I stayed put. I didn't like tobacco.

Suddenly she was back, ducking under the leaves. A fat, green worm wiggled between two of her fingers. I liked the skinny worms Mama used for bait, not that ugly thing.

"If I smash him, gooey stuff comes out."

I squeezed my eyes shut. But I peeked. She tossed that worm a long way from her daddy's green tobacco. After that, we just stood around. She didn't say anything, me neither.

From out of nowhere, a rumbling noise came. Tee's voice sounded, "Whoa, Red. That's a good boy."

We couldn't see her. Oh, no—she had to be walking. She couldn't do that. Mama 'nem would tease her. Then I saw her. Hot dog! She was taller than the stalks of tobacco. Tee remembered to ride on the back of the truck.

Me and Hazel took off to meet her. She was born to drive a horse. I bet she could ride one, too. Sam, Tee, and me could join the circus. Travel everywhere. Be in parades . . . "Dot, come on!" Hazel shouted.

When Tee drove Red under the shelter everybody cheered. Then it was work time for them. Two hands, Cousin Olivia and Aunt Sister Hattie, and one looper, Cousin Marie, got to one side of the wagon. Mama and

Mr. Coggins were the hands on the other side. Aunt Burrell was the looper. The hands lowered the two burlap sides of the wagon. The loopers put a skinny wooden stick on a wooden stand. Then they looped the string, which ran down from the ceiling, onto one end of the stick.

By then, the hands held three huge leaves by the stems in their fists. They flung them at the loopers who snatched them, whirled the string around the stems, and slid them down onto the stick. I was so close and stared so hard, gritty water from the tobacco hit me in my eyes. Boy, did that sting. I couldn't see and rubbing made it worse. Someone grabbed my shirt and pulled me backwards, away from the tobacco. I opened one eye a tiny bit. Hazel stood next to me.

The hands and loopers filled the sticks with tobacco, fast. Cousin Olivia took their stick to the nearby rack and hung it at the very top. When Hazel's daddy took theirs, we followed him. As soon as he got out of the way, we climbed on the wooden racks and acted like monkeys.

Hazel talked just like the hillbilly music Tee listened to on the radio. "This whole rack has to be filled up."

That rack was tall and long. Picking up one leaf at a time would take forever.

We hung around for a while. Then she began pushing dirt around with her bare feet. I gazed at her house on stilts. It stood alone. The closest house was across the red dirt road we came in on. Hazel started drifting towards her house. I followed. A tall, skinny, brown-haired white woman walked towards us.

Hazel said, "Mama, is it alright if I show Dot my dolls?"

"Why yes, Hazel. That sounds like a fun thing for you girls to do."

Hazel grinned at me and took off running. I started after her but slowed down to look at her mother. She had a sweet smile, but her chest kinda sucked in like she had TB. But she didn't cough like her husband.

Still, it would be a good idea for both of them to go into town on Main Street, in front of the bank, and walk into that big white bus with the government's name on it. They took x-rays for free. No TB; fine. If they had it—off to the TB ward.

After I knew her better, I'd tell her. Another thing crossed my mind. This was the first time I'd ever been up close to poor white people. They weren't all that bad. Matter of fact, I could grow to like them. Of course, no self-respecting, colored maid would ever work for them. They just weren't rich enough.

I was so excited about getting to see inside Hazel's house that I followed her right through her front door. She didn't notice so I acted like I did it every day, use white folks' front door. The living room came first. No furniture like rich white people had and not as nice as Mama's. But it was real clean and that's what everybody said mattered, cleanliness.

Hazel's room was right off the kitchen. We could have played right there if we wanted to, but we decided to play outside.

"Dot, I'm taking my favorite doll. You can pick whichever one you want from the rest."

I looked for a colored one; all she had were white dolls. A doll with dark brown hair was my choice.

Tee had told me colored dolls were real hard to find. I was lucky. I had three.

"And get some doll clothes, too. Mama made them on her sewing machine."

I thought they came from Woolworth's. Mama sewed a lot of my doll clothes by hand; she didn't own a sewing machine. She probably didn't know how to use one, 'cause Papa would have given her one.

I decided not to tell Mama about them. She'd work her fingers to the bone to make my pile bigger.

I was lucky on the first day of green tobacco. I found a friend who loved dolls as much as I did. We set up a playhouse under a big tree, around its roots. I decided to go barefoot, without my sandals, like Hazel. She was one year older than me and knew things.

Tee

One day Mama asked me, "Who do you love the best, Tee or Sam?"
I loved both of them. They were my mother and daddy.
"Dorothy Leigh . . ."
I looked at her.
"Who do you love the best?" She raised her voice. "Pick one."
I put my hands between my legs and wiggled, like I had to pee real bad and ran to the bathroom. I counted to five and flushed the toilet. Why did Mama want me to choose? That wasn't nice. We were supposed to treat everybody the same. But that didn't happen in my town.

In a store on Main Street colored people like me had to drink water from an ugly fountain stuck on a wall. Right beside it was a big, pretty new one. Tee said it was for white people only.

I knew something else, too. One time Tee and me were walking to Aunt Sister Hattie's house with the big white letters on the roof. I wanted to show her what I could do. I said, "Tee, watch me skip all the way to the corner."

"Can you skip, Punjab?" She called me that when she loved me a lot. I think she got the name from the funny papers. Anyway, I skipped my very best right past two big white kids playing in their front yard. One of them yelled, "Hey, you little nigger."

I stopped skipping and ran as fast as I could to the corner. But the mean, ugly word followed me, stuck to me. I knew it was bad 'cause one night my daddy said, "Tee, some old white cracker called me a nigger today." He was very mad.

At the corner I was scared. Nobody ever said that to me before. As I waited for Tee, I decided not to tell her. Even my daddy couldn't fix things like that.

I learned more about differences one night at Aunt Burrell's. No one else was there, just us. Since I lived across the street, I visited her whenever I liked. That night, there was a knock at the door. She said, "That must be him. He is right on time, too."

When she unlatched the screen door, a man holding a little kid said, "Here I am, Miss Burrell. I brought Alice with me. That way you can see for yourself."

Aunt Burrell got the man settled in a chair while I stared at a skinny little, light-skinned girl with tiny puffs of hair on her head. She looked real pitiful.

My aunt reached for her. "How old is she?"

"Just turned two. My wife took and ran off. Left me with five little children. I found homes for my four older ones. But with Alice being so sick and all . . .. My boss already docked my pay two times."

Aunt Burrell rocked Alice in her arms. I got closer. One tiny hand slipped out of the blanket. I reached out to touch It; but pulled back in time. I squeezed my hands together. I didn't want to break her on accident.

My aunt took her time. Poor Alice. Mama always said, "Sometimes sick people are already at death's door."

I wondered. Should Aunt Burrell keep her? Where would she sleep? She looked too long for a basket thing. My aunt's place was tiny, only two rooms and one was the kitchen. The toilet was outdoors, stuck onto the duplex on the other side. I hated that toilet, its spring seat stuck up in the air. For a long time, I wasn't heavy enough to make it go down. There was no flush handle. I had to jump down off the seat to make it flush. The noise was loud. Gobs of water gargled down and ran out through a hole at the bottom. It could take me away but I was too fast.

Alice couldn't do that; she wore diapers. Her daddy said so. Aunt Burrell tried to sit her up on the bed. She started to fall. Aunt Burrell propped her up with some pillows. Her daddy said, "I ran out of food. She may be hungry."

Aunt Burrell would give her plenty of food, if she kept her. Still, she might die.

Suddenly, her daddy kissed her forehead and left.

I couldn't run home and tell everybody. Alice might die before they came over. I stayed put.

Aunt Burrell got a quilt from the cedar chest and made a pallet on the floor for Little Alice. I sat down close to her on the linoleum. As soon as my aunt left the room, I lifted one of her hands with toothpick fingers. I was about to touch her hair when Aunt Burrell came back with a bowl of oatmeal. Feeding her was messy. I ran home to tell the news.

By the time I finished, it was bedtime. Tee said, "Little Alice's daddy was too poor to take care of her. Sometimes people, like your Aunt Burrell, take care of babies. That kinda happened to me."

I stopped pulling up my pajama pants. "That's not true. Nobody gave you to Papa and Mama. You always belonged to them. Just like Uncle Rhone."

She smiled. "You're right." Then she sighed. "Too much excitement for one night. Now say your prayers."

I buttoned my shirt. Why was she making up a story like that? Adopted. Then I remembered the prayer thing. She practiced me on that. First, I got on my knees. God didn't listen if you stood up. Then, Tee's scary poem . . . I forgot the words. To keep her from being sad, I said, "I'm big enough to say my prayers to myself. Like Sam does."

"Are you sure, Punjab?"

I nodded, got on my knees, and whispered, "Now I lay me down to sleep. Little Bo Peep has lost her sheep and can't tell where to find them. Amen." And I hopped into bed. Tee was so happy; she grinned and kissed my cheek. "Little Bo Peep" was so much better. God 'nem didn't want me having bad dreams.

Before I fell asleep, I thought about adopted. I knew kids who lived with their grandparents. They would go back to their mother or father or both of them, when times got better. But nobody gave them away to strangers. We weren't supposed to even talk to strangers. Look at what happened to Little Red Riding Hood.

There was lots of talk in the family about Aunt Burrell taking in Little Alice. I heard Mama tell Aunt Sister Hattie, "Why you reckon Burrell would take in a baby so close to death as that?"

"That's her plan. She'll take out a policy on her. When she goes, which looks like any day, Burrell will whip out that thing and collect in no time."

Little Alice didn't die. I was glad. I liked having her around. When company came, they gave her all their attention and left me alone. I hardly ever had to say "How do you do."

Every morning, Aunt Burrell brought her over to Mama's to drink her bottle. A lot of times I had one, too. I liked it. One day, Aunt Burrell mixed up the bottles. I knew it right away. She loved playing tricks. Like the time when I had chicken pox she said, "Dot, go in the hen house let the chickens jump on you. That chicken pox will go away."

I didn't go. I certainly didn't trust her about the milk bottles. She said, "It was an accident." Under her breath, she whispered, "Bottles don't matter; it's the same milk."

I never had another bottle.

Aunt Burrell saved Little Alice's life with Pet milk and big jars of nasty medicines, creomulsion, and cod liver oil. She put pretty little dresses on her, bought her a cute little girl's bed, and gave her a stuffed animal to sleep with. I knew everything that went on. I was there every day, all day, except when it was time to eat.

Aunt Burrell was so proud of saving her, she said, "Tee, I'm having Alice's picture made. Do you want one of Dot, too?"

"What a great idea, Burrell. Punjab, we're gonna get you all fixed up in Shirley Temple curls."

I liked the idea; I saw Shirley Temple dance with Bojangles in a movie.

"You'll have to go to the hairdresser's."

I was dropped off at Cousin Marie's in Little Raleigh. She took me to her hairdresser's house. "I'll come back when you're all cute in your curls."

As soon as she stepped off the porch, the hairdresser lady led me to her kitchen. I remembered Tee's poem about a spider and a fly. The spider invited the fly in and ate him up. I was scared but I had to be polite.

She put a big book on a wooden chair, "Climb up here, honey."

I did.

A big frown covered her face and she took me down. After piling on another book and a pillow, she said, "Upsy-daisy."

I was perched way up high like a bird. It got real hot next to her cook stove. Nobody let me even walk near a hot stove at home.

"Now, baby, don't move."

I almost cried. "Okay."

And she turned to me with a hot, smoking comb. "You're gonna be so pretty when I'm done, your mother won't know you."

"Little Bo Peep . . ."

"After I straighten your hair, I'm putting in those pretty Shirley Temple curls. Now be still."

Smoke was everywhere. She was burning me up. "Baby, hold your ear on this side."

Finally, after a lot of ear holding and clicking of the curling iron, the hairdresser lady said, "There, your Shirley Temple curls are done."

Cousin Marie picked me up. Somebody else in the family would take me home to Tee. I looked at my curls in her big round dresser mirror, a strange little girl had on my clothes. She didn't look like Shirley Temple either.

By the time I got home, I liked them. I pulled the curls . . . they jumped back up. But Tee looked at them funny. "Why are they so loose?"

I was as quiet as a mouse. Before she could ask me more, Sam came home from work. I ran to him. He picked me up, stopped, and said, "What happened to my baby?"

"You don't love me anymore." And I burst into tears.

"Where is your mother?"

I pointed to the kitchen. "Christine, I'll never ever forgive you for messing up my daughter's hair."

"I'm messed up forever!"

The next morning, Tee dressed me up in my blue corduroy jumper and a white starched, short-sleeve blouse with a Peter Pan collar. I wore blue striped socks. She tied a pretty blue and pink ribbon on one of my curls. Last of all, my gold cross, Sam's Valentine's present (Tee got a gold heart), went around my neck. She smiled at me a long time.

Then we went across the street to Aunt Burrell's. Alice looked cute in a white dress, white shoes, white socks, and a white ribbon in her pitiful little hair. We sat together in the back seat. All that medicine Aunt Burrell poured into her worked. But she still couldn't crawl. Off we went to the white photographer downtown. The colored one was in New York until times got better.

At the photographer's, Aunt Burrell said, "Alice goes first. Babies get tired in a hurry."

The photographer put her on a blanket on the floor. She sat up real good for a minute.

Then she headed down. Quickly, he propped her up and took three pictures. He rushed back to lay her on her stomach. Aunt Burrell sprang up like a Jack-in-the-box. "Alice will be sitting up alone."

So that was that.

On my turn, he pulled out a big brown bench. "Dorothy, come sit in the middle."

I was a little scared but obeyed. I swung my dangling feet back and forth. Suddenly, the photographer stopped backing up to his camera, frowned real funny, and rushed back to me. He twisted my head to the side, backed up again, and held up both of his hands. "Don't move." By the time, he reached his camera, I was tired. So, I pressed my hands down on the bench to hold myself up.

"No," he said and shook his head from side to side. Then he rushed over to me and crossed my legs without asking me first. He backed up to his camera and cocked his head to the side like the illy-formed kid on Star Street. Suddenly, he ran back to me. At first, he couldn't talk. Finally, he said, "Hold your hands like I'm holding mine."

I copied him.

"Now put them in your lap." He smiled, cocked his head from side to side, and backed up.

I thought he was ready to take my picture. No. He popped out from behind his camera to look at me. Then stretched out his hand so hard, his fingers came way apart. "Don't move." From behind his camera, he said, "Smile."

I did no such thing.

Lots of times I didn't understand my mother. She acted like she wanted to give me away to anybody who said I was special—different. I was nervous around people. They thought I was shy. I just wanted to stay with my daddy and my grandmother. Any day, Tee might say to her friends or some stranger, "You like Dorothy? You can either borrow her or you can have her. Take her home with you. Let her spend the night. Two nights. Sure, it's okay."

Maybe she was proud of me. Maybe she forgot I was real, not a doll. One time on Main Street we bumped into a friend of hers. I spoke to her nicely. The friend said, "Where did you get Dot?"

What did she mean? Kids didn't come from no store. I waited for Tee to tell her how silly she was but Tee just acted like she knew a secret. I wondered—am I somebody else's child?

Her friend got all happy and clapped her hands. "I know. You raised her up North. That's why she speaks so proper."

She was wrong. I belonged exactly where I was, in Mama's house. I slept with her. Except one time when Tee talked me into spending the night at Aunt Sister Hattie's house. Cousin Marie and Olivia, Aunt Sister Hattie's teenage granddaughter, invited me. I really liked Olivia. She always took me with her to visit her real mother who lived on Star Street. We went every Sunday afternoon even when it was cold outside.

As usual, it was a long walk to Aunt Sister Hattie's house. Once we got there, we had fun just like Cousin Marie promised. I played with Olivia's old toys. At bedtime, we ran to the outhouse one last time before we put on our pajamas.

Olivia said, "It's Grimm's fairy tale time."

The story was about a princess who couldn't sleep. There was a pea in her bed. My cousin talked like the princess and everybody. I loved listening to her. We snuggled up together on the daybed in Aunt Sister Hattie's room.

The princess and the prince got married. Olivia closed the book and got up to put it away. It was too bad her book didn't have pictures. All of a sudden, the room went black. I yelled, "Cut that light back on!"

It came right back on; Olivia held the ceiling light string. I cried. Cousin Marie came a-running. "Olivia, what happened? Did the story scare her?"

"No."

Aunt Sister Hattie grumbled from her big brass bed, "She just started crying. Olivia didn't scare her. Smithie 'nem done ruined that child."

"Now S'tattie . . ."

That's what Cousin Marie called her mother.

Mama, Aunt Burrell, everybody except Tee called her S'tattie, too. I never knew why.

Aunt Sister Hattie said, "I know what I'm talking 'bout. Her grandpa, Alva, thought sugar wouldn't melt in Dorothy's mouth. He did the same thing to Tee, her mother, spoiled both of them rotten. But he ruined . . ."

"Hush, S'tattie. None of that can be helped now."

I cried louder.

Cousin Marie said, "What's the matter, Dot, baby?"

"I want Tee."

They all looked at each other. Aunt Sister Hattie sat up.

"Take me home."

Cousin Marie pointed. "Oh look, Dot, you're making Olivia cry."

I stood on the floor. "Take me home right now."

They ran around getting my stuff together. Nobody got dressed; just put coats on over their pajamas. Olivia looked at me and shook her head. Cousin Marie breathed loudly when she put on her shoes.

I felt better. I was going home to Tee. I could hardly wait to ask Mama to wake me up when Papa's ghost came. I wanted to tell him exactly what Aunt Sister Hattie said. She didn't like Papa. He'd fix her for hurting my feelings, too.

Cousin Marie wrapped a blanket around me. They had me out the door fast. She plopped me down on Olivia's bicycle. That worried me. I couldn't pedal a bike. My legs were too short.

Cousin Marie said, "Dot, hold the handle bars."

I got worried. Big kids said that to little kids, too. Told them, "We'll hold on. We promise." Then they gave the bike a big push followed by, "Pedal! Pedal real fast!"

Lucky for me, Cousin Marie kept her promise. Tee was surprised but happy to see me. Then Cousin Marie and Olivia got on the bike and I waved goodbye.

My mother's family loved gospel singing. Our church, Mount Zion First Baptist and Aunt Burrell's church, St. James, were on different corners of West Thomas Street. Mama said, "They're too high falutin' to sing spirituals. Their songs leave us hungry, itching for something."

They found what they wanted in Norfolk at Aunt Leatha's (Jiggs' mother's) church. I never wanted to go but the grown-ups were all for it, especially Mama who loved to ride. Usually, she, Aunt Sister Hattie, Cousin Marie, Tee, Little Alice, and me crammed into Aunt Burrell's car on a Saturday afternoon. Three hours later, we parked on Wood Street's cobblestones.

Aunt Leatha 'nem lived on the second floor. Not long after we got there, they spread out tons of seafood—oysters, shrimp, soft-shelled crabs—on newspapers, in the middle of the kitchen table. Hands reached in from everywhere. Come night, we slept wherever we could lay our heads.

Sunday mornings, I got in line for the bathroom. It was shared with the family downstairs. As I waited my turn, I could smell fried chicken, browned beef short ribs, fresh greens, homemade rolls, banana pudding with vanilla wafers and golden-brown meringue coming from my aunt's kitchen. Wouldn't eat any of it until after the spirituals and preaching at church.

Except for the seafood, I hated visiting Aunt Leatha; I was scared of her cat. I heard a radio story on the Inner Sanctum Mystery Hour about a killing cat. For most of the visits, I curled up in a chair in the front bedroom. I didn't want that cat sneaking up on me.

I had another reason—the smelly bathroom. Even though I got real thirsty, I only took sips of water.

Last of all, there was no screen in their kitchen window. Flies and moths flew in. A fly swatter wouldn't work. Aunt Leatha 'nem didn't seem to mind. The window was handy for throwing scraps down to the big rats below.

I frowned a lot on those visits; Tee acted like she didn't know me but Mama shook with laughter every time she looked at me. I was lucky Aunt Burrell didn't know how I felt; she would have teased me forever. In spite of her joking and teasing, I liked her. She was funny. One time, Cousin Marie said, "Burrell owns a car and ain't got driver's license the first."

Aunt Burrell said, "Driver's licenses are for people who don't know how to drive. I've driven all my life."

She liked to recite poems by heart. One time, she acted out a poem by Paul Lawrence Dunbar, a colored poet. She said, "I'm doing it right up there in the pulpit in my church."

Tee and I went. I crossed my fingers, on both hands, hoping she wouldn't mess up. She did good in practice. At her church that Sunday afternoon, Aunt Burrell was perfect. Tee said so. It was funny, too. Not like Tee's poems by white men. They were all scary or sad.

One Sunday, Aunt Burrell took me to her church after the regular service. I thought she was religious but she said, "I go for the fellowship."

Tee was helping me get ready. "Dorothy Leigh, you are going to something real special today with Burrell."

If it was all that special, why wasn't she coming, too? She certainly wasn't busy, just resting with Sam. Good for her. I didn't want to rest when there was somewhere to go.

She started plaiting my hair. "You are so lucky . . . going to see an important man from way up North, Mr. Walter White." She tied a blue ribbon on my top plait. "He's the head of the NAACP, the National Association for the Advancement of Colored People."

"I never heard of it. Is he as important as Sister Rosetta Tharpe?"

Tee tried to turn me around, to tie my sash. I didn't budge. She twisted me by my shoulders. "The NAACP is very important to us colored people in the South. Lots of mean things happen down here. White people do awful things, hang colored men, men like your daddy, for no reason."

"Nobody wants to hurt my sweet daddy who brings me presents."

"Dorothy Leigh, there are some mean white folks in this world. They burn crosses in colored people's front yards. Even burn down their houses with them inside."

My almost six-year-old mouth hung open.

She pushed my jaw back up. "The NAACP tries to get justice for us. They want the judge to punish those evil white people who do mean things."

"It's too late then; they already killed the colored people."

"Yes. But the NAACP also wants to make sure nothing like that ever happens again. Now don't you worry, nobody in our family has ever been hurt. Papa's family was freedmen."

"Can the mean white people tell the difference? Is my daddy freed, too?"

Tee was quiet.

"Are my friends' daddies freedmen, too?"

"That's what the NAACP does, protects every colored person's rights."

Rights didn't seem to be for us. The more I thought about it though, I liked the NAACP. It could help us with our city buses. We didn't ride a lot. But one time we moved to the back 'cause a white person came on after we did. If white people wanted to sit up front, they should get there early. I bet the NAACP man could explain that to them. Maybe he could find good jobs for Tee and Sam. Mama said, "Jesus Christ ain't helping one bit."

I was glad she practiced me on saying "How do you do." I'd say that to Mr. Walter White.

In Aunt Burrell's church, I stared so hard at the people on the pulpit, I almost missed the pew. Which one of the men was Mr. White? I couldn't see the man sitting behind the preacher's stand. Maybe that was him. When they introduced him, a white man stood up.

He didn't know nothing. He might be one of the burners, the hangers. When we were riding over, Aunt Burrell said, "Those mean white people would be the police or the sheriff. Coming out at night under white sheets, hiding their ugly selves. I don't trust 'em."

"Is that why you ran over that motorcycle policeman that time?"

She didn't answer.

"Mr. Walter White is really white."

"Like a lot of colored people in town. Get them up North, they pass for white."

I listened to him. Tee was right. He talked about our rights, told some sad stories, and some scary stories. I was sure to have bad dreams.

At the end of the program, I didn't get to say "How do you do" and shake his hand. Too many grownups crowded around him. I was happy though. He wanted good things for us now; not in heaven.

Aunt Burrell dried her eyes with her white, lace handkerchief, pulled me up to a small table near the pulpit, and joined the NAACP.

On the way home, I said, "Is Mr. Walter White colored or white?"

She laughed. "It don't matter how he looks. If he's got a drop of colored blood in him, he's ours."

I knew one thing, he and the NAACP were doing a whole lot more than God. Mama was right about religion.

Me with Shirley Temple curls

Tee & me

Alice

Hattie, Marie & Olivia

(l-r) Roy Wilkens, Walter White and Adam Clayton Powell

Talks with Tee

I was real close to six when Tee began our talks in the kitchen. One day when we were alone, she just started teaching me stuff. I pretended it was our clubhouse. *What can we name our club? Will I learn to bake cookies or make Jell-O?*

No, no. Tee taught me French songs: "Sur le Pont d'Avignon," "Frère Jacques," and "La Marseillaise" - the French national anthem.

"Punjab, when I was in high school, I loved French and Latin."

Although I was proud of her, I didn't know nobody who spoke French. I wondered when our club stuff, the secret codes, and handshakes would start. I didn't ask her; I just waited. Good thing, too. She didn't jump into things like Mama; she took a round-about way. One talk when I was eating a vanilla wafer, she said, "Rhone wanted to name me Mabel Dorothy Christine."

"Uncle Rhone was silly. That was too long."

"Papa stepped in and named me 'Christine.'"

"What did Mama say?"

"Said it was up to him."

Then she got real quiet. I stared out the kitchen window. Watched people walk by on Star Street, counted them. I was up to five when she spoke again like I wasn't there. I wasn't sure if I should listen.

Softly she said, "Before you were born, before you began to kick and play around in my stomach, I read poetry to you."

How silly . . . reading to your stomach. But I didn't say it.

"Punjab, while waiting for you, I always thought good thoughts. Only you know that."

I held my breath. Tee smiled the prettiest ever. I felt warm all over. I was her special present. Right there, I promised to be the best child I could be, forever and ever, amen.

Another kitchen story was about a lady named Laney. I thought she was a family friend or a distant relative. Turned out she was dead.

"When Laney, another one of Mama's little sisters, came to live with her and Papa, she was a teenager. Aunt Sister Hattie raised all their other baby brothers and sisters after their mother died. But Mama took Laney, with her prissy self."

"How was she prissy?"

"Punjab, she dressed up in her Sunday best to cook supper. Everybody teased her. But Laney wasn't studyin' them. To get away, she moved all the way up North to New York City."

"Is anybody else prissy?"

"Well let me think. Hmmm. Yes, there is."

"Who?"

"Rhone's wife, Louella."

"What's prissy about her?"

"She wears real high heeled shoes with the toes out and her face is always made up."

She likes to curtsy, too. I saw her do it in Baltimore.

One time when we visited Uncle Rhone and Aunt Louella in Baltimore, she made a special supper, kidney stew. It smelled awful. I looked across the table at Tee. Her lips made a straight line. She wanted my frown to turn into a smile. I couldn't; the kidney stew smelled like our garbage truck. I watched Aunt Louella put the big bowl of it on the table. Mama, Tee, and Uncle Rhone said, "Ooh, aah."

Aunt Louella was so happy, she curtsied.

Uncle Rhone winked at her and began fixing our plates. "Here's yours, baby."

I stared at the brown, stinky meat with slimy onions and burst into tears.

"What's wrong with my baby?"

"My daddy serves me steak."

Sometime after that, I went up North again. Nobody said where. Just said, "We're going to visit Uncle Rhone."

I didn't want to go there because of the kidney stew.

Mama said, "Baby, don't you want to go see your funny old uncle? Don't you want him to tickle you?"

I buttoned my lips.

Tee pulled me out of Mama's room. Dragged me to the back porch, put her face real close to mine, squeezed my shoulders, "You listen to me, little girl. Mama loves Rhone to death. She sold the farm back in Whitesville to send him money right after Papa died. She wants to visit him, her blood son. You better act nice. Understand?"

I nodded yes.

When we walked back in, Mama said, "Dot, you're going to love this train trip. It will be our longest one yet. We're going farther than Baltimore. Rhone moved all the way up to Boston."

"I don't want to be going to no Boston."

Tee shoved me out of the room.

I was not in a good mood. Maybe I got up on the wrong side of the bed. Maybe I didn't care about drinking icy cold water out of pointed paper cups. Didn't like the cute step the conductor put down for us to get on the train.

Finally, Tee cooled down. "Dorothy Leigh, Mama loves Rhone very much. Papa used to say too much. No matter now. My papa's dead and gone." She was quiet. "Shucks, I guess you're old enough. You know what? Mama always believes everything Rhone says."

It sounded like secret stuff.

"One time Rhone sent her a Western Union telegram from up North. Said he was dead and to send money to a funeral parlor. They would ship his body home."

"Was he really dead?"

"No. But Mama believed it. She started crying and carrying on. I said, 'Mama, you know ain't nothing happened to Rhone. He just wants money.' She said, 'Hush your mouth. How dare you talk about my son like that. He is my blood.'"

"Did she listen to you?"

"No, she said, 'Here, run down to Western Union and send this money so they can ship my boy home.' I told her the funeral director, Stokes, could go up North, pick up Rhone's body and bring it back."

"What did she say?"

"She said, 'Tee, you're so smart. We'll do that.'"

"Stokes can tell when somebody's dead. He knew Papa was dead. Remember?"

"Un huh. While we waited for Stokes' return, Mama cried all the time. In three days, he came back—without Rhone. He wasn't dead at all."

"What did Mama do?"

"Thanked me for saving her money and cursed like a sailor. She swore to never trust Rhone again. Now, Dorothy Leigh, don't ever say bad words like Mama. You hear me?"

I nodded yes.

We headed back to Mama's room. On the way, I remembered how much I loved riding the train. When we walked in, I said, "Mama, let's not go to Boston. Let's go down to see Papa's family. Like you and me do all the time. Can we, Mama?"

She kept quiet.

"Edith is lucky; she gets to live with her Grandmother Dorothy." I kissed Mama. "She lets her do whatever she wants. I really like Edith. We sing 'O Holy Night' just like angels. Remember, Mama?"

She smiled.

"I promise, Edith and me won't make faces behind Aunt Thalia's back—even though she does look like a witch."

Mama's lips twitched.

"When you make us visit, we'll just sit nicely." As I stood up, I said under my breath, "I bet Aunt Thalia wasn't no schoolteacher either; she's mean. That's why me and Edith don't like her."

Tee said, "Dorothy Leigh, Mama wants to see Rhone. He's in Boston. So that's where we're going."

She didn't spare Mama either. "Now you see how you have spoiled her. She thinks she's grown."

Mama stared at Tee and walked out of the room. I was hot on her trail; Tee yanked me back. "You just sit your little self right down. I'm not finished with you, young lady."

A few days later, Aunt Burrell drove us to the train station. While Tee and Mama sat in the tiny colored waiting room, I walked to the door, peeked into the white folks' side. It was as big as our church. The coloreds and the whites had the same long wooden benches but they had more. Even their lunch counter was nicer. I was looking for more differences when I heard the big wagon loaded with trunks, suitcases, and boxes, going down to the tracks.

Hot dog! Our train was coming. Sure enough, the train's whistle sounded. I ran back to Tee and Mama. A porter helped us board the train. I didn't tell Tee she was wrong about Boston; it was not up North, only New York was.

She said, "Punjab, we'll be changing trains in Washington, D.C. That's where President Roosevelt and his wife live in the White House. You remember . . . we listen to his fireside chats on the radio."

Much later, just before we got off the first train from our hometown, Tee said, "Dorothy Leigh, we're about to cross the Mason-Dixon Line. From this point on, everything will be different. We're almost up North."

I got excited. I had no idea what the Mason-Dixon Line was. I didn't know which things would be different either.

Mama hugged me. "Now we can sit wherever we want to."

"Can we make a Mason-Dixon Line for our buses?"

They looked at each other and back at me.

"That way Mr. Walter White can spend his time on the burnings and killings."

They didn't have an answer. I went back to looking out the window until the outside was hidden. We were in a tunnel. Soon the train stopped. It was an inside place. At home, it stopped outside. Tee was right about the Mason-Dixon Line. We grabbed our suitcases, picked up the shoe box with the rest of our lunch—a fried chicken leg, two deviled eggs, some goodies, and hurried off the train.

We followed the other people. It was a really long walk, past our train and another train on the next track. As we walked along, I felt funny; not like myself. I looked up at people's faces. Tee was right; things were different. Coloreds and whites rushed along side by side; not touching. They didn't speak to each other, just bunched in together. The ones who got off first, got to be at the head of the line. It didn't matter how much color anybody had.

I wished someone had showed me that Mason-Dixon Line when we crossed it. It was more important than a street corner. It took away meanness like a dust rag.

I wanted to skip but it was too crowded. In no time, we came to a beautiful place. I must have been dreaming. It was the most wonderful thing I'd ever seen in my whole life—lots of shiny, gold handrails, wide stone stair steps, beautiful lights, fat round posts, hard floors—like a castle. There were tons of stores and places to eat. Colored and white people went every which a way. There were bunches of soldiers and sailors. I stopped and stared.

Tee reached back for me. "This is Union Station."

She found out where to catch our next train, the one to Boston. Just before that, she needed to go upstairs. For Mama's sake and her slow walking, Tee had us wait right where we were with the suitcases.

She ran over to climb the nearby stairs. She stepped on the first stair step—it brought her back down to us and vanished. I had never seen anything like it before in my life. Tee didn't give up; she ran up two stairs. Back she came. Another time she skipped one of the stairs; It didn't work either.

The people on the stairs kept coming down to Tee. She couldn't pass them or break through the crowd. Nobody else was having problems.

I squeezed Mama's hand. "They've got things all backwards here at the Mason-Dixon Line."

She nodded but kept staring at Tee.

I said, "Maybe we don't need a Mason-Dixon Line back home."

A man coming off the stairs told Tee, "Go to the other one, the up escalator."

Escalator? They were mixed up. There was no such a thing.

Tee yelled to us, "I'm going to the 'up escalator.'"

We laughed about that all the way to Boston. Escalator. Back home, we only had elevators in a few stores and in the hospitals. But as coloreds, we only used the store elevators. Colored people ran them. At the hospitals, the colored wards were always in the basement, at street level, or in a nearby one-story house called the colored ward. No, we didn't know a thing about escalators.

Later, on that Boston train, whites and coloreds sat in the same car. Nothing happened at all. Nobody melted away. Nobody grew long noses. Nobody.

Laney & friend

Passenger car

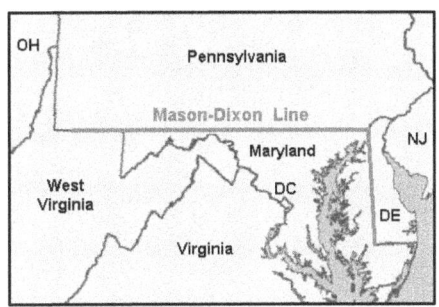

[3]*Mason Dixon Line Map*

Luggage wagon/cart

[4]*Union Station, Washington, D.C.*

³United States Department of the Interior, Public domain, via Wikimedia Commons, GIF, commons.wikimedia.org, *https://commons.wikimedia.org/wiki/File:Mason-dixon-line.gif,* (accessed April 17, 2023)

⁴Jack Boucher, Public domain, via Wikimedia Commons, photograph, commons.wikimedia.org, *https://commons.wikimedia.org/wiki/File:21._INTERIOR,_WAITING_ROOM_-_Union_Station030030pv.jpg,* (accessed April 17, 2023)

Partiality

Long after our Boston vacation, our secret club met again in Mama's kitchen. Tee talked about dead Laney. I didn't want to hear about her but it wasn't polite to say that.

"Laney didn't like any of these people."

"What people?"

"Her family, her sisters and brothers. Laney got as far away from them as she possibly could, all the way to New York." Tee was quiet for a while. I stopped watching her and started to leave the kitchen. But she slammed the muffin pan down on the sink drain board, rumbled through the cooking ladles and spoons. "The rest of them followed her."

"But not Mama, not Aunt Burrell, not Aunt Sister . . ."

"Enough of them did."

I buttoned my lips.

"When Laney died, they all split up her things. Nice things. Beautiful shoes, fancy dresses, expensive jewelry, a real fur stole. Aunt Sister Hattie got Laney's wonderful brass bed with the four great, big balls."

"She still has it; she sleeps in it every night."

Tee banged down a pot on the stove. "Nobody offered me anything."

"Sam will buy you pretty things, just ask him. You'll see. And I'll ask Aunt Sister Hattie if she wouldn't mind . . ."

"She was my real mother—Laney."

She cried real tears, while I stood there not knowing what to say. She was still crying when I asked, "Why didn't Laney take you up North, to New York, with her?"

"Papa and Mama wouldn't let her have me. Said I'd be too much of a responsibility."

"Nobody can take a baby away from her mother."

"After she made some money, Laney came back for me. But Papa wouldn't let me go. She went back to New York by herself. She still couldn't take care of me. She was a hairdresser."

Olivia, my teenage cousin, once told me, "Everybody loved your granddaddy. He used to take care of me while my grandmother and Marie worked."

I almost shared that with Tee but she started talking again.

"Mama said Papa just spoiled me something awful. Anything I wanted, toys, pretty dresses, candy, anything. One Christmas eve, I said, 'I sure hope Santa Claus brings me that walking and talking doll tomorrow. Papa rushed out of the house, rode his bicycle downtown before the stores closed. Next morning, there was the doll under the Christmas tree."

Everything but your real mother.

On another kitchen talk day, Tee said, "We didn't have any colleges in town. Everybody drove up to Durham or Raleigh or Elizabeth City. I found a college up North in Delaware. I wanted to get a long way from here."

"Is Delaware in New York?"

"No. But it's not far from it. I wanted to become a nurse."

"Just like the nurses where Sam is an orderly." Tee would have looked real nice in that blue cape with the white cap on her head and white dress.

"I was going to college. That's what Papa's family did—go to college."

"Mama's family, too."

"No. Nobody on her side went to college. They didn't have a lot of money. Some of them never even went to high school."

I tried to think of something to say.

"Anyway, to earn college money, I began working as a maid after school."

"You were smart, Tee."

"Each time I got paid, I gave it all to Mama to save for me. Things were different back then. After 1929, the banks weren't safe. I worked hard to make money for college."

"Was Uncle Rhone going to college, too?"

"No. He hated school. He just liked playing football. Papa and Mama were so proud of me. Mama even told the white lady she worked for about my college plans. That woman said, 'Smithie, whatever you do, don't send Christine to college; it will just ruin her.'"

I said, "Why would she say that? Did Mama pay her any mind?"

"No, she didn't. Mama said, 'That old white woman has her two sons in medical school but she doesn't want you to get a college education. The hussy.'"

I was real quiet, this was a different kind of meanness. It didn't have mean words.

Tee laughed—not the kind of funny laugh that made me want to join in with her. She seemed a long way away. I tried to call her back, "Tee, oh Tee . . ." but nothing.

"You can still go to college. Sam and Mama can take care of me."

Still nothing. I wanted her to come back. I waited just like a secret club member should. This happened a lot. I wondered if I would ever hear the end of the college story.

Finally, one kitchen talk day, Tee rushed through the old parts and said, "When I was about to graduate from Booker T. Washington High School in 1936 and go to Delaware to study nursing, Mama had spent all my money."

"That was mean."

Tee grabbed the skillet, banged it down on the hot stove, cocked her head to one side, rocked it back and forth, and said, "If my son doesn't go to college, nobody goes to college."

We never had a whole bunch of money. Oh, we always had food and a roof over our heads. Tee said, "Mama doesn't have to worry about money; Papa left her his pension. She rents out two rooms and has her florist business. When colored people die, their family comes to Mama for floral arrangements or wreaths."

I knew about that and the rooms. My daddy's Aunt Lucy talked to Mama. "Mrs. Best, could you see your way clear to let my sixteen-year-old daughter, Darlene, live with you and finish high school at Booker T.? It would look so much better when she gets a job up North to have that school on her diploma. We'd pay you something, as much as we can, and bring you fresh vegetables, a ham, some chickens. And when Ernest, my husband, slaughters a hog or a cow, you'll be first on the list for meat, sausages."

Mama agreed. Darlene fit right into the family. She acted like she was Tee's little sister.

They laughed and talked a lot. Darlene found a tall boyfriend, Johnny, in school. She didn't want her daddy to know about him. One Sunday evening when he was visiting, her folks came into town. Uncle Ernest walked right up to Johnny and said, "Who you piping, young man?"

Although I didn't understand what that meant, when Sam left the room about to burst out laughing, I did, too. Johnny left, too, I saw him from Tee's window. Right after that, I heard Darlene's bedroom door shut. Sam hurried back to the living room.

"Guess we'll be on our way, Sam, can't stay long tonight,"

"Sorry, you're leaving so soon, Aunt Lucy, Uncle Ernest. Maybe next week, you'll visit longer."

My family always came up with ways to make or save money. In addition to her own business, Mama helped out a nearby white florist. Tee came up with an idea, too. "Mama, I want to start my own kindergarten."

I stopped ironing my hair ribbons. "What is a kindergarten?"

She didn't answer just kept on talking to Mama. "I would enjoy teaching children. Can I rent Rhone's old bedroom for my kindergarten?"

"Sure you can. That room is perfect—large and next to the bathroom. Honey, you don't have to pay me one red cent." And she laughed real hard. "I can't wait to tell my friend, Bet. Your own kindergarten. That'll certainly get her."

I said, "I never been to kindergarten."

"You were having too much fun for that."

I cried. "I don't want to go to first grade. I want to go to your kindergarten."

"Punjab, you have been in my school all the time. You were my only student."

Tee's Kindergarten class - graduation day on steps of Mama's Victorian house

[5] *In my future, Booker T. Washington High School*

[6] *Front entrance of Booker T.*

[5] *Booker T. Washington High School Rocky Mount, NC, photograph,* museumofeducation.info, *http://www.museumofeducation.info/images/btw-building-108a-400.jpg,* (accessed April 17, 2023)

[6] *Front Entrance of Booker T. Washington High School Rocky Mount, NC, photograph,* museumofeducation.info, *http:// www.museumofeducation.info/ images/door-36-300.jpg,* (accessed April 17, 2023)

Happy Birthday

I met my first boyfriend in first grade. My mother brought us together at my seventh birthday party. Some of my new friends from school were invited. My favorite, Doris Kay, came. I was crazy about her and her three little sisters—Janet, Mary Jane, and Baby Sally. She only had to cross the ditch and walk through the short cut between the duplex and Ida Lee's shotgun house.

I also invited Donald Randolph, the best-looking boy in my class. His family and friends called him Bunny. Nobody told me why but I guessed because he looked so cute in knickers. Even better than they looked in Montgomery Ward's catalog.

Tee made a delicious, three-layer pineapple cake with see through icing. Before the icing got hard, she decorated it with pretty pink and yellow candy letters and seven yellow candles from Kress.

My friends brought me so many pretty presents, I hardly knew what to do first—play on my swing set or open their gifts. I picked the gifts and ripped the paper off the biggest one. Tee said, "No."

Just then the doorbell rang. I counted; everyone I invited was there. It rang again. Tee had given me permission to open the door for my party guests. When I did, there stood my teacher, Miss Brown. At first, I thought she was lost but there was a present in her hand. "How do you do, Miss Brown."

I really thought she should be home resting. Little kids like us tired her out. She was old; maybe a hundred. She had short brown and gray fuzzy hair, white skin, and a pitiful little smile on her skinny lips. She was nice; just not young.

Suddenly, Tee was beside me and surprised, too. Without even a hello, she said, "I need to get the game" and ran from the room. I gave

Miss Brown a comfortable seat and prayed Tee would come back fast. She did—with an empty Pepsi Cola bottle.

Why? Even one Pepsi wasn't enough for all 12 of us. An empty one? She smiled. I crossed my fingers and hoped to open at least one present before my classmates took them back and went home.

Tee shouted, "Everybody come and sit in a circle on the floor."

All of us except Miss Brown obeyed.

"Girls on this half of the circle; boys over there."

Tee knelt in the middle of the circle, put the bottle on our painted oak floor, and twisted it real hard. It spun like it would never stop. By the time it slowed down, I was dizzy. Maybe that's what she wanted—to hypnotize us. Maybe she knew how to do magic tricks or how to conjure, to work roots. I didn't see any fun in spinning a bottle. Especially since none of us kids had our own bottle.

Tee said, "Dorothy Leigh, you are the birthday girl. You get to go first. When it stops, you kiss the boy it points to."

My mouth dropped open. Kiss a boy? I couldn't look at my friends and especially not at Miss Brown. The girls giggled; the boys made faces. I had to obey my mother. As soon as I spun it, I crossed my fingers hoping the bottle pointed to a handsome boy.

It did—to Bunny. He jumped up, walked closer to me, and stopped in front of me. I closed my eyes, like they did in the movies. Our lips touched quickly. We fell in love like a prince and a princess right there in Mama's living room, and it was perfectly okay with my mother.

My party set up a lot of things. First of all, my mother's present was a sailor girl's dress. Just like a real sailor's suit except there were no pants and I had a red tie at the front. There were white lines around the collar and near the bottom of the dress.

Next thing I knew, Bunny wore a sailor's suit which looked real, to school. He didn't say so, but I bet his parents bought it in Washington, D.C. where they lived without him. He lived with his aunt, his uncle, and his grandmother.

Not long after my party came Booker T. Washington High School's homecoming parade. I didn't know what homecoming meant.

I knew Tee graduated from Booker T. and Sam didn't go to high school at all; just finished eighth grade and found a job. His father's parents who raised him, still had leftover children. I felt sorry for my daddy growing up without his parents. I wondered who picked him out of his other six brothers and sisters. I wondered why his daddy didn't take some of them?

"Why did your parents leave each other?"

"They didn't love each other anymore."

"Why?"

"That was grown folks' business, Dorothy Leigh."

Anyway, I'd seen lots of parades right downtown: Ringling Brothers, Barnum and Bailey Circus, and Christmas. When Miss Brown asked Tee if I could wear my sailor dress in Booker T.'s homecoming parade and represent Abraham Lincoln Elementary School, I asked, "Represent, what does represent mean?"

"You and Donald Lyons . . .."

"Bunny."

"You and Bunny are the only ones with sailor suits. She thinks that would look very patriotic for the parade."

"I want to do it. I want to represent. Hot diggety, we'll be like twins." The whole town would see us.

On parade day, Bunny and I held each end of a wooden pole with the school banner hanging on it. At the beginning, I smiled across at him and he grinned back. I pretended we were in a wedding, our wedding. From somewhere way up front in the parade, a whistle sounded. The tall boy in the white suit and tall hat was the major of the parade. When he blew his whistle, the drum players beat their drums fast and loud.

I smiled at Bunny again. It was a good thing he was with me. Else, I might have told Miss Brown, "I can't do it. The school banner is too heavy." I wouldn't even get to see the four girls in short skirts and white boots prance like pretty little ponies.

At first, I was strong. Then my legs got tired. I wanted to go home. My face hurt from smiling. By the time we reached Main Street, I hated my sailor dress. I was never wearing it again for my school or my country.

But I loved Bunny more than ever.

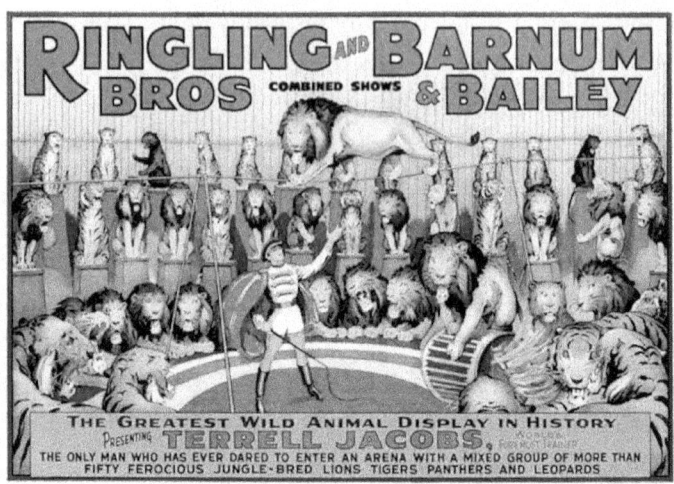

⁷Ringling Bros - Circus Poster - Allentown PA

⁷Self Scanned, Public domain, via Wikimedia Commons, photograph, commons.wikimedia.org, *https://commons.wikimedia.org/wiki/File:1939_-_Ringling_Bros_-_Circus_Poster_-_Allentown_PA.jpg, (accessed April 17, 2023)*

Follow Your Hunch

When I ran the numbers for Mama and Aunt Burrell, I got to play a little bit with the numbers lady's daughter, Barbara Ann. One day, she said, "I saw you and Bunny in the parade."

"You did?"

"Yes. His aunt, Miss Coon, is my mother's best friend."

"Miss Coon?" I sure hoped she didn't look like a raccoon. Sometimes Sam shot and cooked them.

"They go everywhere together in Miss Coon's big, black convertible car."

I couldn't make up my mind one Sunday after Sunday School. Should I go home and play with my toys or stay for church with Tee and get an ice cream cone after? But I didn't like church—it took too long. Besides, I would miss the best part about Sunday, Miss Maudie's candy store. Tee always gave me money for the collection plate and a little bit for candy on the way home. The big kids told me "Just put the little bit in the plate; keep the rest for candy."

"But..."

"It's your reward for going to Sunday School."

I decided to stay for church with Tee that Sunday. As my friends waved goodbye, I wondered if I had picked the right thing. I could be home playing with my toys. Tee was never on time, on purpose. That way people looked back and saw her outfit. After church, she always bought me an ice cream cone.

Finally, she came. Heads turned to look at her as we walked in. The usher put us near the last row of pews. I slid back in my seat, the choir started singing the song before Reverend Underwood's turn. Softly, the swinging doors opened. Who was coming even later than Tee? Barbara Ann's mother and a short lady stood there. Miss Coon, I bet. They looked real sharp standing next to the usher. I was right to stay for church.

Mama told me, "Dorothy Leigh, always follow your hunch when it's hard to make up your mind."

My hunch told me, "Stay for church with your mother." And I did even though I'd miss Miss Maudie's candy store.

Hers was the only store that just sold candy. It used to be her family's garage but they now had a store door with glass at the top, windows, and real smooth walls. The concrete floor was painted gray. Kids were her best customers. A bell tingled when we entered. She didn't have to get up from her telephone desk in her Mama and Daddy's house. She only had to reach out, part the dark-red curtain that hung between the store and the inside of the house, to see who was there. A good thing, too; it gave her time to hide or destroy the evidence in case the customer was the law.

Weekdays and Saturdays, Miss Maudie handled the numbers. Numbers took a break on Sundays. Sometimes I took Mama 'nem's numbers to her instead of to Barbara Ann's mother. Changing up was Aunt Burrell's idea. She never told me why. Maybe it was for luck or maybe to fool the law.

On Sundays, Miss Maudie's candy store looked like Sunday school. We were all there, gazing into her glass showcase crammed with boxes of penny, nickel, and ten cent candies: Cracker Jacks, Tootsie Rolls, Sugar Daddies. Everything a kid could want. She even had baseball diamond square cookies in a big, fat jar on the counter. They weren't my favorite. I just wanted my turn to buy one of her delicious sour pickles.

When I ordered it, I kept my eyes glued on her. First, she got a small, brown paper bag from her stack next to the pickle jar. She acted like it was a fancy bag for earrings or rings. Next, she gently lifted the long fork or her bamboo tongs. I never wanted her to use the fork; it made holes in the wrong part of my pickle, the sides. That just spoiled everything. Delicious sour juices oozed out when I sucked the top of the pickle. I had to eat a lot fast. It took seven whole days before I got another one. But I couldn't tell Miss Maudie to use the tongs.

"Is this the one you want, honey?"

"No ma'am . . . the one under it."

She tried again, always checking with me before forking it or squeezing it with the tongs. "This has to be it."

I nodded yes. By then, my mouth was so watery, I couldn't speak. I couldn't watch her pull it from the big jar. I turned my head and swallowed. "Anything else for you, sweetie?"

"No, ma'am."

If I had extra money, a peppermint stick was added. By then, I couldn't wait. The smooth end of the pickle was in my mouth in a hurry. I bit off a little bit. It was so sour, water squeezed out of my eyes. When I could see again, I eased the peppermint stick down into the pickle. Finally, I sucked sour juices through peppermint sweetness. It was wonderful.

Sometimes I wondered if Miss Maudie made any money; she looked like she ate a lot of stuff herself. She was really big, not just pleasingly plump. I never saw her anywhere except the candy store, in the little room off the candy store, or on the front porch fanning with a pretty Japanese fan. Even though she lived with her parents, they couldn't tell her anything; she was grown.

She kept herself fixed up: makeup, black pencil stuff on her eyebrows, red lipstick and matching fingernail polish, sparkling diamond rings, jingling silver and gold bracelets, pearl necklaces, and fancy hairdos. She acted like June German happened every day and she had to be ready.

I got a little nervous in church. I still had the extra money I kept back from the Sunday school collection plate. Tee might get mad if she saw it. I had to keep my little red purse shut. Reverend Underwood said, "Let us bow our heads in prayer."

My eyes closed all the way.

"Amen."

I looked back. The usher stepped off down the aisle with Miss Coon and her best friend behind him. He checked the rows behind us for empty seats. "Please don't let there be any seats for them." There weren't.

He came to our row—his white gloved hand shot up in the air. The ladies almost crashed into him. He waved his hand over the next row. They stopped ahead of him. Hot diggety! There were two empty seats in front of me; nowhere else in that row. I crossed my fingers. *"Please Lord, don't let the folks in the first seats slide down the row. Make them impolite."*

The Good Lord worked his roots; Miss Coon 'nem had to squeeze past them. Her red lips whispered "excuse me" to each person she climbed over. She was kinda pretty, round like Tee; not skinny like Barbara Ann's mother. She didn't favor a raccoon one bit. Before sitting down in front of me, they smoothed out their straight skirts in time with each other.

Bunny's aunt wore a black suit, a black pillbox hat with a veil, and a fur stole around her shoulders. Barbara Ann's mother copied her. Their stoles' four brown foxes' eyes stared dead at me.

I swallowed my scream.

Secrets

As a little girl, I thought secrets wanted to be told. They went in my ears, ran to my mouth, and slipped out. Mama told me one, "Promise not to tell Tee."

"You don't have to worry 'bout me telling nobody." I crossed my heart and hoped to die. I kept it all day. When Tee came home, Mama grabbed my hand in hers, real tight.

Just before she sent me out to play, I squeaked out "hello" to Tee. Outside, as long as I kept the secret, Mama didn't care if I played with strangers or monsters or caught a cold in the winter air. I got close to the street, walked on the big tree roots. Mama was wrong about them; I didn't fall down and skin my knees once. At least not so anybody could tell. I scuffed my Poll Parrots in the dirt. Mama didn't care. I wasn't telling the secret.

After supper, when Tee and I were alone, I said, "I know a secret."
"About what?"
"About you. But I can't tell you. It's a secret."
"Oh, is it a good secret?"
"You betcha. Ask me something about candles."
"No. I don't want to spoil the secret."
"Candles on your birthday cake with all your friends."
"That . . ."
"Shh, it's a secret."

The secrets I kept the best were the ones I wasn't supposed to hear at all. The ones I eavesdropped in on. I learned one big secret when I was just passing by.

It was on a regular day. After playing in Mama's room, I went looking for Tee. Mama and Sam were not at home. I heard Aunt Burrell's voice coming from the kitchen. She was loud at first until Tee said, "Remember little people have big ears."

I got the feeling she meant me. I tiptoed and hid myself behind the bathroom hallway door, across from the kitchen. Aunt Burrell said, "I couldn't believe my eyes."

"Where was I?"

"I can't rightly say. It's been a while."

"Go on."

"I'd just popped over that afternoon. Walked in the front door like usual. Only that day, I didn't go straight out to the kitchen."

"Why not?"

"Something just told me, 'Don't go through the dining room to the kitchen. Cut through the spare bedroom. You'll get to the back porch quicker.' It might have added, 'You'll never regret it.' So that's what I did. Thank the Lord."

A chair moved on the kitchen floor. I got as flat as a pancake behind the door. Heavy footsteps came closer. It had to be Aunt Burrell. My hiding place was not good. She was near the door. I held my breath. Whew. She went past the hallway. Good.

I still didn't breathe loudly. She was tricky. The porch screen door creaked open. Aw, she was spitting out snuff juices. I was safe. She went back to the kitchen.

"I saw Smithie aiming a gun."

"What? Where did she get a gun? Aiming at what?"

"I'm trying to tell you . . ."

"Doggone it, Mama's temper will be the death of us all. Usually, the things she does, don't hurt anybody. Well, maybe their feelings. Feelings heal or you just try and forget whatever she said or did. Course there was the time she took the scissors and cut her hair real short to hurt Papa."

"Yeah, he loved her hair. That was not to hurt him; it was to punish herself."

Tee said, "Punish herself?"

"Do you remember when she did that?"

"Yes, when me and Sam told her and Papa about our secret marriage. Papa took it well. Mama just left the room humming a hymn."

Burrell said, "You were her last chance to get everything right; she felt like she failed Laney all over again."

As a pot hit something, Tee said, "That's what's wrong with this family. You just won't let go of the past. We had to get married. Simple as that. Only we're still in love."

"I know."

"None of you even noticed my condition. Mrs. Kornegay did and she arranged a wedding ceremony right there in her living room."

"Uh, huh."

"It was real pretty, Burrell. Me and Sam stood in front of her fireplace. As the late morning sun streamed in through the French doors, we said our vows."

"Hmmm."

"She went out of her way to be kind. That was something for a white woman. Am I right?"

"True. True."

"She made a bouquet out of pretty pink roses from her garden, tied them with a white ribbon. The justice of the peace came to her house just for us. Paid him herself and never docked our pay one red cent."

"Smithie could have done the same thing right here. God knows, she knows flowers."

"The point is no one else stepped in to help us—only her."

"Only her."

Tee said, "Made me forget all about her earlier remarks."

"You would have been the first on our side of the family to go to college. That would have been something. You were always so smart."

"I finished high school. When are you going to finish your story?"

"After I spit."

She hardly settled into the kitchen again before Tee said, "What is this gun business? What was she aiming at anyway?"

"I came on out to the back porch from the middle room. I planned to turn into the kitchen. Lo and behold, I spied Smithie out of the corner of my eye. She was too quiet. I stepped back for a better look. She was at the screen door."

"What was it?"

"Lucky, I had the presence of mind not to yell. I followed her gaze. That's when I saw him."

"Saw who?"

"Sam."

"Burrell, what are you saying?"

"Bless his heart, he was out there chopping wood. Just as innocent as you please, Tee."

"Oh, no, Burrell. Don't say that. Don't . . ."

"I hurried to her as quietly and as quickly as I could. Reached out, grabbed Smithie, and commenced to wrestle that gun away from her."

Tee cried out loud.

"Once it was in my hands, I said, 'Have you lost your fool mind, woman?'"

"Oh, Sam, my Sam."

"She said, 'Leave me alone. I'll kill the son of a bitch. Messed up Tee . . .'"

Messed up? What was Mama talking about? Tee wasn't messed up. It seemed all three of us were holding our breaths. The emptiness scared me. I started to cry. I wanted Tee to hold me real tight. I wanted her to tell me it was just a story. But I couldn't go to her.

I stood there in the corner. Big tears rolled down my seven-year-old face. I didn't like Mama anymore.

New York

When I was about eight years old, every morning Mama woke up mean, screaming and yelling. At the time, I cried a lot about everything which would have been good if I were a movie star.

Her meanness always caught me off guard like a clap of thunder on a summer day. When it hit, I wanted to hide. One time, I couldn't. I was still in my single bed, snuggled in between the folds of a red-and-white-striped flannel blanket. I didn't like sleeping between two ironed bed sheets. Couldn't stand the way the top sheet touched my toe nails. Outside, all the leaves were off the trees. Summer was gone. Pretty soon we'd start the stove, bring in scuttles of coal and arm loads of wood, open up a few of our canned jars of food.

One morning the slamming of doors woke me up. I knew what it meant.

"I know I put my watch right there on my dresser last night. Like always. I wake up this morning and it's gone."

I scrambled out of my warm spot. My feet hit the cold hard, linoleum floor. I squirmed back into bed, into the warmth, and curled up into a ball. I tried to look like a bunch of bed stuff, hoped Mama wouldn't notice me.

"Somebody is gonna answer for this. And I know who took it, too. That son of a bitch."

On her last words, I curled up even more. Who did she think would steal from her? Certainly not my daddy. He didn't steal from nobody. He already had a watch. But he was the only man living in Mama's old Victorian house with us.

"Heads will roll over this. I may have let other things slide; but not this. You hear me?"

It was Saturday. Everybody was home but nobody answered her. Most days, Mama found whatever she accused us of taking, later; some place she'd put it. She never apologized for anything she said or did. After a bad start, we got through the day. I always made a wish tomorrow would be better.

My daddy got fed up with her. He said, "Christine, I'm going to New York—to look for work. I got family up there; I'll stay with them until I can make enough money to send for you and Dorothy Leigh."

I thought I would burst open with excitement. While they told Mama our plans, I daydreamed about going up to the real North, way past that Mason-Dixon Line. Straight to New York, to live in our own house.

When Sam left, Tee and I cried a lot. I knew he would work hard, save the money, and send for us. 'Cause one night after getting on his knees to pray, Mama said, "Sam, who do you pray for, son?"

"Me, Christine, and Dorothy Leigh."

Mama laughed at him like his idea was silly. Like she knew how things went.

While he was away, two things happened. First, Tee shared our plans with everybody she knew; I didn't tell anyone. One neighbor said, "Tee, you might not want to move to New York."

"Why not?"

The neighbor got real close and hissed like a cat. "'Cause lots of couples' marriages break up due to them moving up North."

It sounded silly to me. At my age, I doubted a lot of stuff I heard. Sometimes I thought I could see through people; hear the part they didn't say. I never told Tee what was going on in my head.

I waited for her to tell the old biddy off; but she didn't say nothing back to that heifer. That's what Mama would have called her. I wanted to tell her that to her face. Face all scrunched up all the time. Always looked like she was smelling something stinky. One of her sons had killed his brother over nothing and got away with it.

At the time, Mama said, "Police don't care nothing 'bout colored people killing their own kind. Saves them the trouble."

I kept waiting for Tee to say something to the old biddy. Surprising me, she nodded her head in agreement. This was the same woman who once said, "Tee, you're getting fat; your hips are starting to spread out a bit. Husbands don't like fat wives. You better watch yourself, dearie."

The second thing that happened was Mama started going blind. It came on suddenly. She couldn't read her mail. Tee read it to her. She got lost in the house. Tee made me guide her. I didn't mind. I liked being in charge of a grown-up.

Soon after that, Mama's temper calmed down. I started to mention the changes in Mama to Tee but I didn't want to rock the boat. Actually, I wanted to ask Mama, herself. I decided to let sleeping dogs lie. She looked the same but she might be playing 'possum. With no outbursts from her, mornings were wonderful. Blindness cured meanness.

Then Mama's teasing and joking stopped, too. At nighttime, she prayed on her knees. During the day, she said the Lord's name a lot; like she was religious. Jesus, the Lord 'nem probably didn't even want to own up to creating her.

I decided to see if she really was blind. I stared at her a long time. She didn't say a word. Still, I wasn't satisfied. I did one more test—tiptoed around the room. She called out like she had lost me, "Dot."

I didn't answer.

"Dorothy Leigh."

Finally, I answered like I was in another room. Next, I stomped my feet, acted like I was back in the room with her. She passed the tests; I kept on guiding her around.

Then came a day when Mama cried out, "I can't see nothing at all."

Tee rushed over to Miss Laura's house to use her telephone, to get Mama in to see Dr. Armstrong.

When it was time to go the three of us walked slowly to West Thomas Street to catch the bus. We never did that; always saved that money for other things, a loaf of bread or something. Tee figured the bus would be safer and faster for Mama.

When it came, I got on first, put the coins in the slot, watched them land in the bottom. It reminded me of the time Mama pretended she lost her money and cried out, "Oh, Lord, I can't find my money."

Some kind soul on the bus had run up and paid her fare.

As I turned around, I saw Tee and Mama sitting right up front. I joined them. No white people got on when we got to their neighborhood. We kept our seats all the way downtown.

At the corner of Main and West Thomas, we got off and walked across the railroad tracks to the block of colored businesses. Dr. Armstrong's office was upstairs. It took a long time to climb to the second floor. We didn't wait long in the reception room for Mama's turn. Tee went in with her.

I stayed and looked at the magazines. Pretty soon, Tee was saying goodbye to the doctor. Mama still looked blind. I hurried over to help guide her. The receptionist didn't give us another appointment. We headed for the stairs.

I waited but Tee didn't tell me what the doctor found out. Nobody ever told me nothing. "Dot, help me get Mama down the stairs."

Those stairs were real steep and skinny; I didn't want to be first. Mama was big; she might fall and crush me. I hesitated. Tee said, "Here, let me be the leader."

Once we were on solid ground and headed for the bus stop, Mama said, "What kind of an examination was that? I couldn't even see the chart; forget about letters."

"Now, Mama, he did look into your eyes but didn't see anything suspicious. Remember? He said it all might just be nerves."

"I knew we should have seen a white doctor. Told you that in the first place."

Although I remained quiet, I agreed with Mama. Dr. Armstrong could have given her a prescription. I could have had ice cream while we waited in one of the two colored drugstores. Mama was right. A white doctor would have given her a cane, or a pair of shades, maybe even an eye patch. Everybody knew he had more stuff than a colored doctor. Heck, she was blind; I tested her.

For the first time, it struck me—how would Mama manage without us? Nobody else in the family could take care of her like we did. The thought of Mama wandering around in the darkness, of being alone, was not pleasant. I didn't say anything. It might bring us bad luck.

To take away some of the ungodly thoughts I was having, I reckoned since Mama still got Papa's railroad pension, she would do just fine. She could hire someone to live with her. I felt so much better.

Nothing changed after that visit. Mama went on being blind; Tee and I went on helping her. A few days later, my daddy called on Miss Laura's telephone. I ran behind Tee to hear his voice. We couldn't afford to let me talk, too. I was laughing and giggling all the way, my daddy was calling with good news. Usually, he wrote. I had waited all winter to hear him say, "Come to New York."

I beat Tee to Miss Laura's and waited on the porch for her. When she got there, Miss Victoria stood at the door grinning and holding out the telephone. Tee took it and said hello. Next thing I knew, she was explaining Mama's condition. She went on and on. I wanted to squeeze her arm and say, "Find out when we are leaving."

"So, Dot and I won't be joining you just yet."

I wanted to snatch the phone away from her.

"Not right away, not while she needs me so much. You understand, don't you, Sam?"

I stood there quiet as she spoiled everything.

Sam must have been chewing her out; she didn't talk for a long time.

I wanted to holler to him, "Tell her 'no'. Tell her you don't understand nothing."

Tee said, "Yes, honey. Of course, it is wonderful you've saved all that money."

She listened again. I crossed my fingers, wanting my daddy to win, to move us out of Mama's Victorian house. I looked away from Tee, right into Miss Victoria's pursed lips. Her hands pushed and yanked yarn around two knitting needles. She gripped them so tightly, her knuckles bulged. Miss Laura, her mother, sighed, shook her head, rose from her rocking chair, and jabbed the dying fire in the fireplace. It didn't matter spring was just around the corner—the old lady's bones got cold.

Embarrassed about what was happening to my family, I turned back to my mother. It seemed like forever before Tee's turn came again. Sugar wouldn't melt in her mouth when she said, "But just think how far all that money can go down . . ."

He didn't let her finish; she had to listen.

When her turn came again, she said, "Oh, no, honey. I certainly don't mean that. We both know up North, up there in New York, is the best place for our little family."

I stopped listening. At first, I was disappointed. Then I was angry at my mother. She knew my daddy wanted us in New York with him. She knew how excited I was about going. She also knew my daddy's life was in danger in Mama's house.

Mostly, I didn't understand disappointing him. She had promised.

Tee was still on the telephone, "Yes, Sam, yes. I have two weeks. I love you, too. And thank you so much for working so hard and saving money for us. Goodbye."

I wanted to run back home and cry. I couldn't. Tee had to thank Miss Laura and Miss Victoria. Still, we couldn't leave; Tee told them a little bit about her conversation with my daddy—like she was paying them for use of their telephone. I looked away.

Tee said, "If it weren't for Mama and her condition . . ."

Miss Laura said, "She still 'blind' or can she 'see' her way clear yet?"

"Nothing has changed really. I feel sorry for her; she's usually so independent. You can only have one mother . . ."

"Or husband for that matter," Miss Victoria interrupted. "Of course, don't mind me, I've never been married. A real good man is hard to find these days."

Tee said, "Yes, ma'am. Thank you so much for letting Sam call me on your phone. In two weeks, we'll either be headed up North or I'll be welcoming him home."

I wondered what it would be like to live in a different house?

Man of the House

One weekday evening just before dusk, a Star Cab Company driver pulled up in front of Mama's house. From my perch on the back of the living room sofa, perfect for watching the comings and goings on Howell Street, I stared in disbelief as Sam, my daddy, stepped out of it. At first, I was too stunned to speak. He was supposed to be in New York. I yelled to Tee in the kitchen, "Sam's home! Sam's home!"

"Oh, Lord. My husband's come back to me. Sam! Sam!" And she ran through the dining room untying her apron strings as she went. In no time, she was out the front door, across the porch, and on the front walkway before he stepped on the dirt sidewalk.

"What's all the commotion about? Who's here? Tee? Dorothy Leigh, what's wrong? Is somebody hurt?"

"It's Sam, Mama. My daddy's come back." Although I felt a tiny ache growing inside me, I ran outside to welcome him home.

Mama said, "Thank you, Jesus."

Tee and I were so happy to see him, we smothered him with hugs and kisses. "Seeing" didn't include Mama, she was still blind which was a good thing. It proved Tee had told the truth about her condition.

Slowly and with no fanfare, we settled into a pattern that included Sam's return to his hospital job and his handyman jobs. I overheard some mention of seeking new or additional employment. He told me nothing about his New York job. As much as I fancied moving to New York before his short adventure there, I never once asked his opinion of that city or his kinfolk. All talk of New York was sealed away, never to be opened. I began to think I'd dreamed it up.

Even though our New York plans didn't work out, something good came out of it. I had time to inspect what I'd almost left behind. For one thing, I developed a new opinion of Miss Victoria. Before, all I thought about her was what I saw; and she showed me nothing. I wasn't alone in my thinking.

As cruel as it was, she was the joke of the neighborhood; never to her face. Her head was way too small for her wide body. She reminded me of a penguin and walked like one, too—took short steps, arms out from the sides of her body. To top it off, her lips beaked a little. She was an old maid. Absolutely nobody envied her, but as Mama always put it, "Don't hold me to that."

By the time I came along, she was ancient and still living with her mother, Miss Laura, just like we lived with Mama, I wished we didn't. Mama was back to her old self—the mean one. And could see better than before. It all happened shortly after my daddy returned. Not right away but little by little. First, she said, "Dorothy Leigh, do you have the ceiling light on, honey? It seems kinda bright in here."

My ears perked up. She hadn't mentioned light to me for months. She no longer called me to guide her down the front steps. I'd been so excited about Sam, I hadn't noticed. Maybe Dr. Armstrong was right; the blindness was her nerves. Or maybe, Mama faked it to get what she wanted—Tee taking care of her. I started to mention it all to Tee but quickly changed my mind. It would just make for more bad blood.

Besides, our little family was doing okay. Sam did pick up more handyman jobs on the side. Tee continued her kindergarten but had switched to a new lady, Mrs. Wilson for afternoon domestic work. There was very little to look forward to. People in general had a whole bunch of time to pick on others, like Miss Victoria

On our street, her mother, Miss Laura, was the richest. Her name even sounded rich. I knew two other Lauras—my mother's cousin and Stella Dallas' daughter on the radio. Stella's Laura married a rich man and ignored her poor, working mother. Mama and Aunt Burrell listened to Stella's problems every weekday.

Miss Victoria's mother owned most of our street. She collected rent from at least six families which included Aunt Burrell and Britches' family in the duplex, Aunt Burrell's friend, Felicia and her mother, my daddy's friend, the only family on the block who had a black and white television set with rabbit ears. Aunt Burrell cloaked for her own married brother who kept company with Felicia. Aunt Burrell either loved sin or was willing to participate. As for Mama, she didn't care for Felicia or her mother—their purple and pink petunias were far too pretty.

Since her mother's money didn't make Miss Victoria beautiful, she took matters into her own hands. One hot summer night, she rocked on Aunt Burrell's front porch and said, "Have I told you about my new boyfriend?"

Aunt Burrell and Mama got real quiet. I pretended to be playing but listened. I knew a lot about boyfriends; I still had Bunny from first grade. Miss Victoria continued. "We have to keep everything a secret; but I can trust you, Burrell, and your sister. You see he's married. So, we have to plan our dates real carefully."

Aunt Burrell said, "That can be a problem. How did the two of you meet?"

"Oh, I was substituting at a new country school and he was my ride for the day."

"So, he's a teacher."

"No. He's the principal. So, you can imagine just how careful we have to be, under the circumstances."

Aunt Burrell said, "It was kinda like love at first sight."

Miss Victoria laughed and said, "Exactly. That first time he gave me a ride to his school, he rushed around to open the door for me. Such a fine gentleman. We looked into each other's eyes for a long moment. I tell you, Burrell . . . ."

Her romance didn't remind me of any of the movies I'd seen with my mother. Aunt Burrell 'nem just nodded. Occasionally, they'd ask her to go back over some part that sounded odd. When she explained, they'd look at each other funny.

Aunt Burrell said, "I bet this will surprise your sisters."

Miss Victoria's two sisters lived up in Washington, D.C. and came home in long, black cars. On Sundays, they wrapped up in fur coats and matching hats. Some Sundays, they threw fur stoles over their shoulders; Miss Victoria walked next to them in her old, gray, wool coat.

Miss Laura, their mother, believed in education as a way up in the world. With it a Negro could escape the South, be somebody. She educated her three daughters to make it so. Miss Victoria could teach school but all she did was substitute. No one had ever heard of the schools who used her services. I don't know what her sisters did but they always brought expensive presents like a tall pyramid of silver with a million tiny glasses, for Mount Zion First Baptist Church. Even I was impressed. They understood religion.

On sacrament Sunday, music played softly as our deacons removed the monogrammed linen which covered the pyramid. All that polished silver and sparkling tiny glasses blinded us. The ushers saved our eyesight by gathering around the table. The deacons handed them trays of grape juice filled glasses (Jesus' blood) and plates of small uncooked white crumbs (his body).

Then the ushers turned in unison, faced the congregation, and walked up the aisles serving the people. It was such a good show, I almost clapped. They passed the glasses right in front of me without so much as an "excuse me." All because I was a kid and hadn't been saved.

My chances for being saved didn't look good. Daily, I was being led astray by my very own grandmother and her sister, with their numbers. Now that I was older, Aunt Burrell also shared her pearls of wisdom with me. One day she told me and an older neighborhood boy, "Clarence, you and Dot should get married and have children. They would be some pretty brown-skinned babies with your light skin and Dot's chocolate mixed together."

I wondered why my parents even let me be around her. She was far from being pure of heart. Nothing could get Aunt Burrell or Mama through those pearly gates.

In April of 1945, something really, really sad happened. It wasn't sad just for my family, our friends, or our neighbors. It was a crying time for the whole United States. Our beloved President Franklin Delano Roosevelt died. In our neighborhood, people were hugging each other, shedding real tears. I'd never seen anything like it before in my life.

All the radio stations carried it. Tee said, "I declare this is the end of any hope for equal rights in the United States."

I said, "We still have Miss Eleanor. She may be better than him."

Nobody bothered to tell me to be quiet.

Two days after he died, we gathered around our radio to listen to our beloved President's last trip from Georgia back to Washington, D.C. His coffin didn't come through Rocky Mount; it went through Salisbury instead.

The white undertaker had him ready for viewing fast. Colored people never had anybody ready that soon. Heck, we held a body up to a week or more before the funeral to give everybody time to get home.

Nobody in our family or neighborhood could afford traveling to Salisbury to wave goodbye to old FDR; especially not for just a few minutes with no funeral to go along with it. It wasn't like we had a whole bunch of rations for gas; World War II was still going on.

Tee said, "We showed our respect the only way we could."

Aunt Burrell said, "Wonder what that Truman gonna do for us."

Nobody had any answers. After all the funeral business, our lives went on as usual. Mama laughed, "Could have told y'all, white folks would still be making the decisions."

I tended to side with her; she was usually right in her fashion.

The rest of spring just went along regularly. Then early one morning our doorbell rang. My daddy was already at work. Tee was preparing for her kindergartners. I was about to leave for school. I rushed to the front door, peeked through the white lace curtain on one of the double doors, right into a bosom—Miss Victoria's.

She never ever came to my grandmother's. Tee was right behind me. She said, "Good morning, what brings you out this nice day?"

Miss Victoria caught her breath. "Christine, honey, you come on over to our house, right now."

"What is it? Is something wrong with your mother?"

"No. This is your chance; a chance to get a place for you and your husband and your daughter."

I grabbed my school stuff.

Tee turned, looked back towards the kitchen where Mama was.

Miss Victoria grabbed her hand. "You have to come now. The tenant in the Wells' house is moving out, as we speak."

Tee stayed rooted to the floor.

Finally, Miss Victoria whispered, "Don't you want to get away from your mother's ranting and raving?" And she charmed Tee off the porch, down the steps, and onto the walkway.

I followed.

They walked side by side towards her mother's house. As we crossed the street, she said, "Of course, you want a better life for your daughter, a peaceful life."

I nodded.

"I have the Wells' phone number up North. All you have to do is call them. You can be in your own place before nightfall."

Like magic, we were standing in their front hallway. Miss Laura handed their telephone to Tee. While Miss Victoria called out the numbers, my mother said them to the operator. Then we waited for her to place the call.

I was shocked. Tee was making a long-distance call on Miss Laura's telephone. Nobody got to do that.

As we waited for an answer, I crossed my fingers.

Tee spoke into the phone, "Hello, is this the Wells' residence? Good. This is Tee, Christine Best, Smithie's daughter. Yes, ma'am. Miss Hopkins let me call you because your tenants are moving out right now. My husband, Sam, and I would like to rent it, if you haven't promised the house to anyone else. Yes, ma'am. It would be a fine place to raise Dorothy Leigh. No, ma'am. This coming weekend wouldn't be too soon for us to move in at all."

It was broad daylight that Saturday morning when we started moving our stuff out of Mama's old Victorian house. We created such a flurry. We looked like chickens with their heads cut off—jumping around in all directions. Miss Victoria brought over the rental house key early that morning. Sam put it on his key chain and said, "Christine, get ready, honey bunch."

In the midst of our happiness, there was one evil spirit—Mama. "The damn ingrates are trying to sneak away. After all I've done for them. Don't even have the decency to look me in the eye. Trying to steal from me, too. I won't stand for it."

We didn't care what she said, just piled our things into Sam's car. Actually, the car belonged to both of my parents. It was a sore spot between the two of them. Sam made the decision to buy it, by himself. He went to the bank and withdrew the money from their savings account. Tee knew nothing until he drove it home.

She didn't argue, just suffered in silence, and glared at him a lot. Told me, "Dorothy Leigh, let this be a lesson to you. When you get married, always have separate accounts."

I promised to do that. Of course, I didn't tell her how excited I was about our black, four-door Chevrolet. My daddy looked important in it. It suited him.

We didn't have much furniture to move, just my parent's bedroom suite. Not even a bed for me. We certainly couldn't borrow one from Mama.

Bed or no bed, we were leaving. I concentrated on what was going on at the moment. Tee and Sam were wrestling their mattress onto the roof of his car. Their matching chest of drawers ended up on top of that. The dresser would come later. The inside of the car was jam packed. Tee and I had to walk down the dirt sidewalk, carrying the bed rails between us.

We made quite a parade for the neighbors and anybody passing by. We didn't care. In fact, we acted like we were moving to a palace or someplace special. My mother and I grinned so much, our faces ached. We sang some silly songs and marched along.

All the while, I thought we are headed for the ugliest house on this street. It was struggling to hold on to its orange paint and losing. It fit right into its spot—next to a ditch where weeds and crab grass grew on the other side. Some scraggly roses were next to the dirt driveway. They didn't count; Mama never grew them.

Our new home squatted down diagonally across from the railroad tracks. There was only one next door neighbor, on the right; a two room, shotgun house which looked like it had never been painted in its whole life. Both houses were very close to the dirt street. The dirt sidewalk was our front yard. Nobody walked on it because we were the last house. Only two more houses were on the block, one on the other side of the shot gun and a white house across the street from it.

Nothing blocked our view of a bunch of different sized, murky-red, stinky buildings just across the railroad track from us. On moving day, the smell wasn't noticeable at all. The buildings made up the cotton processing plant. Mama and I took a shortcut one day to Falls Road through the plant's property long before we moved to the end of the street. It was okay to do that walking or riding.

I ran ahead of Mama and peeked inside the first building. I'd never seen so much cotton in my life. It was up to the ceiling and sloped down like snow on a mountain. I wanted to roll around on those balls of cotton, climb to the top. What fun.

On the plant's main road, Mama and I came to an open pit area, with one wall and a shelter over it. The pit was cement and filled with black, boiling hot water. I could see the steam. We watched men drop big cut trees into it. They were sucked in. No bark was left on the trees when they pulled them out. Mama said, "This is a dangerous place. A man fell in on accident one time. He was cooked alive."

I grabbed her hand and held it tightly.

By the time Tee and I reached our rental house, Sam had unlocked the front door. I ran straight to the kitchen. There was no stove which didn't bother me. I still wasn't crazy about food. It would be nice though to eat some of Tee's fried chicken. I even ate two vegetables now, broccoli and asparagus. Not at home; in the new white lady's kitchen where Tee worked.

At Mama's we mostly ate collard greens, mustard greens, green peas. Not to my liking but I was crazy about okra. I liked its pod shape and tiny, round seeds. And I didn't have to chase it around my plate like green peas. My favorite food was liver and onions.

As we moved in, I began to worry about a bed for me. There was no heater either. Come winter, we would freeze to death. My parents were poor planners. Papa would have made sure I was comfortable and happy.

Did they know what they were doing? Could they take care of me and themselves? Staying with Mama didn't seem like a bad idea. She liked me a lot. And I'd have a bed. Maybe my own room; Tee's room was empty now. No. I had to move, too. I belonged to them. Their feelings would be hurt. Besides, I wasn't a traitor.

Tee yelled, "Punjab. I have a surprise for you."

I found her in one of the bedrooms.

"Ta da! Your own bed." She pointed to a roll away, fold down, bed thing that looked like it used to go on a porch.

I didn't know what to say. I wanted a real bed. Tears welled up in my eyes.

She didn't even notice. She was too busy playing house. I didn't like being independent one bit. Brushing away my tears, I watched Tee make up the cot's thin mattress.

"Punjab, come and test your new bed."

I tried real hard to like it, but if I could have found a way, I would have run back to Mama's. She'd gladly take me in. Probably brag about it. Buy me candy, anything I asked for. No. I couldn't let her win. Not after she pretended to go blind to keep us from moving to New York.

I sucked it all up, smiled, and looked on the sunny side. I wouldn't have to sleep in a room by myself; I'd be right across the floor from my parents' bed.

Lucky for us, a round oak kitchen table and one wooden chair came with the house. There was a built-in cupboard, too, but we didn't own any dishes. We didn't have an icebox either. My parents didn't seem to mind at all. I stopped thinking about what we didn't have.

That night for our first meal, we ate tuna fish sandwiches, cans of sardines with vinegar and hot sauce, and crackers. No vegetables were in sight. Living without a cook stove was fine. I hoped our next meal would be tomato or banana sandwiches with mayonnaise. I loved them.

Sam sat in our only chair and winked at Tee and me. She walked around the table to him, put her arm around his shoulder, "Sam, you're the man of this house."

He grinned and pulled her gently to his lap. He never did that at Mama's house.

Making Ends Meet

The next day, Tee's kindergarten stuff was moved to the ugly house's small back room. It was a straight shot through the kitchen to the bathroom.

We were not only missing church but working on Sunday, too. Other good things were happening. With no cook stove, I got to eat all the Pork 'n Beans I could hold. They never put in enough wieners, but I loved them anyway, hot or cold. They reminded me of putting in green tobacco, which we'd be working in again in less than two months.

Actually, I didn't work unless somebody needed to go to the outhouse. Then they called me and Hazel, the farmer's daughter, to spell 'em. We were real slow but the grown-ups praised us anyway. On Fridays, her daddy always gave Hazel and me a dollar each.

We had worked for that old sharecropper for the last three years. I was almost ten years old. Tee no longer drove Red, the horse, she was a looper. Mr. Coggins still smoked and sounded like TB. I never got up the nerve to tell his wife about the bus with the x-ray machine.

Darn. Mr. Coggins didn't know we'd moved. Mama wouldn't tell him; she'd give Tee's spot to someone else. Mama held grudges. Tee said, "I need the green tobacco money. My kindergarten is closed in the summer. I'll only have my domestic paycheck."

It was not the time to ask for a real bed. If we ran out of money, it was back to Mama's. Everyone would know we failed. I decided not to worry; that was grown folks' business.

On Monday morning, breakfast was peanut butter and jelly. Tee gave me money for lunch in the school's basement cafeteria. Usually, I ran home for lunch.

After breakfast, Tee said, "Let's go back to Mama's. I'll meet my students out front and we'll all walk back here. It'll be like an outing for them."

She was always cheerful about things. It made me angry when anybody hurt her feelings which her family did a lot. Mama was no help. All she was good for was promising her family her Victorian house when she wanted a favor.

I loved waiting with Tee. She was way more fun than my teacher. "Tee, can I stay until almost the last minute?"

"Okay. But you can't loiter along the way. Hmmm, I wonder how Jean is doing up in Philadelphia."

"What do you mean? She's fine. We're still in the same grade."

"Yes, well she was in the hospital for a while. She's been real sick."

"Does she have polio?"

"Nothing that bad; she has breast cancer."

Breast cancer? Only one girl in my class had breasts. "What is cancer?"

"Oh, Dorothy Leigh, you ask too many questions. She just didn't take care of herself."

Tee didn't want to talk about it. Jean couldn't take care of herself; her grandmother did that. At least it wasn't polio. "Tee, how can Jean have . . ."

"Dorothy Leigh, go to school. We'll talk later."

My friend Jean visiting from Philadelphia at Eastertime – red factory in background

The short cut across the street from Mama's took me to Middle Street and from there to the school yard. I started looking at things along the way. Suddenly I remembered it was the first day of practice for wrapping the maypole. I wrapped it last year, too. I flew to school.

Mrs. Neville, the teacher who helped Mr. Eggars, the principal, was in charge. She put Larry, the cute, curly-haired, brown-skinned boy, with me. I liked looking at him. He had a lot of red in his skin and high cheek bones.

At practice, we went in and out and over and under, weaving the beautiful ribbons. They were tied at the top of the pole. It looked so pretty.

With only a little ribbon left in our hands, we went in the opposite direction to undo the colorful pattern we had made. Mrs. Neville would have us speed up once we could do it well. We had to beat the other two elementary schools on May Day.

The idea came from Germany where our enemies lived. Somebody in the United States liked it, so we did it, too. Those Germans may have been doing evil things but we loved their maypole.

After practice, I hurried home. I was careful, walked on the other side of the street from Mama's house. Didn't want to forget and turn into her walkway. If she happened to be out front, I would look straight ahead. If she spoke, I'd say, "Good afternoon, Mrs. Best."

When I reached her house, she was nowhere in sight. I went on to our rental. Funny, after only three days, it looked better. By the end of the week, it might be beautiful. Two big trees separated it from the street. It was missing something—flowers.

Too bad we had fallen out with Mama. She knew how to pretty up a place with petunias, snapdragons, dahlias, sweet Williams. A little water to their roots, some dirt, and a final drink on top—it would be the prettiest house on the street. A delivery truck pulled out of our driveway. I hurried inside calling, "Tee, Tee."

"I'm in the kitchen. Come see our surprises."

I found her standing in front of a small, black cook stove. It looked like a toy and didn't have a warming cabinet like Mama's. "It's wonderful."

Tee said, "I know. Did you see our new icebox?" She pulled me back into the empty dining room, in the middle of the house. The room had a slanted floor, four doors, and two inside windows to the kitchen.

"Isn't this the best icebox you've ever seen, Dot? When the ice in the top melts and drains to the pan below, your job will be to empty it."

I nodded yes.

Back in the kitchen, she said, "We're all set, Punjab. Neighbors brought over pots and pans, even a cast iron skillet. Burrell showed up with glasses and dishes."

"Wow."

"It's been hectic. I called my job, told her not to expect me today. Now you run round to Davis Grocery with this list. Brown's is much too high; let him bleed Burrell to death."

I was scared; I'd never grocery shopped before. I started to worry.

"Dorothy Leigh," Sam called from outside.

I hurried out to him. Before I gathered up the wood he had chopped, I said, "Thanks so much for the wonderful icebox and the stove."

"Cute, ain't they?"

I kissed him on the cheek then picked up the wood and headed for the kitchen. As I worked, I thought this is really it—independence and no turning back now.

"Dot, look at all the goodies Mama just brought us."

All the stuff hid her. Tee acted like we were family again. Even though I wanted a bed, I was staying right there in that ugly house.

Since we had our own place, Mama already treated us better. Being independent worked. Course we had to come up with more money for rent and lights. Tee said, "We have to work real hard."

I didn't; I just had to get excellent grades.

A few weeks later, Tee said, "Sam, honey, we don't need all these rooms. We'll rent one of them. That's easy money."

"You right, Christine."

In no time, the front bedroom on the ditch side of the house was rented. Ruth, a country school teacher, moved in with her husband and their little girl. They came with their own stuff—a bed, a chest of drawers, a chair. We just needed to buy them a heater. They had bathroom and kitchen privileges, plus space in the kitchen cabinet and icebox.

Tee enjoyed Ruth. They belonged to the same pinochle club, "The Gay Senoritas." Most of the members were school teachers. Because of her kindergarten, Tee fit right in. They took turns meeting in a different member's home each week.

By renting to Ruth and 'em, our rental seemed like a little village. Because of them, I got my own dark-brown, full size iron bed and moved into my own room, the middle one on the ditch side. A door separated me from Ruth's family. My other door opened to the dining room with our brand-new white chrome table with red trim and four matching red chairs.

I was just settling into my room when Tee said, "Dot, you're getting a roommate."

"Who?"

"Zellie Mae."

She wasn't a kid; she used to be one of Uncle Rhone's girlfriends. We all liked her. Mama and I liked watching her shout at the Sanctified and Holiness Church. She pranced around beating a tambourine, flashed her high heel shoes with the toes out, swished her dresses. I liked the stuff she wore. Sharing my bed with her was okay; it was just that nobody asked me about it.

In the end, I was glad except I didn't like sleeping on the scary side of the bed, next to the window. So, I snuggled up real close to Zellie Mae. Before she came, strange animal noises, creepy footsteps, crackling branches frightened me. I kept my head covered up. Something evil, like the wolf man, might drag me out through the window while everyone slept. Next morning, I'd be long gone. Buried. Or a vampire could come, suck my blood. I always checked my neck when I woke up.

We were doing great money-wise but our living room was empty except for my parent's old arm chair, Tee's piano, and a black gateleg table. A sofa and a coffee table were on our wish list. We had to make more money fast. Tee's turn to host the Gay Senoritas was less than a month away.

Last month's money went for three heaters for my parents, the renters, and me. Mine stood in the corner next to my window. Its chimney which stretched to the ceiling, reminded me of Abraham Lincoln's hat. Unfortunately, we still didn't have enough money for living room furniture. Money was so tight, we couldn't even buy it on time.

To the rescue came my daddy. He had a plan—bootleg liquor, white lightning. I overheard him telling Tee. I got excited. We'd be rich in no time. But I couldn't talk about it to anyone, including my parents; it was illegal, against the law. Folks got arrested for making it, for selling it, and for drinking too much of it. Hot dog, we were starting to live dangerously. A real holy deacon in our church was a bootlegger. He owned a nice brick house and a black Cadillac. I could hardly wait to get started.

Sam began right away . . . brought home liquor in canning jars. They looked like water lined up in the cupboard. I wanted to ask, "Why can't we fill some of those empty brown bottles with the pretty labels? They always look good in the ABC store."

Sam went there to buy liquor when they were going to a big dance.

I liked the word liquor; it sounded so illegal. My tongue did tricks when I said it. Living in sin was exciting. Sam was good at it, too. He brought it home with no cops chasing him or breaking into our house without a warrant.

I overheard him say, "I'll sell it by the glassful."

Perfect. Our big, round, oak kitchen table could seat six. I'd sit with them, like Tee used to do when Papa had important people over for dinner. She said, "Mama never wanted to eat with them 'cause she felt she wasn't educated enough. She made me do it instead."

I wasn't all the way educated yet, but I knew how to hold a conversation. All of my years of eavesdropping paid off—I was a great listener.

Sam was such a good worker; we'd have a lot of customers in no time. They'd bring their friends. On June German night, people would stop by, have a drink or two. I'd see the ladies dresses up close. We'd be rich in no time.

Finally, liquor day arrived. My labels weren't ready for the bottles; I couldn't decide which ideas to use and I couldn't ask anybody's opinion. I watched Sam bring in customers. Tee wouldn't allow me near the kitchen. None of the men just dropped by like at a store or a café. In less than a month, it fizzled out.

I never found out exactly why Sam's business failed but I had my suspicions. Probably had a lot to do with my mother's lack of enthusiasm. Mama always said, "Another person's bad vibrations can poison everything."

Street's End

I started having fun in our new home. Right away, I learned how to swing across our ditch on a skinny tree limb to the opposite side. It was higher and the best limbs were over there.

I slid down the dirt slope, hopped across the nearly dry ditch, scuffled on hands and knees up the other side, wiped my hands on my dungarees, grabbed the limb, and flung myself into the air heading back. I was louder than Tarzan. It was more fun than the swings I still snuck rides on in the city parks.

I took up walking on the rails on the railroad track. Trains hardly ever came by. When they did, they were like snails. By practicing every day that first summer, I could walk almost a block without falling off. It was so much fun balancing like that. I might have been in training for the circus.

That year, I celebrated my tenth birthday in the house at the end of the street. It was the best ever. Tee made it more like a carnival. Not only did she invite my classmates, she included her friends' kids, too. We bobbed for apples, competed in suitcase races, peanut races where we loaded as many peanuts on a spoon as we could and carried them to another point using only one hand. The winners of any of the games got prizes.

Three more kids lived on my dead-end block: two sisters, one older than me, and their cousin, a boy. I invited them to join my Deed-A-Day Club. I think I read something like it in *Highlights,* a children's magazine. We needed money. I said, "Don't worry. We'll make a play, make a ton of money. Besides selling tickets, we'll sell Kool-Aid and cookies. Right there in Tee's kindergarten room."

We didn't have a play or a library to get one. Our library at the high school was all the way across town; the closest one was for whites only.

So, I wrote one. I was lucky I didn't have to hand write four copies of my three-page play. Our first roomer, the country school teacher, used to have me make copies of worksheets for her students.

It was a flat box with hard jello stuff inside. Tee had one. It was fast and easy. I copied each play page on a master which had a purple back sheet. Rubbed the master onto the jello, pulled it off, rubbed on a clean sheet of paper and pulled it off.

Shazam. I had one copy of page one of my play. I did that three more times before cleaning the jello and rubbing on page two's master. The other page followed. So much faster than handwriting each copy.

In no time we were ready for rehearsal. Afterwards, we made tickets and sold them to kids on Mason and Star Streets. The day before our show, we prepared the treats. The play was a success. We made almost fifty cents. We never did any deeds; we started swim lessons instead.

Since lessons cost twenty-five cents each time, my mother paid for mine and their grandparents paid for theirs. For a few weeks, we walked all the way across town and back. I got so good at swimming, I dived off the high diving board one morning. Everything was fine until I caught a cramp. The life guard saved me. I quit swimming as did my neighbors.

We took up card games: tonk, pitty pat, smut, and whist. Sometimes we played jacks or pick up sticks all day. Early afternoons, we bathed and walked down to West Thomas Street for ice cream cones.

Before we knew it, August was almost over; after Labor Day, school opened. I never wanted to go back even though education was the answer to escaping the South.

Living at the end of the street changed my mind about the joys of being a grown-up. I dreaded the idea of nylon stockings. I was happy with warm, colorful or white socks. Just buying a pair of nylons was a problem for dark-skinned Negroes like me. In the Main Street stores, I watched Tee try it. A white saleslady (coloreds worked there only as elevator operators or in the back) who guarded the nylons behind the counter said, "Now let me see. This color, tan, should be perfect for you." She put the box on the glass counter, removed the lid, opened the top of one stocking. "Just slip your fist into the top."

Tee did so and shook her head.

The game was on. The saleslady chose different boxes.

Over and over, Tee said, "No." Finally, her lips formed a straight line.

I was annoyed, too. In fact, I developed an attitude about white salesladies.

This one said, "Tan's the closest we can get for your skin."

Tee sighed and paid for the too light nylons whose back seams had to be worn straight on her legs.

Except for that frilly, white, lacy garter belt, I didn't look forward to nylons.

My mind changed about marriage, too. I was not in any hurry and my parents only saw college in my future. Sam said, "Christine, I've found the one for Dorothy Leigh. I drove the Lane family to their son's graduation there. Hampton Institute. That's where my daughter is going when she graduates from Booker T." And he pulled me onto his lap.

That all seemed years and years away. Meanwhile I thought about seeing Bunny, my true love again. It was almost summer. Ever since the end of first grade, he lived in Washington with his parents. I only saw him for holidays and vacation. But the minute his daddy parked at Miss Coon's house, Bunny hightailed it to Beal Street to pick up his half-brother, Aaron, his best friend, James, and the three of them came to my grandmother's house. Of course, he no longer wore knickers, but he was still cute. We never talked about marriage or love. We hadn't kissed since my seventh birthday party. I didn't need to; just being near him, in the same room was enough.

Not only did Bunny find me after we moved to the end of the street, that Easter he showed up alone. Like always, he spoke to my mother. This time, he said, "May I take Dorothy to see a movie?"

I just about fainted. Tee didn't. "No, maybe next year."

Her answer stung. I wanted to die when I learned days later he took Bettie Jean. She was an ex-classmate of ours who had joined her mother in New York. I was doomed to be an old maid like Miss Victoria. I would rot away in the South.

Tee's promise of "next year" took two more years. I was almost thirteen the Sunday afternoon of our first date. I put on an aqua sheath dress with a rounded neck and a zipper up the back. None of that frilly stuff Tee always chose. I was excited. I'd never even walked down the street with a boyfriend in my life. *Would we hold hands or just walk close together? Would we kiss in the movie?* I floated into the living room where Mama and Tee were sitting.

"Dot," Mama laughed, "you look like a snake in that dress."

I broke from the room in tears. Tee said, "Dot has Sam's shape."

In my room—I no longer had a roommate—I examined myself in my pretty round mirror trimmed with a ruffled, yellow material. Tee made it herself, without a sewing machine. She was right. With no curves, no breasts, no hips—I was the spitting image of my daddy. But I couldn't cry then; I was about to go out on my first date with the boy of my dreams.

Good. I heard Mama leaving. I hoped she didn't bump into Bunny on her way home. She had no idea how important everything was. None of this had ever happened to her.

I recalled Tee's advice for handling situations like mine: "Think good thoughts, Punjab."

That's what I did for a minute. Then it hit me—I'd never been to a movie on a Sunday. It wasn't the Southern Christian thing to do. Not in broad daylight. Neighbors would see us.

Since all was quiet, I wandered back to the empty living room and waited there, closer to the front door. I'd yell to Tee as we left. Thank goodness, Sam wasn't home. He'd want me to give him a kiss in front of my date.

There was a knock on the screen door; we didn't have a doorbell like at Mama's. The front door was open. It was Easter, an April Easter with pleasant weather. I rushed from the living room into the hallway. As I neared the door, I saw the love of my life, my knight, in a long, tan trench coat. Bunny.

He was so handsome, dressed up like a Northerner. We just stared at each other for a moment. From behind me I saw Tee rushing to us. I wanted to push open the screen door, grab Bunny's hand, and run.

I looked again; she was grinning broadly. I almost turned back to Bunny, but noticed the closer she got, her grin seemed to slide off her face. She never said a word, just stopped dead in her tracks.

"Good afternoon, Mrs. Burston."

"Dorothy Leigh can't go to the movie with you."

Where did that come from? Why was she being so mean? I flew to my room. I couldn't face him ever again. How could she do that to me? How could she let us get our hopes up so high? How could she embarrass me?

Later that afternoon, I heard her on the phone with her girlfriend on our party line. "I couldn't help myself. I just couldn't let Dot go to the movie with Bunny. He looked like a grown man in that trench coat."

As I grew older, I tried to understand harder stuff. War still mixed me up. Tee tried explaining it again. All I knew was we were in a new war in Korea. Tee didn't call it that. "The news says it is not a war; it's a conflict. President Truman started it all by himself. It's about the 38th parallel. He told someone not to cross it and they did."

Later, Mama explained it to me. "President Truman was mad somebody was messing with his friends, so he said, 'To hell with Congress.' Sent troops hisself."

I understood. My friends stood up for me; I never learned how to fight. So that's how we got the new war in Korea. Milton, one of our Star Street neighbor's sons got killed early.

Aunt Burrell said, "His folks are making their old house look good with the money Uncle Sam gave them for killing Milton."

Something important happened one day when I was in sixth grade. Mr. Edgars, our principal who looked a lot like Chinese people and never smiled, announced over the intercom in our classroom, "Miss Perry, please send Dorothy Burston to my office."

I almost fainted, I was that scared. A boy in class said, "Oh, Dorothy, you better hurry. Nobody keeps Mr. Edgars waiting; not even the Lord."

When I reached his office, two other girls, Jackie and Barbara Jean, were there. I hoped we'd see him together. I asked, "Why did he send for us?"

No one knew. While I tried to look brave, Jackie, the oldest, slouched in her seat like she was bored. That didn't fool me. Barbara Jean, who was younger than the two of us, pretended to be calm. I knew they both dreaded seeing Mr. Edgars as much as I did.

Shortly, he roared from his office, "Come in, young ladies."

At least it was a polite roar. I gave a little smile. He got right to the point. "I picked the three of you because you always keep up with your class work and you're smart. I need someone to answer the telephone, to greet any visitors when I'm away, and to escort special visitors around the school."

Boy was I happy we'd finally gotten a telephone; I had experience. Mr. Edgars impressed me. Rather than cry about not having a secretary, he found a solution. If we were to make strides, as Negroes, time was precious. The grown-ups always told us that. He knew those white people would never give him a secretary. Like Aunt Burrell said, "There's more than one way to skin a cat."

His offer was interesting. It was a chance to be out of the classroom. Sure enough, education paid off, not always in money. This was worth it. We'd be almost as important as Mrs. Neville.

He asked, "Would you be interested in doing that? Being a representative for Abraham Lincoln School?"

Jackie, whose daddy taught at the high school, said, "I would like to represent our school."

I had to be next; I was a year ahead of Barbara Jean. "Yes sir, I'm interested."

Before I could congratulate myself for not copying Jackie, Barbara Jean grinned from ear-to-ear and chirped, "I'd love to." She sounded like Mr. Edgars had offered her a new bike, not a job. Her enthusiasm pushed a sourpuss like him over the edge. He smiled. "Perfect."

Right then I realized the importance of being experienced in Northern ways. Every summer, Barbara Jean visited her mother up North. While she dressed like the rest of us, she had an air about her that was Northern, carefree. I pledged if offered even the slightest opportunity in the future, I would say, "I'd love to."

Fall of seventh grade when I turned thirteen, my daddy surprised me with the prettiest blue and silver bicycle from his favorite store, Firestone. My bike had everything . . . twin silver, small airplane-shaped lights on the front fender, a great seat, another seat over the back fender for a friend. I rode better than most girls and a few of the boys.

One Sunday, as soon as we left church, I led three of my friends on a bike ride on one of my daddy's routes. I knew it was a long way from home so I said, "Don't change into dungarees; just wear your dresses, grab your bikes and meet me at my house."

We rode for a long time before we reached our destination near a white boys' reformatory school. Some of them jeered at us; but they couldn't get out. We pedaled on by. In less than a mile, I said, "It's time to head back home."

Nobody complained about how far we'd gone. To save time, I said, "We're taking the short cut; crossing over to the main highway."

In no time, we were there. Traffic was whizzing past in both directions. "On the count of three when there's a break in traffic, we charge across the northbound lane to the far lane which will take us back to Rocky Mount."

By some miracle, a break came. I yelled, "Go! Go!" We pedaled as fast as possible to the far lane. There was no time for relief; we kept moving like crazy on a skinny strip of a dirt path next to the highway. A steep drop-off threatened us on our right. Any break in the line of cars found us on the highway which angered the drivers. They laid on their horns. Others pulled towards the center when there was no oncoming traffic. All in all, it was the worst idea I'd ever had.

I became frightened. I wished we'd taken the long way but we couldn't turn back. I imagined our paper's headlines, maybe even Raleigh's *News and Observer*: "Four Negro Girls Riding Bikes on Highway Squashed to Death."

I couldn't let on how scared I was. It was too late to cry. We had to push on and for God's sake, don't fall down. At one point, I yelled as I dismounted, "Walk your bikes!"

None of us mentioned that trip—ever.

Turned out, I didn't have my first date until February of my seventh-grade year. And it wasn't with Bunny; it was with James, his best friend from Beal Street. He escorted me to our Valentine's Day Dance in the multi-use room. Since it was winter, it got dark real early. This time, Tee had no complaints about anything. James was sweet but not as cute as

Bunny. Nothing against James, but I vowed to never marry a boy from the South.

However, I was excited, I was thirteen years old and had a date for my first dance. I made myself as pretty as possible without lipstick and rouge. Tee wouldn't allow the very things I'd craved all my life. She seemed determined to deprive me of a lot of things I liked. That evening, handsome James gave me a heart shaped box of chocolates; my first ever from any man other than my daddy.

We danced together until seven o'clock that night. Neither of us mentioned Bunny. Not even when James walked me home through my short cut. Not even when he kissed me lightly on my lips at the front door.

Behind Lace Curtains

One summer evening while eavesdropping on my mother and her friend, Verna, on our front porch, I heard the best reason in the world for never getting married. It was about our next-door lady in the shot gun house. It was so real, I could see it. Tee said, "Late at night, every night, Louise crosses the street in her white slip, barefoot."

Verna asked, "Whatever is she doing out like that?"

"Wait."

Verna put in her two cents, "That husband of hers drives Louise crazy."

"Whatever. She sneaks out in the middle of the night, traipses across that dirt street—just as pretty as you please—to visit the bachelor in the back bedroom."

"Shameful."

"She climbs through his window. Do you hear me? Don't want to disturb his daddy in the front bedroom."

"Hush your mouth."

Tee said, "Some women will go to any lengths to play hide and go get it."

The next day it was hard speaking to Miss Louise without asking her if the rocks in the dirt street hurt her feet at night. I couldn't walk barefoot at all. I had more questions. Did she enjoy the game with the single man? On warm days, did she just sit there on her tiny porch and daydream about it?

I studied her. She never gave anything away—always as sweet as pie to her husband, pampered him, had his supper ready on time, and fixed herself up real pretty after a day of doing absolutely nothing. Shucks, her makeup was good enough for June German. It was something to see. I knew then and there, marriage was tricky.

Three more things bothered me. I wasn't sure why they happened. First, Little Alice was playing at my house and ran back home to get a game. People didn't lock their doors in our neighborhood. If they did, the key was always under the front door mat. Back doors were left open to let in the cool breezes. Alice's room was on the back; she returned in no time, empty-handed. I asked why.

Catching her breath, she said, "I heard Cousin Marie in my room. I peeked inside. She was in my bed with a man."

"Oh, Alice, that was nothing to run from. She and her husband probably got tired of waiting for your mama to get home, decided to rest a bit."

"It wasn't her husband."

"Take me to your room."

At her house, we tiptoed up to her bedroom. Sure enough, there they were. When Cousin Marie called out his name; it didn't sound anything like her husband's.

I came across these things by accident. I never searched for trouble of any kind, but when I was close to thirteen, my own mother took me to it. One Sunday night, just before Ed Sullivan's *Toast of the Town* came on, she insisted I run an errand with her. I didn't want to. Ed Sullivan's special guest was Sammy Davis. She said, "Dorothy Leigh, cut off the television and let's go."

At the corner, we turned on to Star Street. We never did that together. Tee was quiet. We walked like we were late for something important. She never once called me "Punjab" either. She just pulled me along onto Tillery Street. We sped past Davis Grocery Store, hit West Thomas Street, then stopped. She looked up and down the street. For what, I didn't know; there was no traffic.

We were on the corner next to Ford's, a café across the street from my friend's house. It wasn't as popular as White's; but it was okay. Tee dragged me across the street.

I said, "That's Sam's car parked right over there."

With no hesitation, she walked straight up to his gray Plymouth, opened the back door on the sidewalk side, and shoved me in ahead of her.

As she closed the door behind her, I settled into the back seat. She pulled me down to the floor. "I can't see anything from down here."

"Hush."

I shut up for a pretty good while. Then I said, "Sam's probably inside Ford's having a beer with his friends."

"Yeah, I bet he is—with his girlfriend."

I popped up; Tee returned me to the floor. I wanted no part of what was happening. She had tricked me. I looked back at her. She sounded like she had a cold. A few minutes passed before she said, "If we hurry, you can still catch a little of Ed Sullivan."

We never saw my daddy.

The last thing to really convince me I didn't want any part of being married was a shocker. I was watching television in my parent's bed. The living room doorway was straight ahead. I could see our set under the front window. It wasn't a large set but the black and white television from Firestone had a real clear picture.

I was enjoying *Father Knows Best* when it struck me— Tee had been gone from the room a long time. She was missing all the funny parts. I went to find her. She wasn't in the bathroom or the kitchen. I decided to check on our tiny back porch. I pushed open the screen door and yelled, "Tee, Tee!"

From the darkness came, "Go back inside, Dorothy Leigh."

She didn't sound like she needed my help. She used her "do as you are told" voice. My eyes, however, had adjusted to the night. As I slowly closed the screen door, I picked out two figures—Tee and a man. They stood real close, holding onto each other.

My daddy was tall next to my mother; this man was short. I knew him. He lived around the corner, on Star Street.

I was shocked. What was I to do? My father wasn't home, which was good. I made a decision; I'd better get back in the house as fast as my two skinny legs would take me. I did and waited. *Father Knows Best* was off. I stared at the television. My whole world was falling apart.

Tee didn't rush back into the house. That was good in a way; I wouldn't have been able to look at her, especially not to talk. When she did come back, she acted the same as usual. I didn't know what to say. I neither clung to her nor avoided her. I just was.

Later, during our day to day lives, when I saw that man in the neighborhood, I was very respectful. I didn't want him to think I knew anything about him and my mother.

Along about that time in my life, I became especially annoyed with Mama. After school I returned to an empty house. Tee's kindergarten was done for the day. She was at her domestic job; wouldn't return until around six or seven o'clock. My daddy always stopped by around four o'clock. I pretended to be super busy when he drove up. He was always finding jobs for me to do. Usually, he only spent about twenty to thirty minutes chopping kindling or doing something else. Then he returned to work.

None of what he did at home seemed pressing. I never said anything. In fact, he pretty much took off from the hospital whenever he wanted. Went and did handyman jobs at the hospital owner's house. I had at least an hour after school before he stopped by. After a long day, I enjoyed the calm and the freedom. I'd fix a snack, change my clothes, watch a little television, then tackle my chores. Homework, if I had any, was done in the evening. I liked my routine. I felt like an adult. Nobody bossed me around. I was comfortable.

Then one afternoon when the weather was still pleasant outside, the whiny singsong of our metal aqua and white porch glider disturbed my peace. It needed oil. A little scared, I tiptoed to the living room window. There sat Mama, as bold as you please, swinging back and forth. Odd. She always announced her arrival. Well, if she didn't say anything to me, I wouldn't say anything to her.

This went on for a couple of days. She always arrived before my daddy and left when he drove up. I bet she still bore a grudge against him.

I mentioned her behavior to Tee. Included the way she always left, like she didn't want to see my daddy. I didn't bring up the time she tried to kill him. A couple of days later, Tee and Mama were arguing. Coming in late, I didn't know what all the fuss was about. As I entered the kitchen, Mama pulled herself up from her chair and said, "Mark my word, she'll have a baby before she's sixteen."

I couldn't get out of the way. The words hit me all over. What was she angry about? I felt sorry for whoever it was. Somehow, I avoided her rocking body as she strode through our house and slammed the screen door.

"What was that all about?"

"Nothing to worry your pretty little head about."

In spite of Tee's words, Mama disturbed me.

Me and the house that Miss Louise visited frequently at night

Sam's Plymouth in front of ugly house

Tee's kindergarten class

Tee's graduating class

Forties metal porch glider

Next

My first day of high school began with trepidation. Maggie and Bob, two sophomore neighbors ditched me at the north entrance to the building. Over her shoulder, Maggie yelled and pointed, "Take the stairs to your homeroom."

Before reaching them, I was caught up in a whirlpool of strangers. The staircase vanished. I yearned for my old elementary school's separate lines of boys and girls lead by helpful classroom teachers. Then as suddenly as it had begun, I was out of the eddy and alone.

As I cowered there, a parade of grown-up looking girls in skinny skirts and perfectly ironed blouses sauntered by. Their necks had white pearls or colorful scarves. Pretty gold hoop earrings peeked from beneath freshly curled hair or flashed near clinched ponytails. Their faces were beautifully made up in stark contrast to my clean, Pond's Vanishing Cream face.

A few of them stared up into the slightly hairy faces of older looking boys. One boy even had a mustache. Their voices sounded deep like my dad's. Here and there, a few naïve-looking people hung on for dear life; I squeezed in with them.

We climbed to the second floor. I arrived at my homeroom and sat down next to a girl on the front row because she smiled at me. She whispered, "Nick is our homeroom teacher. That's short for the devil. And she's an old maid."

A bell sounded. From up high on a platform in front of us came, "You are my charges for the next three years." Nick introduced herself.

In a crisp, bossy way she was helpful, but real fidgety. I watched her shift stacks of papers back and forth before the next announcement. "When I call your names in alphabetical order, come get your class schedule."

Once that was done, she said, "These students will remain here with me for first period." Eight names were read.

When the passing bell rang, I watched my new classmates and a few from my old school exit to freedom. So far, there hadn't been much to like about high school. I hoped second period would be better.

After roll call, Old Nick clicked her heels and took off. Algebra turned out to be a higher arithmetic, with sentences instead of numbers. It was obsessed with cars, trucks, and trains leaving point A to arrive at point B at different speeds and start times. It seemed a rather pointless waste of the brain.

When the period ended, I sprang from the room. I knew where I had to be for the next two hours. Outside the door, a stampede of students forced me to a halt, pressed me up against a hard, metal wall. Lockers. Old Nick said we'd each get one. "Buy yourself a combination lock as soon as you can; people are not always honest around here."

My minutes were ticking away. I needed to hustle but I couldn't. Eventually I arrived at another set of stairs. The trip down was tedious and cramped. By the time I arrived at my second period class, I only had energy enough to gasp, "Present."

In only one day of high school, I learned each teacher came with a different set of whims which had to be satisfied. The physical education teacher expected me to undress and shower in front of not only her, but thirty or more strange girls, without a shower curtain. There was no way around it.

High school placed other obstacles in my path. Our required classes weren't enough; "extracurricular activities" had to be added. Failure to do so would put me in a poor light. I chose band and choir.

At the appointed time, I showed up at the band room. My cousin Olivia, now in college, had spoken very highly of the director, Mr. Woods. As a clarinet player, she got a band uniform, a seat on the bus, and everything.

I was ready and hopeful. I liked the sweet music played on a flute. I also enjoyed the way an oboe seemed to talk, to carry on a conversation with the other instruments. I settled on the flute; its weight was ideal for parades.

Mr. Woods said, "Which instrument are you interested in playing?"

"I'd love to play the flute."

"Do you own one?"

"No. I'd love to play a clarinet, too."

In a few minutes, he began distributing instruments. He didn't use the alphabetical system. 'Cause a girl from across town whose last name began with a "p" got the only flute.

Mr. Woods called everybody in the band room except me and Ann, my classmate from elementary school. His system was confusing. Our last names were at opposite ends of the alphabet. What we had in common was we were skinny, short, and not very strong. When he called us, we rushed to him.

The instrument room was a large, almost empty closet. All that was left were Mr. Woods and two big brass things, one in each hand. He thrust them at us as we crossed the threshold. We each caught one. I almost collapsed under the weight of mine. Brushing his hands together, he said, "There, you two girls will play the baritone horns."

Baritone horn? Where's my clarinet? Why was he picking on us? In all our weekly music classes in elementary school, I never saw a lady play a baritone horn. I wanted to let Ann know what I thought of the whole mess but she was hidden by her instrument.

He aimed us in the direction of the band room. I crushed the huge baritone horn to my chest and walked blindly forward. In the band room, someone steered us to our section. By then, my horn was up to my face. I peered through the open space near the three buttons. Not nearly enough buttons for all the treble or the bass clef notes. It would be a miracle if I produced any music at all.

In a few days, I showed up for choir. We all knew Miss Butler, the director. At one time, she was the traveling music teacher for all three Negro elementary schools. Her voice was so lovely, she appeared on the Arthur Godfrey television show. Regardless, the white school board would not expose their lily-white children to her, even though she looked more like them than us.

Aunt Burrell was right about that ounce of colored blood. It didn't make a lick of sense to me. Southern white folks were peculiar.

I was happy we had Miss Butler. In the choir room, we all got to singing. After a few minutes, she frowned. "I'm hearing an odd voice."

She walked closer to us. My singing dropped to a whisper. Just a few more people and she would be right in front of me. In an effort to relax, I reminded myself: I am a Negro. Every Negro can sing. We can sing without one ounce of training. I had seen it over and over in movies.

Oh, I knew Miss Butler couldn't hear odd notes from me. Still, I was nervous. Guilt started popping out on me like chicken pox. When she was only two people away, the intercom blared. "Please send Dorothy Burston to the auditorium. Mrs. Armstrong wishes to see her."

I flew from the room with no idea who Mrs. Armstrong was or what she wanted.

In the auditorium, a lovely lady with the most beautiful, Northern accent ever greeted me. It was a joy just to be in her presence. "Dorothy, here is the script. Please go up on the stage and read the cripple's speech on page 11."

I read as never before.

"Now, Dorothy, please move about the stage."

She called out stage positions. I followed her directions. Then she smiled and said, "I'd like to cast you in the Christmas production."

I wept silent tears. I didn't know why she had sent for me but I'd likely been spared possible humiliation. Sometimes that's the way root working happened. I might never find out. So, I dismissed it and thanked my lucky stars.

From that moment on, I adored high school. True, Mrs. Armstrong had the same last name as the doctor who killed my grandfather. I didn't hold that against her; she married into that family. I was crazy about her. She was the answer to everything.

Acting was my forte. It was so easy. I understood it all. As the cripple in *Star Song,* I followed directions, stayed in character, limped about the stage, filled my big eyes with real tears. Crying came natural to me. Except for Mrs. Armstrong's nephew, Kenneth, I was the youngest in the cast.

We performed *Star Song* first in our school auditorium. Then we traveled to our area's television station. A bus transported the stage flats, props, costumes, and cast. I didn't get to ride on it; Mrs. Armstrong put me up front in her powder-blue Cadillac with the huge fins. I liked that car. After the production, telephone calls and telegrams arrived for our principal. We were a huge success.

Drama became my thing. A drama clinic was scheduled in the fall at Fayetteville State College in Fayetteville. Mrs. Armstrong picked me to play the role of the sole girl in the three-person cast of "Heat Lightning." Very exciting as both boys were seniors. A one-act play, it was set in a small bus station on a stormy night. The action was fast paced, the situation tense, and the curtain closed on my perfect scream. The applause was wonderful on both the high school and college stages.

Although I was always an above average student, I made sure I stayed up with all my classes. Nothing should stand in the way of my being excused whenever the goddess called. In March, the regional drama festival was held in our auditorium. The best performances went on to the state level. Our production, "Auf Wiedersehen," a one-act play about the Jewish incarceration in Germany, featured my favorite senior actress, Essie Mae. I played her niece. As a first-place winner, we moved on to the state finals at Shaw University in Raleigh.

The judges for all productions were college level professors from private or state universities in North Carolina, Virginia, West Virginia, or Washington, D.C. By the end of my freshman year, I was nominated for the International Thespian Society and awarded a letter. I had found my niche; I was happy.

Freshman year in general went pretty well. I was super busy, so much so, I didn't fall in love until March. My first romance at fourteen was driven by me. I decided to no longer be in love with the cutest and especially not the smartest boy in my class. I wanted a boyfriend with rough edges and found him, Mike, in my own homeroom.

Unfortunately, Old Nick, my homeroom teacher, was aware of my choice. One morning, she said, "Dorothy, please come up to my desk."

"Yes, Miss Davis."

She spoke in a whisper. "Dorothy, I know your mother. And that is not the kind of boy she wants you being interested in."

Stunned, I nodded and returned to my seat. After school, I talked to Mike. "Which church do you go to?"

He said, "Travelers' Rest."

I winked at him. That Sunday morning, with a friend in tow, I showed up two pew rows from the pulpit and grinned as Mike passed the collection plate.

By April, I was out of love with him and smiling at Mrs. Armstrong's nephew, Kenneth, who bumped into me on the staircase. We started meeting there. At the time, Kenneth was courting a sophomore.

It didn't really dawn on me that we were starting a courtship until she said, "Are you in love with Kenneth, my boyfriend?"

"No." It was all just fun at that point. However, pretty soon, our names were linked together. After school, he walked me half way home, a real commitment considering he lived just down the hill from Booker T. and had an afternoon paper delivery route. The courtship moved along to Sunday evening visits in my family's living room, movies together at the Center, and good night kisses on my front porch. Towards the end of spring, a girl named Pimp broke up our romance.

I had known her younger cousins for a long time but not her. One afternoon, Barbara Ann and I were walking past Pimp's duplex when she called out, "Hey, you two. Why don't you come up on our porch and talk for a while."

We stood there dumbfounded. Neither of us could ask "why" but we couldn't come up with a reason to say no. Almost in unison, we said, "Okay."

We were barely seated when she said, "You girls have to plan."

Barbara Ann and I looked at each other. Plan what? We tried not to look dumb. "Just go on and do it. You'll never regret it. It feels good."

We were totally lost.

"You both know Peter. He lives around the block. Just as handsome as he can be."

We nodded yes. She was right about Peter.

"Peter and me. Oh, I'm telling you. Real good. Besides, if you do it while you real young, later when you get married, your husband won't have such a hard time breaking you in."

We had read the little Kotex booklet the teachers gave us in sixth grade. But we'd never heard the whole thing explained the way Pimp did. She acted like we were almost too late. Although it sounded really nasty, my curiosity was aroused.

Before I realized it, Easter vacation arrived. My mother, my friends, neighbors, everybody went to the falls on Easter Monday, a school holiday.

Kids my age had outgrown the egg hunts at Miller's Grove on West Thomas Street. Besides, the falls area was far more exciting than any old grove of trees. There were boulders to climb and paths to explore. The falls was the place to be.

I decided to lead an expedition. I liked that word. We would walk the narrow, two foot wide, cement ledge of the concrete wall which held back a lot of water. The cotton mill was next to it. Sometimes water flowed over the ledge. Although I didn't know the water release schedule, I was pretty sure it wasn't Easter Monday; too many Negroes were hanging around the large boulders below.

Finding four followers was easy. Off we went. Within a few steps onto the ledge and a closer view of the gate across it, I discovered a problem. A fat padlock hung from it.

Darn. It was too late to cancel the expedition; my people were lined up behind me. "There's a padlock on the gate. Instead of opening it and walking through to the other side, we'll simply hold onto the smooth part of the gate, swing out over the water and land on the other side. Copy me."

Since no protests came, I yelled, "Onward to the end of the ledge!"

"Yes!" They answered.

Cavalry troops in western movies came to mind but I advanced. There was no other choice, nobody could squeeze around me. If anyone tried, one or both of us would either crash to the boulders below or drown in the deep, dark water.

I almost panicked recalling my helplessness in the swimming pool a few summers earlier. I stopped thinking about it, became more careful than ever. In three more steps, the gate was less than an arm's length away. I reached out, grabbed the fat edge, and swung out over the dark water. My eyes focused on the ledge on the other side of the gate. Gratefully, my foot touched solid concrete. I brought my remaining hand and foot to brief safety.

There was no time to relax or to catch my breath—my party awaited my directions. "You can do it. Get set! When you're ready, swing around the gate and come to me!"

As each one landed successfully, I inched farther down the ledge. Once we were all on the same side, the expedition carefully continued to the end of the ledge, a block away. A few times the enormous boulders below made me catch my breath. That's when I looked to the other side, to the water; it appeared to have risen to a close to overflow height.

Near the end of the ledge, our jumping off point, I grew nervous. True, I'd looked up and seen the big boulder at the end before we ever took off on our expedition but was it close enough to jump down to? *Careful, they mustn't smell my fear.*

When the last member of my party jumped down to the big boulder, I decided to never include others in my adventures again. The responsibility was too great.

By May, I'd forgotten all about Easter. I was still in so love with Kenneth. Although I didn't exactly plan my experiment as instructed by Pimp, I didn't prevent it either. One spring day, everything just seemed to fall into place. It all began with Kenneth telling me at lunch time how much he loved fishing. He said, "I have my own rod and reel."

"You do? I like fishing, too." I'd never dipped a pole in any water. "I was raised on Tar River."

Kenneth said, "I fish in it, right across from the swimming pool. I'm going there this afternoon."

"As soon as I run home and change my clothes, I'll join you."

His fishing spot was behind the Girl Scout cabin, one of the many leftover buildings from the WPA or WWII. In elementary school, I had been a Girl Scout; had begged to be one. Two years later, my friends were dropping out of it. I pleaded to get out, too. Tee wouldn't let me. I was a Girl Scout all the way to eighth grade.

Now a year later, I hurried home, crammed my lace trimmed, white cotton slip into my dungarees. Pulled on a button up shirt, and tied on my Keds tennis shoes. "Tee, I'm going for a bike ride."

I pedaled back across town to join Kenneth. Once in the river area, I walked my bike across the tall green grass. On the very edge of the thick trees which hid the river from view, I struck out on the worn, dirt, pine needled, foot path; headed for the river.

Kenneth was exactly where he said he'd be. His rod was propped up, waiting for a nibble.

We kissed. At the river's edge where all was quiet with only the two of us, it was true love. We went from there. Kenneth forgot all about fishing as he watched me unzip my dungarees and pull up my slip. In his turn, he unzipped his pants, unbuckled his belt, and drew closer to me. We sank down to the damp ground ever so gently.

Kenneth eased my dungarees down around my legs and slid down my panties. All was quiet while he slid on a rubber. Then lowering himself, he put his penis between my legs. I was surprised; I wasn't in the least bit afraid. Rather I was anxious to get started, ready to feel real good. Like Pimp had said. Slowly, he started trying to enter me. It hurt.

There was the rustling of leaves. A male voice said, "Hey, little brother, what are you doing, huh?"

Kenneth froze.

It was his big brother. They called him "20", his football jersey number. Their parents had just bought him a brand-new, blue-and-white 1954 sleek Ford Fairlane. He was everywhere in it. He stared at us, stroked his chin, stopped, and stared some more.

I was petrified.

Slightly behind him, taller than 20, was his best friend, an army vet working on his high school diploma. I wanted to die; somewhere deep down inside me, I thought I might.

Kenneth knelt straight up between my legs.

From the corner of my eye, I looked at his stocky, boisterous brother, a high school junior. Then looked straight into Kenneth's eyes and begged silently, "Please don't let anything bad happen to me."

He remained where he was.

His brother's friend said, "Let's leave, 20. We got some things to do. Remember?" But 20 said, "Get up little brother. Let me get a piece of that."

Kenneth stayed where he was. I hoped it was for my protection. I wanted to pull my slip down over my thighs but thought better of it. The air itself seemed ready to explode. Anything could trigger it.

In desperation, I watched 20 swagger towards us, unbuckling his belt as he advanced. He sneered. I wasn't sure if it was meant for Kenneth or for me.

Kenneth's voice began low, gently, as if to a child who was about to do a dangerous thing.

His brother shook his head.

"Aw, 20, go on about your important business. Leave us alone."

Suddenly I remembered where we were—the muddy Tar River. I stared up at Kenneth.

He didn't look back. His eyes were glued on 20.

His brother tilted his head to one side, stroked his chin again.

From behind him, his friend said, "Come on, man, let the kids do their thing."

He ignored his friend, reached for his zipper and forced the teeth apart.

I squeezed my eyes shut. In the silence, the damp ground beneath me was so chilling, I longed for the sun which filtered through the canopy of trees.

"20 . . ."

"Yeah, yeah, you're right. Let's go."

The ledge and metal chain-link gate at the entrance to the falls area where I led the four-girl expedition on Easter Monday

Stumbling Blocks

By mid-May of 1954, the country and especially the South was confronted with school integration. With three years of high school yet to go, I regarded it as a personal threat. That brand-new white high school was closer than Booker T.

I didn't dislike change. In general, life as a Negro in the United States, and in the South in particular, wasn't pretty or fair. We survived some rough times. Integration couldn't just walk in and make everything equal in one fell swoop. I especially didn't want it messing with me. Any Negro with an ounce of sense knew anything the white man gave or granted to us would certainly be covered with sores, problems, and stuff we couldn't even imagine.

Nobody I knew wanted to go over to their old white schools and be treated like dirt. No doubt about who would be doing the going. Their kids would not be coming to our schools in our neighborhoods.

Unbeknownst to them, we had secret weapons—our teachers. Whether or not they would go with us was unknown but they had instilled in us a motto: "You have to be a hundred times better than any white person to even get noticed. Don't ever forget it"

Mama said, "Any fool knows they'll get rid of the Negro teachers. How white people can twist things around in their heads is beyond me." She spat.

All that spring, I dreaded the idea of integration. Before long, all talk of it quieted down. I relaxed, started thinking about earning some money for college. I needed a job. Green tobacco work was out. Mr. Coggins and my family had parted ways. Nobody ever told me why. For all I knew, he may have died.

'Round about July, the tobacco factories opened up. When Tee went to apply, I tagged along and got hired. I didn't look like an eighteen-year-old; but there I was, working on the belt. I stood to one side of a big flat basket placed on a rolling trolley, at least 40 inches round, waist high, stacked with at least two bundled, burlap wrapped bags of yellow cured tobacco. My partner stood across from me. As stemmers, we were to strip each tobacco leaf from its stem in one quick downward motion. It took me two to three pulls to release the gold leaf. Then I fed the crumbled offering to the conveyor belt next to me and grabbed another leaf.

There was no instruction. Nothing—pulling grass dolls, climbing trees, carrying kindling into the house, or working in green tobacco—had prepared me for the factory. My tender hands ached. My knees buckled. Except for walks to the toilet or water breaks, my feet stayed in one spot with occasional shifts of my weight.

The greedy belt rolling by ignored my youth, demanded more leaves. Pleased or not, it accepted my puny offerings, and carried them up a ramp to a big, rolling barrel of a thing. There, the feeble tobacco was tossed every which-a-way, steamed, dropped, and sent through a series of overhead, metal tunnels. No amount of impromptu singing of "Amazing Grace" or "Down by the Riverside" from my co-workers changed the order. Repeated itself . . . again and again.

Aside from the physical demands of the job, I worked nights from seven to seven. At dawn, I stumbled home, bathed, ate, and slept the whole day—just to return in the evening to do it all again. I saw no friends; did nothing. Three whole nights later I was fired.

By the end of the week, my desire to go to college forced me to find other work. That Monday before dawn, I arose and got dressed. In minutes, I made a small lunch and quietly left my sleeping parents. The sun was peeking out when I headed for the very corner where Tee tried to ambush my daddy. There, I began my vigilance.

The street was bare. I wished for a farmer in need of help. I dared not sit down; I might appear to be lazy.

There was a prime example of laziness on television, "The Amos and Andy Show." I was proud and happy to finally have that all Negro weekly show. I even asked my mother if I could have the doll, Amosandra, whose father was the sensible Amos, owner of a cab company.

I received it for a Christmas present. Once I showed it to my cousin Brit's mother and grandmother, I couldn't pry the doll away from them. They idolized Amosandra, created a wardrobe for her, and displayed her on their big bed. The NAACP scorned the one-sided portrayal of our people on that television show.

When I thought about it, I agreed—my daddy worked hard all the time. I never saw any Negro man as dumb as Andy.

I let Brit's mother and grandmother keep the doll.

Not to appear lazy, I stood up real tall that morning chanting "looper" which paid better than a hand. I yearned for employment. After a while, a lone car packed with workers approached. As it pulled to the curb, a lady leaned out of the front passenger window and called, "Dorothy Burston?"

"Yes ma'am."

I never said that to any white person and only to a few colored ladies. I bent the rule of Miss Exum, my seventh-grade teacher: "As long as you say 'Yes, Mrs. So and So' or 'No, Mr. So and So' to white people, you don't have to say yes ma'am or yes sir."

I loved her for that. None of my Northern friends ever said "ma'am." To tell the truth, I cringed each time my parents or my grandmother said "Yes ma'am" to white people.

The lady in the car who called out to me was Mrs. Boone, a fellow actor's mother. They lived one street over from where I stood. Her son, Herman, and I had been in a few plays together in high school. He had just graduated. His little sister, Alice, had attended my mother's kindergarten. Oh, yes, I knew Mrs. Boone.

"Can you hand tobacco, baby?"

"Yes ma'am. I can loop it, too."

"Y'all hear that? Exactly what we need, a looper. And I know her family."

As I squeezed into the car, introductions were made. We drove off to that white man's farm. When we got there, I stored my lunch with theirs and began my first looping job. At dinner time, we knocked off, washed up, and went to the farmer's kitchen—to a feast.

As a teenager, I ate practically anything. My favorite foods—fried chicken and fried liver smothered in onions—were on the table. Also, platters of ham slices, and bowls of cooked vegetables, hot rolls and pretty potato salad. Other stuff I wasn't crazy about but tasted them. The best was sliced red tomatoes and crunchy green cucumbers in a peppery vinegar. For the rest of the season, I ate other people's cooking, white folks included, and loved every bit of it.

By fall, Kenneth and I had cooled down to a friendship. The river's edge experience just destroyed any love interest. We never even mentioned it. Much to my relief, no rumors circulated about my behavior which would have been devastating.

I made the band, got a uniform and a hat. Some of my tobacco money paid for the white shirt, white buckskin shoes, and white socks. My fellow baritone player, Ann, and I were so excited, we lugged our horns and school books all the way to her house to practice. I still had five more blocks to my house. Mr. Woods began whipping us into parade shape, up and down the streets around the school. My position was on the right-hand side, the first row behind the drum major. Tee 'nem could easily find me.

Since Ann's house was in front of Mangrum's tobacco warehouse (where I'd seen my first June German) her street was paved. We lined up on opposite sides and marched like the whole band was with us. Our music summoned no spectators, not even her parents or sisters or brother.

The first football game half time show was my test. I had to play my instrument, remember the different positions for forming letters or figures, and arrive at my spot on time. Through it all I struggled with my bulky uniform whose pants required suspenders. But I was in the marching band.

I also appeared in plays with the theatre group. That year we did three one-act plays of which I appeared in two of them: *Behold the Man* and *The Monkey's Paw*.

Sophomore year was shaping up into a lot of fun, even though Old Nick still ruled my home room and my algebra class. In the spring, she had enrolled me in typing and shorthand 'cause someone at a convention she attended made extra money on the spot for her skills. I would have preferred wood shop; but it was for boys only.

At home, Tee surprised me. "Dot, I found a job for you. You can earn some extra change cleaning house for Mae, on Saturdays."

It was her childhood friend who had recommended her for membership in The Gay Senoritas' pinochle club. Although I wasn't crazy about the prospect, I appreciated the chance to add to my college fund. Saturday morning, I skipped my household chores for a few hours and walked to work. It was late afternoon when Sam learned of my job. All hell broke loose. "If that's the only way she can earn extra money, she won't have any."

Later, I overheard Tee telling her friend, "Sam said Dot has enough chores at home."

School was even better than freshman year. I had Spanish with my theater teacher. The very first day, I learned to say our pledge of allegiance in Spanish; I doubted I'd need it in Spain. However, if Mrs. Armstrong wanted me to learn it . . . well. I was happy with my sophomore routine; Old Nick wasn't. "Dorothy Burston, bring your schedule up here, please."

With a quick eye, she examined it. "Aha." Furiously, she erased whatever it was with pleasure, held it up to fan away eraser crumbs, and wrote quickly. Eyeing the results, she smiled to herself and pushed it back to me. "Your mother wants you to have French. You need it for college."

If that was the case, I had no qualms.

In a way, as wonderful as Mrs. Armstrong was, she complicated my high school life. It wasn't her fault there was no class period for theater and she always called me out of band. It got so bad that I cringed whenever the intercom interrupted our playing. Often it was for me. Regardless, it was a small sacrifice to be called by such an exciting and clever lady.

Even her vocabulary was impressive. Words like "facetious" flowed from her lips. When she sent for me, I faked being annoyed, stashed my instrument in the storage room, and as quietly as possible, trespassed through the resumed band practice. Avoiding Mr. Woods' flying baton, I humbly left the room. Once out of sight, I skipped to the goddess.

The day I long sensed was coming, came. Mr. Woods called me into his office. "Miss Burston, you have to make a choice between band and dramatics."

His bluntness was appreciated. "Yes, sir. I will."

At home, I mentioned nothing to my mother. I simply left the next morning, books in one hand and my heavy band uniform on a hanger in the other. I walked the long way to Booker T.'s band room with occasional switches of hands and refused help from my two upperclassmen neighbors. It was my cross to bear. How ridiculous he was to place band on the same level as theater.

Contrary to what he offered, theater presented me with possibilities to engage not only my mind in problem solving, but provided chances to explore other possibilities without exposing myself to failure or danger—I was always someone else. When the curtain went down, I returned to being me. And at that point, an exhilarated me who welcomed the applause for my performance.

Even the tediousness of repetitive rehearsals was thrilling. Capturing a character's meaning, interacting on stage with fellow performers, sensing when Mrs. Armstrong's directing worked, hearing her approval and delight—sometimes brought tears to my eyes.

Probably the most magical moments in theater came when I either waited in the wings to enter or when I was on stage as the curtain opened. I was in a different world, one I wished to acquaint my audience with. I was rather possessive in that sense; I wanted them in the palm of my hand. As a young, petite Negro high school girl, it was a powerful feeling, especially in the heat of the persecuting South.

No. I would never sacrifice the stage with its brilliant spot lights, magical make up, clever costumes, and interesting characters—for a chance to carry around a huge instrument, keep a straight line, produce loud music, wear a big, heavy, old uniform, and step lively in wide shoes wearing two pairs of socks. That morning when I entered the band room, Mr. Woods sat at his desk in his office.

"Good morning, Mr. Woods. I made my decision. Here's your uniform. Thank you for letting me play in the band; it was fun."

That spring, he surprised me, "Miss Burston, there's a seat for you on the bus to the band festival at A & T College in Greensboro."

I accepted.

When summer arrived, I joined the crowded half-circle of anxious Negro female faces in front of the white boss at the China American

Tobacco factory. Being short, Tee insisted we move to the front. Exactly where I didn't want to be; the boss might remember firing me last year.

He greeted his favorite returnees by name. Enviable exchanges took place before the chosen entered the hallowed tobacco factory. With them in position, he started on us. Tee was picked early. Looking at me, he said, "You'll be a sweeper."

I'd never swept anything in my life except our house, our front porch, and our dirt front yard. That first night, as the stemmers prepared to feed the belt, I pushed my first broom and began clearing the floor around each of their tobacco stacks. Later, my mother whispered, "Occasionally, see if any of the stemmers need anything, like water, or snacks from the vending machine."

One night weeks later, our boss stopped me as I was headed outside to the park for a midnight lunch. "Would you like to earn some extra money?"

"What do I have to do for it?"

"Climb up into that drum and pull out all the tobacco trapped in the little holes."

I looked at the drum; then stared at the switch mounted on a nearby post.

"Oh, I'll stand right there by the switch. You don't have to worry about that."

I wished Tee could advise me but she was outside already. After a moment, I decided if I was old enough to get hired, I was— "Yes, I can do that."

"I'll be right back with the ladder."

With him gone, doubts hounded me. What if someone came by, cut on the switch while his back was turned. I wanted to change my mind. Tell him the truth. I'm only fifteen. Get fired. No. I need the money for college.

"Here's the ladder. There's five dollars in it for you."

I climbed up the ladder, crawled into the huge, gray, metal drum with all the punched out, nickel sized holes on its insides, peeked out the other end which sent the tobacco into a narrow tunnel, and began snatching pieces of tobacco wedged in the holes. It took only a few minutes. "I'm done."

He paid on the spot. I rushed outside to join Tee. No need to bring it up then.

I made it to my first payday and promptly gave her money to put away for college. As crazy as I was about my daddy, I didn't ask him; he liked cars too much. With my remaining earnings, I saw a movie, ate treats, bought a *Seventeen* magazine. There wasn't a single Negro girl anywhere in it but I pretended it applied to me anyway.

One day I learned of a bus trip to Sea Breeze, the Negro section of Virginia Beach in Norfolk. I paid my fare. The trip, sponsored by Ann's family, was an all-day thing, leaving early Sunday and returning later that night.

I was on my own. No family, best friend, or boyfriend which didn't bother me a bit. I knew my way around Sea Breeze. I'd been there lots of times with my relatives. I was ready to have some fun. Out of nowhere, a soon to be senior eased into the empty bus seat next to me. I knew him or rather I knew of his sisters. They were real smart and popular when they were in high school; now they were in college. His name was Billy.

It was like we'd been waiting to meet. He lived on Happy Hill, too, about six blocks away from me. The beach was perfect for us. We did everything together—rides, games. It was so much fun. And I liked him. He was cute, not too scholarly and was on the basketball team. Not as a starter or even second off the bench, but he had the cutest legs on the team. We laughed and talked about anything.

By August, something really horrible happened. Worse than the summers of protecting myself from polio to escape that iron lung. That horrible thing involved a fourteen-year-old Negro boy who was killed by some white trash in Mississippi, a colored person's hell. I was shocked. Although, I still was amazed when a Negro man was slain, I was stunned at the level to which any human being would sink to kill a Negro child.

According to *JET* magazine, Emmet Till, from Chicago, was visiting relatives for the summer when a young white girl claimed he made a pass at her. When her husband returned that night, she told him the made-up story. He and a relative went hunting for that fourteen-year-old boy. They dragged him out of his uncle's house and threw him in the back of their truck. Later, Emmet was found shot in the head. Barbed wire was wrapped around his neck. His body, tied to a heavy factory fan, was in the Tallahatchie River.

In a Mississippi courtroom, those two white men were found not guilty of murder.

That was it for me. I was getting as far away from the South as I possibly could. Southern white people were crazy, mad. A lot of times, their women lied about colored men making passes or whistling at them. I began to wonder if the white men were in some way jealous of colored men. It was all very evil. They must be the devils religion preached about all the time. I didn't want to breathe the same air people like that breathed. I wouldn't even return for June German.

My third year at Booker T. began with school integration stalled in Rocky Mount. White people had no intention of letting black and white children sit together in the same school. I fervently hoped we would remain separate and unequal until I graduated. I was so close to the end.

Curriculum wise, trigonometry replaced algebra. At first, I thought that was a good thing. Although I sensed some value to the study of it, I was not thrilled. But I loved every bit of English. I had finished French I and was enrolled in French II. Oh, how I wished my mother could have replaced me in that classroom since she loved it so much.

The United States was now threatened by a Senator McCarthy who was worse than any foreign enemy. Like a bloodhound, he hunted down anyone he deemed a communist. Once he had the scent, he wouldn't let go; he persecuted the poor victim in the courts. He, along with members of the House Committee on Un-American Activities, disgraced people and deprived them of their livelihood. What a madman. I saw him in action on television.

Tee said, "Thank goodness, Negroes can't get caught up in that. We don't have any important jobs and we certainly don't know any government secrets. At least, we won't get blamed for any of this."

Were we surprised when the committee on un-American activities called in our very own Paul Robeson, the singer and actor. Right away we knew that was pure jealousy. He was too brilliant for words. Smart as a whip. On a full Rutgers' scholarship, he made the All-American football team and graduated valedictorian of his class. And Lord, could he sing. His rich, deep voice was heard in concerts all over the world. As a Columbia University law student, Mr. Robeson played NFL football and earned his law degree.

Years later, I read about his appearance on Broadway as Othello with Uta Hagen and Jose Ferrer. As a teenager, I often read the theater critics reviews in the Sunday *New York Times.* It didn't matter that I read them a day late on Monday evenings when Sam brought the used paper home from the hospital. From the *Times,* I recognized a lot of the actresses and actors who appeared on television in Westinghouse Playhouse 90 or Lux Video Theater productions. I daydreamed about seeing my name in that paper.

I talked to Mama about Mr. Robeson. She said, "Dot, it don't pay for a colored man to be too gifted or smarter than a white man. They'll tear him down every time; even if they have to lie to do it."

Once while Mr. Robeson was visiting in another country, they asked his opinion of Negro rights in America. He said the United States was doing a poor job. Our government was some kinda mad at him—telling the truth like that. Next, he spoke up for workers' rights all over the world. The Russians liked him.

Aunt Burrell told me, "If there's one thing America can't stand—it's a foreign country treating Negroes nice."

Lots of foreign countries loved Negro artists. Writers like James Baldwin, singers, dancers like Josephine Baker were waving goodbye to America and moving to Europe where the people couldn't get enough of us, especially in France. I was glad Old Nick had switched me to French. I could go there, if up North didn't work out.

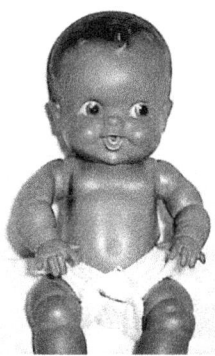

Amosandra

Miss Exum

Booker T. Washington High School Marching Band
I'm in 1st standing row, 3rd from right

THE PLAYBILL

FOR TROUPE 403

The National Thespian Society
<small>(Devoted to the Advancement of Dramatic Arts in the Secondary Schools)</small>

Booker T. Washington High School

THE BARRIER
BEHOLD THE MAN
THE MONKEY'S PAW

THE BARRIER
A Play in One Act
By John McGreevey

CAST
(In order of their appearance)

MEG HUGHES	DOROTHY BURSTON
DR. GEORGE HUGHES	DAVID DUNN
LIEUTENANT CARTER	DONALD ARMSTRONG
BRADY	JAMES NELSON
PAUL WILSON	JOHN PRESTON BRYANT

Scene: Dr. Hughes' comfortable living room in a small midwestern town. One evening in the present.

THE MONKEY'S PAW
A Play in One Act
By W. W. Jacobs — Dramatized by Louis N. Parker

CAST
(In order of their appearance)

MR. WHITE	JOHN PRESTON BRYANT
MRS. WHITE	DOROTHY BURSTON
HERBERT	DAVID DUNN
SERGEANT-MAJOR MORRIS	DONALD ARMSTRONG
MR. SAMPSON	JAMES NELSON

Scene I. The living room of an old-fashioned cottage on the outskirts of Fulham.
(The curtains will be pulled to denote the passing of time.)
Scene II. The White living room. The next morning.
Scene III. The White living room. A week later.

DONALD ARMSTRONG (Lt. Carter and Morris), a Senior, has been a member of the Thespian Society since in Sophomore year. During his Sophomore year he appeared in STAR SONG as the Roman Centurion, Lucius, and as the man at the door in JACOB COMES HOME. He was the Centurion in NO ROOM AT THE INN in his Junior year. This year he was Gaius, the Roman Centurion, in two performances of STAR SONG, and tonight he is appearing as Lt. Carter in THE BARRIER and Sergeant-Major Morris in THE MONKEY'S PAW. A diligent and enthusiastic worker, Donald has played an important role in making the productions of Troupe 403 a success.

DOROTHY BURSTON (Mrs. Hughes and Mrs. White), a Sophomore, made the Thespian Society at the end of her Freshman year for her outstanding roles as a slave in NO ROOM AT THE INN, as the Girl in HEAT LIGHTNING, and as Elsa in AUF WIEDERSEHN. This year she starred as the slave in STAR SONG, and tonight is appearing as Mrs. Hughes in THE BARRIER and as Mrs. White in THE MONKEY'S PAW. Dorothy's keen perception of the dramatic values in a play and her instinctive feeling for good theater give promise of future dramatic successes for her.

I'm in a scene from "The Monkey's Paw" rehearsal in high school

Two Students Win Honors At Festival

Two Booker T. Washington high school students, Dorothy Burston and Maceo Knight, were awarded top honors at the North Carolina High School Drama Festival held at Shaw University Friday and Saturday.

Tobacco Factory Entrance and Loading dock.

⁸*Paul Robeson*

⁹*James Baldwin*

¹⁰*Josephine Baker*

⁸Gordon Parks, Office of War Information; cropped by Beyond My Ken (talk) 07:13, 3 February 2011 (UTC), Public domain, via Wikimedia Commons, "Paul Robeson," 1942, https://commons.wikimedia.org/wiki/File:Paul_Robeson_1942_crop.jpg, (accessed April 17,2023)

⁹Allan warren, CC BY-SA 3.0 <https://creativecommons.org/licenses/by-sa/3.0>, via Wikimedia Commons, "James Baldwin," 2022, commons.wikimedia.org, https://commons.wikimedia.org/wiki/File:James_Baldwin_37_Allan_Warren_(cropped2).jpg, (accessed April 17,2023)

¹⁰Studio Harcourt, Public domain, via Wikimedia Commons, "Joséphine Baker en 1940, photographie Studio Harcourt," 1940, https://commons.wikimedia.org/wiki/File:Baker_Harcourt_1940_2.jpg, (accessed April 17,2023)

Realizations

My junior year was moving along nicely. I was acting and loving it. Billy and I were deeply in love. We went to movies, he put his arm around my shoulders until it cramped. I got to meet his older sisters when they were in town. Although, I'd never considered having even one sister, I looked forward to a future together with Billy and his family. But just when our relationship seemed at its best, we would break up. Rocky Mount was too small and our high school was less than a thousand, I saw him talking to other girls. I smiled and bore it. To make up for his absence and pretend to be doing just fine, I talked to other boys. In a short time, we'd be back together.

By then, our relationship had already progressed to a higher level of involvement. It happened one night in his neighbor's car which Billy drove often. I always trembled when he touched my arm. Just to hear him say, "Dorothy," made my heart beat faster. I was eager and so was he. By the time he put on protection, I wanted to scream. He went slowly. I wanted him to charge ahead, to make me feel real good. I whispered, "Billy, take off the protection, let me really feel you inside me, just you."

"No. I could never forgive myself if you got pregnant."

So, I missed the thrill.

Later, on the way home, we listened to music from Randy's Record Shop out of Gallatin, Tennessee.

I never knew how he found those rural lanes. We were all alone; or so I thought.

However, one warm evening, he and I were swinging on my front porch. Without warning, Tee joined us. Billy popped up.

"Sit down, Billy. I have something to read to the two of you."

She began by painstakingly unfolding a sheet of notebook paper. Then she cleared her throat, and read a nasty description of Billy and my youthful lovemaking. Silently, I prayed for "Yours truly" or "Sincerely yours." Tears pooled in my eyes, threatened to overflow. To curtail that, I stared wide-eyed, unblinking, across our dirt street, beyond the railroad track to the ugly cotton mill buildings. I tried to propel myself from the porch to the mountain of cotton contained in the first one, to sink in deeply.

She stopped. All was quiet. I blinked. Tears rushed down my cheeks. My mother stood there boring holes into our teenage bodies. Billy and I started talking together, stumbled over each other's words, denied everything.

Tee never interrupted us, just carefully and tediously refolded the letter along its original creases. "I'm not going to show this to Sam. Instead, I'm going to trust you both. But I'd better not hear any more of this. Do you understand, Dorothy Leigh, Billy?"

He quickly replied, "Yes ma'am."

Even I chimed in loudly, "Yes ma'am."

One day out of the clear blue sky the rumor began that Mrs. Armstrong was pregnant. I refused to believe it but soon it became painfully obvious. I got scared; I might escape integration but not a pregnancy. Helplessly, I watched my world crumble like a stack of blocks. It had happened before when I was a second grader but very little was at stake then. Before the end of my junior year, Mrs. Armstrong was gone. I mourned because I never got to play "Camille" and die dramatically from tuberculous, as planned earlier that year. I placed my copy of the script in the same box as my favorite girlhood paper dolls, my Superman comics, and struggled to move on, to mature.

Although I continued to perform, the joy went out of high school. Her replacement, a single, middle aged, unmarried woman with no visible outstanding qualities that I could detect, arrived. Her introductory production was the Christmas play which she proposed staging in a series of ramps with no backdrop, no scenery, no nothing. I was cast in a decent role. However, where the theater was concerned, for the balance of my high school experience, the magic was gone.

Senior year flew by quickly. Billy had graduated then moved to Detroit to work with his brother-in-law in his construction business. I wasn't dating anybody. I just focused on graduating and going away to college. I was elected secretary of the senior class; my old boyfriend from freshman year was president, and James, my seventh grade Valentine's date was vice president. My highlight was the Jabberwocky.

It was Mrs. Armstrong's sorority's fund raiser for college scholarships. Senior girls were chosen to run for Jabberwocky Queen. The one who raised the most money won the crown and a $500 scholarship. When asked, I was eager to run. To my good fortunate, Billy returned home in time to help me gather business ads for the sorority's souvenir program. He borrowed his neighbor's car to drive me to companies. Since two of his older sisters had once reigned as queen, I felt confident of success.

After weeks of work, Billy joined the Air Force and left for Texas. He didn't even see me crowned Queen. On Jabberwocky night, my long white gown sprinkled with sparkling rhinestones and fluffy chenille balls was gorgeous. It was my first strapless. I sat on stage all during the program as the performers presented their songs, original skits, or modern or ballet dances for my pleasure.

In spite of its opportunities and experiences, I didn't really enjoy high school. If I'd had my druthers, I would have skipped being a teenager altogether. It was too traumatic. There was barely enough time to get used to one thing, one age, before something else arose. Out of the whole experience, I surprised myself with only one real regret—high school senior day.

Each spring, seniors from across the state were invited to A&T College in Greensboro. Before the three-hour bus trip for my class, our counselors belabored the rules of good conduct intended for trouble makers; not for me. When we arrived on campus, the day was more beautiful than either of my previous band trips there. Maybe that was because I was practically a coed, only a piece of paper stood in my way.

I strolled the campus with Ann, from my old band days, and Helen, a childhood friend. We were carefree and cute when up rolled a butter-yellow, long, sleek convertible with the top down. Its whitewall tires glided over the asphalt road and stopped just beyond us. With great effort on my part and a squeeze from Helen, the three of us continued our stroll.

It bore three good looking college men clad in the current rage—banlon sweaters. Still, I'm unsure about what lured us, but magically Helen was in the front seat between two handsome devils. Bringing up the rear—Ann and I languished like parade princesses in the back seat. Between us, Sam Cooke's look alike sparkled. At any moment I expected him to croon *You Send Me.*

Revving up the convertible's engine, Carl, the driver, committed cardinal sin number one—sped off campus. Red brick buildings flew by at the speed of a film strip gone awry. My eyes widened. My heart did flip flops. I leaned over to look at Ann. Her fear raised mine. Resuming my position, I read Helen's hunched, defeated back. We were in deep trouble.

Our pictures would be plastered across the front page of the *Baltimore Afro-American* or the *Pittsburgh Courier* newspapers. The story would be too big for just our home town paper. Heck, we might even make *Jet.*

Carl asked, "Any of you young ladies want to see Bennett College?"

It was the all-girls' school I'd erased from my list of potential colleges. I declined their scholarship early. But if it would help Ann, Helen, and me now, I'd reconsider. I deeply regretted not paying attention to our counselors.

By silent agreement, Ann and I left the decision making to Helen. She was closer to the driver. Besides, I was afraid I'd burst into tears if I spoke at all. Helen said, "We'd like to go back to A & T. We can't be gone too long. Our teachers will be looking for us."

That's when our "Sam Cooke" spoke up for the first time. Until then all he did was smile. "You three girls just don't know how lucky you are to have us to break you in."

That statement opened his mouth to filth. I swear I saw two small horns pop out of the top of his head. When the car came to a stop sign, I prayed he wouldn't stand up. I couldn't bear seeing his tail.

The three of us were begging to return to the campus. The college men viewed us with disgust and dropped us at the front gate. I was relieved; those pine tree lined streets were scary.

Back on campus with our hearts securely in our chests, we went in search of our female counselor. For the rest of the afternoon, we clung to her like shadows.

Six weeks later, it was graduation night. To my good fortune, white people had stalled integration. It was a relief to have remained at Booker T. After graduation, I looked forward to another four years without direct confrontation with white people. None of the four colleges offering me scholarships had white students to my knowledge. They did, however, have white teachers on their staffs.

Mr. Hubbard, our male counselor, struggled to get our attention. I paused in mentally rehearsing my valedictorian speech (an honor for which my grandmother could have eaten me up) to listen. Mama ignored the fact my honor was shared with Gwen, the girl who got the only flute our freshman year.

The call came to line up for the processional. As practiced, I was in direct and final contact with Emma Jean, the across town girl who acted like she hated me from day one of high school. By all rights, we should have been the best of friends; one of her older sisters was my play mother in elementary school and her brother was my cousin Brit's friend in high school. Although Emma Jean never came right out to say why she disliked me, I suspected she resented her boyfriend being friends with me.

Her feelings came to a head our senior year. With lockers assigned alphabetically, she was next to me, on my left. Her swinging locker door could leave bruises on me. She always apologized like it was the first time ever.

Graduation night, I marched off to the auditorium behind her. We waited at the door for our cue to enter. In that small gap of time, Emma Jean spun around and hissed, "You really shouldn't be valedictorian. I worked in the office. I looked up your grades. Gwen's were higher than yours."

I was stunned at both her snooping and her revelation.

With a smirk, she turned back to face the auditorium.

No time remained to discover the truth of what she said. I desperately needed something to get me through the night, something to restore my confidence—to make me less of an impostor. I recalled Gwen in a chemistry test studying her hands before writing down her answers. Other times, she pulled something from up her sleeves. Could they have been answers? At the time, I'd wondered if she was cheating, but I wasn't a snitch and I never cheated.

Then there was the sympathy side. Like my mother years earlier, Gwen worked in some white lady's house after school. To top it off, she and I were members of the same girls club, as was the salutatorian. Both of them were acrosstown girls. Maybe I was in the way of what the staff really wanted—two acrosstown girls in the top spots. Here I was a Happy Hill nothing.

The cue came for us to begin the processional. The audience rose. The first person stepped off. The curtain opened on the farce, our pre-written speeches handed to us by the assistant senior advisor weeks earlier with the command, "Memorize them."

I knew how to write, to compose a speech. Maybe she didn't trust me or my classmates. Maybe it saved her time. Since it was the last thing to do before escaping to the North, I said nothing.

Emma Jean's shocking information devastated me. What was I to do? But wait . . . somebody on the staff knew or believed I deserved to be valedictorian. Or maybe it wasn't done in fairness to me. Was this Shakespeare's "tangled web?" All of the teachers, except one from Happy Hill, lived across town.

I was almost at the stage and still unsure of what to do. Should I stand up and deliver "my speech" or decline? I continued to the stage and sat down. A few speakers and music preceded me. I searched for my proud parents in the audience. If they only knew what was going on. Meanwhile my mother was in her glory.

What about my grandmother? In spite of her blind act, her wrath, she always wanted Tee and me to be recognized as important. Could she ever live down the embarrassment of my decision if I decided not to speak? I almost laughed; Mama would be amused at my turning the tables on this valedictorian plan, if indeed, such a plan existed. But as a whole, my family would hurt terribly for my one moment of truth.

Scanning the audience, my eyes came to rest on my mother's white employer, Mrs. Wilson. She sat there proudly with her two little granddaughters. I was their example. As a Negro, I liked her well enough. And I recognized how my people always wanted white people to see us at our best. Inadvertently, her appearance placed me in the position of paying dues for future acceptance of other Negroes.

It was a "tangled web." No one could help me, except Aunt Burrell. I imagined her saying "Dot, go on. Take the valedictorian prize money. Forget about truth; it rarely if ever gits you anywhere and makes more people mad at you."

She wasn't there in person, but I used her thinking. I sure hoped the prize money was worth it. Applause carried me to my seat.

As Gwen spoke, I fantasized about being at Howard University, my college of choice in Washington, D.C. I was on my way. Not only was their scholarship offer of $300 bigger than the other colleges, they were farther up North than my daddy's choice, Hampton Institute, in Virginia. I had yet to reveal my decision to either of my parents.

Finally, all speeches were done. It was awards time. This part would include announcements of any scholarships including the ones received as the result of national testing earlier that spring, Mrs. Armstrong had invited me to her home to help me request acting scholarships from her contacts in the theatrical departments at Howard University and Hampton Institute.

At the time, aside from the honor and money to be gained, I didn't suspect how valuable those announcements would be to me on graduation night. As I sat there on stage after receiving my valedictorian award and acknowledgement of my college scholarships and acceptances, I watched as every possible prize for achievement in many categories went to Gwen. Thanks to my acting skills, I maintained a stoic expression on my face.

By the end of the ceremony, I was emotionally drained. As quickly as possible, I returned my rented cap and gown, found my parents, and asked to be taken home. I told them nothing and they didn't ask.

That summer, three significant things happened. First, Billy's sisters engaged me in discussions about possible majors when I arrived at the college of my choice. They wanted me to know about the financial benefits of becoming a speech therapist. I was thrilled at the attention and the advice which was given without casting aspersions on a theater major.

Second, Billy's mother invited me to work with her at the country club, the white folks' private golf course. By then I was in love with his family as well as him. There would be no tobacco factory for me. His parents picked me up and delivered me all summer. For the first time in my life, I was a waitress, the same type of job I'd tried unsuccessfully to get at the Trailways Bus station. Only the rich white people tipped better at the country club. I wasn't even fired when I dropped a whole tray of glasses, or when I had no idea how to bake an apple pie, or when I didn't know what a crème de menthe was.

And third was really news—my co-valedictorian, Gwen, was married in a private ceremony in her grandmother's living room five days after graduation. Her baby was due in September.

Frankly, I found that cruel even for the Lord.

Me as Miss Jabberwocky

Straps added to Jabberwocky gown for Debutante Ball a month later

Booker T. Washington High School graduate, Dorothy Leigh Burston

Leaving Home

On a September morning in 1957, Sam, Tee, Mama, and I turned onto Church Street business route 301, in Sam's black 1949 Ford. He said, "Traffic's really bad this morning. We'll just take it easy. Got three hours of driving ahead of us."

Locals like us avoided Church Street. Except for today; we were headed north.

As we crossed the city limits, Sam floored the gas pedal, "Now we'll make some time."

I waved goodbye to the last remnant of home, our small airport, and settled in for the non-stop drive to Virginia.

"Sam, are you as excited as I am?" Tee asked.

"Of course, I've looked forward to this day ever since I drove the Douglas family to their son's graduation at Hampton. Now it's our turn to take Dorothy Leigh."

"Amen," Mama said. "This is a glorious day."

Tee said, "It's a real good school, Sam. You were smart to pick Hampton."

"I don't know about all that. I just knew no daughter of mine was going to no college up there in Washington, D. C. That city would be too much for her to handle."

It hadn't been as simple as all that. The only thing that had saved me on graduation night after all that mess, had been the realization of going to Howard University in Washington, D. C. It represented more than just a college; it was my ticket out of the miserable South, my release from the ills of a small town. I could rid myself of the gossip, the back biting, the jealousy. In only three months, I could finally breathe freely. At least that was my thinking the day after my graduation. Actually, I thought it up until Sam said, "Dorothy Leigh, we need to get you a foot locker to take your stuff to Hampton."

Without a word, I fled from the kitchen. When I reached my room less than twenty steps away, I slammed my bedroom door, probably for the first time in my life. Heck, it was the first time. When I discovered Sam had opened my mail—the very first love letter ever from a boy, from Bunny my love—I hadn't slammed my bedroom door. I had remained quiet and obedient as Sam stood there explaining his disdain for the letter's contents. When he had left my room, I'd merely sprawled on my bed while everything inside me died.

But this was different. As reluctant as I was to go against my daddy, I had to. No way was I going to a college with institute in its name. I didn't care if it was in Virginia. That was still the South and I wanted no part of it. Gaining strength, I rose from the side of my bed and spoke in the voice which so often had carried my performances to the very last row of the high school auditorium, "Sam, I want to go to Howard. It has a better theater arts department than Hampton. Mrs. Armstrong has already spoken to their theater arts chairman. Howard is what I've always wanted."

"Dorothy Leigh, you are a little country girl. You'll get into trouble in that big city. No telling what can happen to you there."

"Sam, honey, why don't the two of you sit down and talk about this a bit. I'm sure they are both good schools. Dot will do well no matter where she goes. At least listen to what she has to say. After all, she'll be the one going to college."

Actually, I was shocked to hear her speak up. Usually, she tried to get me to change my mind about things.

"She has no business in a big city like that. Just asking for trouble."

"Sam, what if I had a chance to try it out for a few weeks. Just to see how it goes this summer. My friend, Evelyn, has a big sister who lives and works there. She says the two of us can get a summer job at Woolworth's or try and get on at the post office where she works. We can stay with her. She has a small apartment in the city."

"Absolutely, not. If I don't agree to a college campus where you can live in a dorm, I'm certainly not sending you to work in a five and dime store and make you the responsibility of some young girl. Just think about what you are suggesting."

"Okay. Forget about the summer job thing. Will you at least talk to me about Howard University?"

"Let me tell you something, Dorothy Leigh. From the first time I saw Hampton, it represented quality to me. A place I felt my daughter would be protected. No big city life there. Responsible people looking out for my precious child. I didn't bring you up to throw you away at the end. Besides, I've been dreaming about this for eight years. I know this is the place for you. Mark my words."

I burst into tears and ran from him. Nobody followed me. Neither of them cared about what I wanted.

From the back seat, I watched him grin at Tee, then flash me his Clark Gable wink. I turned and gazed out the window at miles of boring farm land. Even the Burma-Shave signs lost their appeal.

My plan to land at least on the Mason and Dixon Line when I went away to college was squashed. There they sat as Sam always said, "Just a couple of kids ourselves."

Traitors, that's what they were, bosses who snatched up Virginia like the ring on the carousal.

My letter of regret to Howard University tore at my very soul. No turning back. The whole town knew where I was going. Before we took off, a neighbor yelled, "Make us proud, Dot."

One day, Sam and Tee would regret their decision. I could see them—when things went wrong—looking bewildered, wringing their hands. Mumbling, "Maybe Howard wasn't such a bad idea."

I planned to do only enough to get by. I no longer wanted to be the best. I'd show them how I really felt about the "institute," such an awful name. I preferred "university." Fast dancing would be the first thing I'd study. Any other self-respecting Negro girl could fast dance, not I.

And I planned to attend every cultural thing the institute offered. I deserved it after being cooped up in that godforsaken little town of ours. I'd learn to smoke, too. Shucks, Sam smoked all the time: Pall Mall, Phillip Morris. My lipstick would be thick and red. Above all, four whole years of fun loomed before me.

Satisfied, I relaxed. In spite of my disappointment, I loved going out on my own, leaving my parents' rule. No more eating their food, following their orders. I was grown-up.

My mother edged closer to my daddy. She practically cuddled with the man. It was nauseating. I rolled down my window, took big gulps of fresh air. Actually, I wanted to break my silence but didn't want Mama's teasing. Maybe in a few miles . . ..

Before I knew it, we were in the drab town of Hampton, Virginia. It was even smaller than back home. I ached for Washington, D. C. "This is beautiful, Sam," Tee said.

"I told you so."

We crossed over a small bridge; the water grew broader in the far distance. Nearby, it lapped away at some huge rocks along the shore. A brick building, hidden by trees, appeared then disappeared. I leaned in between my parents hoping to get a fuller view through the windshield.

Tee said, "Mama, ain't this pretty?"

"Praise the Lord, Tee. You and Sam done good."

Sam steered our Ford to the entry. His laughter collided with Mama's "Thank you, Jesus."

I turned back to find her eyes overflowing with tears. Hampton took my breath away. Sam slowed down so we could stare at and read the words on the curved brick entry: Hampton Institute, established in 1868. Beautiful deep-pink flowers bordered it. Mama said, "Azaleas."

No one challenged her.

Slowly we followed the winding road and were welcomed by widespread green lawns, towering trees, a few charming white cottages. Ahead, a large grassy circle accented a stately Colonial Williamsburg looking building. I knew. I'd been there on our seventh-grade field trip. At the time, it disturbed me seeing colored people even pretending to be slaves. True, they were paid and went home at night. But I told myself, this is a picture to guide me farther away from the South.

Sam said, "On graduation day, the students march around both sides of this circle, in caps and gowns, meet at the top of the circle. Then they climb up those stairs in twos, and go in that building for the ceremony."

Mama started humming "Bless Be the Ties That Bind." She stopped and said, "One day, if the Lord spares me, I'll see Dorothy Leigh do that."

Tee was silent.

I was overwhelmed. Hampton made me proud of my people. It outshone all the other campuses I'd seen. I forgave my daddy—everything. I pictured the parade of graduates. This man with only an eighth-grade education, wanted all of that for me.

We turned right, left the circle behind us. Shortly, we parked in front of a tall, ancient to me, gothic looking building which seemed to go on forever. A park sized green lawn rolled down to the water where a sailboat glided by like a swan. Sam opened his door, got out, and shook out the cramps of the long drive. Tee got out, too. Sam pulled out a cigarette.

Mama and I were alone in the Ford. Neither of us spoke. It was the end of our long journey, a parting of our ways. Months might pass without hearing her all-consuming laughter or catching sight of her rocking walk. For as much as I disliked her at times, I cherished her even more.

The car trunk creaked open. Mama stared at me and looked away. I sat there reluctant to put this part of my life behind me and afraid to move forward into my new world.

Taking in a deep breath, I reached out and gripped the door handle. Before pressing down on it, I glanced over at my grandmother. She winked at me; I winked back and opened my door.

I narrowly missed hitting a tall guy hurrying down the steps of the building to the sidewalk. Before I could apologize, he was gone. Drawing closer to the trunk of our car, I saw him single-handedly grab my largest piece of white Lady Baltimore luggage and swing it to the sidewalk. Hampton had men; not the boys of high school.

In no time, all three pieces of luggage lined the curb. Last minute tossed in stuff was divided between my mother and me. As we turned to enter the building, the two men tackled my heavily packed footlocker.

Sam's new helper yelled, "The dormitory mistress' office is at the head of the stairs."

We joined Mama at the entrance into Virginia Cleveland Hall, the freshmen women's dormitory. Inside, the walls of the vestibule reached to the floor above. The tall staircase was accented by light pouring in from a huge window across from it. Everything was trimmed in dark brown wood. A tall set of double doors was on our left.

There appeared to be only one landing, four steps above the floor. It was a long climb to the floor above. Tee and I exchanged glances. Could Mama make it? At age 65, she claimed to be unable to do many things. As we pondered the advisability of her climbing, she strode past us.

The climb was slow. Sam and his tour guide caught up to us. The younger man said, "Sir, you see these stairs here? Hampton men, students enrolled in the trade school built them, way back. In the late 1800s."

Sam said, "They did good work. The railings look sturdy."

"Hampton's own choir raised most of the money to build this hall. Can you believe way back then the choir toured Europe? They must have really showed off."

We all voiced our amazement.

He said, "Have you ever heard of Dorothy Maynor?"

I yelled back, "Oh, yes. She's an opera singer." All those years of black history paid off.

He laughed. "She studied right here at Hampton; climbed this same staircase. Of course, she didn't sing in that original choir that raised all that money for this building. She came around much later. But Dorothy Maynor was a Hamptonian, like me. Like you'll be, too."

Finally, we were on the second floor. Mama wasn't even winded. I smelled food which I couldn't readily identify. My fellow Hamptonian said, "The double doors below in the vestibule, lead to the freshman dining hall."

At the moment, all I wanted was to meet my roommate but registration into the dormitory came first. Tee, Mama, and I waited in the lobby while Sam and the college guy returned to the car for my luggage. The lobby was a large room with imitation leather seating groups in orange and turquoise scattered about. While I got Mama settled into a square orange seat, Tee got in the registration line, just off the lobby. When I joined her, she was talking to the family ahead of us. Just then it was their turn.

"Where are they from, Tee?"

"New York."

Poor thing got dragged all the way down to Virginia. Surely her parents could have found a school up North. On the other hand, maybe they wanted her to have an all-Negro experience for a change.

Finally, our turn came. There was a matronly woman waiting for us. On her desk, a small sign read: Assistant Dormitory Director. After a few questions, she checked her sheet and announced, "You'll be on K corridor. The young lady who just left is your new roommate."

My assigned room, K-7, was just around the corner, down a long dark corridor, to the newer portion of the dormitory, and on the same floor. We headed in that direction with Mama. Sam brought up the rear with my luggage. My new home was just around the corner at the end of the corridor next to the communal bathroom. I could see the line-up of washbowls as we passed the doorway. A few more steps and we walked into the room and met the New Yorkers.

The room itself was nothing special. I'd stayed in two separate college dormitories while still in high school. The two pale-green metal beds, one large gray metal desk with two chairs, and two chests of drawers made up the furniture. Brownish curtain panels hung at either side of the very large window which was directly across the street level courtyard from the office. A single white, globed light hanging from the very high ceiling, cast a faint glow on the dark-brown, polished floor tiles. It was nothing like home.

I was barely adjusting to everything when Sam said, "Christine, it's time we hit the road. It's a long drive on those two-lane highways."

True, they had put my belongings on my half of the room, had given me my money to pay my tuition, room and board, and had wished me good luck, still I found their leaving a bit off-putting. Sam held my hand and guided me back to the lobby. Tee and Mama followed.

Once there, Tee said, "Come here, Punjab. Let me kiss you good-bye."

Next, I went to Mama and hugged her real tightly. As she kissed me on my cheek, her tears wet my face.

With my daddy, I wrapped my arms around him and tried to squeeze all the love I would need to sustain me and keep me safe.

Then they started their descent down the beautifully constructed long staircase Dorothy Maynor had trod, and left me alone with strangers.

My freshman year at Virginia-Cleveland Hall

My New York roommate and me

1949 Ford Fordor Sedan

Mama

Hampton Institute, 1868
(Hamptonian Yearbook 1960)

Entrance to Hampton Institute
(Hamptonian Yearbook 1960)

Rules, Rules, Rules

My freshman year at Hampton was so crammed with rules, home seemed like the land of the free. The sun barely sank before nine o'clock curfew. Lights out at 11 p.m. A talkative matron patrolled the dorm at night. My roommate and I feigned sleep to avoid her. According to the dean of women, cleanliness was next to godliness. The dormitory director and her assistant inspected our rooms on a regular basis to ensure her orders were followed. We signed in and out when leaving the campus. The few freedoms granted by my parents, were snatched away.

The only thing I controlled even halfway, was religion; so, I never showed up for church. My parents were informed but neither of them mentioned it to me. I did, however, have to appear at 6 pm each Sunday evening for vespers in the graduation building. Seats were assigned alphabetically. Empty seats were reported by an upperclassman posted in the balcony.

With so many rules, some begged to be broken. Not by me; I wasn't jeopardizing anything. However, there were others who lived on the edge when it came to curfew. They couldn't help themselves; enticements were plentiful. Every branch of the U. S. military was within yelling distance of our campus. On weekends, the fire escape at the end of K corridor, the only unlocked entry, was busy. The Lord placed all that temptation on our doorstep and said, "Let me see you deal with this."

A distinct dichotomy played out those days around me and in my history class. Off campus, white Southerners waged war on integration; in class, Columbus landed in the new world. Virginia's governor closed all public schools; the Indians were massacred. A classmate's younger sisters and brothers were being taught in neighbors' homes, churches, wherever. Virginia's governor announced state funding was available to white people who set up private schools.

The importance of that Mason and Dixon line was nailed home and I was trapped. White people were losing their minds, acting like the South was being invaded by hostile forces instead of granting equal opportunity to Negroes. They begrudged us everything.

A fellow history classmate from Baltimore needed a tutor. Her hometown and Philadelphia were the dance capitals of the East coast. I said, "Sure. I'll tutor you in history. You teach me to fast dance, including the latest, Birdland."

Each afternoon, she came to my room. After history came dance. The steps looked so simple broken down. I learned to fast dance in the middle of K corridor and didn't care who watched. Her history grades improved.

One of the fun things at Hampton was the steel band composed of guys from the West Indies. While they played and sang, we snaked around the campus dancing. Oh, yes, I was crazy about Hampton.

On a serious note, I was enjoying my written communication class. Unlike high school, verb tenses and literary memorization were things of the past. Instead, we wrote. One of my pieces, *My World of Paper Dolls,* included a note from the instructor, "Your piece shows some style."

I thought I was doing well in all my classes, even the one I didn't like, math. It met three days a week (including Saturday) at 7 am. My brain didn't function well that early. I sat in the front row nodding. When the grades were posted at mid-term, a "C" was next to my name. I wobbled outside, sank down on the steps, and cried in disbelief.

That's where my knight in shining armor—a guy I had never said two words to, in or out of class—found me. He was on the swim team. Through my tears, I noticed how cute he was, all brown with neatly trimmed, wavy hair. When he spoke, I almost swooned. His New York accent was better, prettier than my roommate's. I stopped crying.

Bruce, my knight, said, "I'll tutor you. Help you raise your math grade."

He had so much going for him: smart, handsome, and of West Indian heritage. I accepted his offer. We arranged to meet in the small individual corrals of our Huntington Library. That late fall, we worked every day. We started eating dinner together in the evenings. Then we had our first kiss behind the chapel.

After two or three more times in that almost holy spot, an anonymous letter arrived for me. Hand written in pencil bearing no return address. I read it. It sounded familiar. At first, I couldn't place it; then it hit me. I was in my boring biology class and almost said out loud, "I got it." That letter was identical to the one sent anonymously to my mother three years earlier about me and Billy.

Lo and behold, that same person was writing again. This time to me. He or she had beaten me to Hampton. How did I know? 'Cause I was the only freshman from my hometown attending Hampton; the eleven other homies were upper classmen. After a series of eliminations, I arrived at a probable suspect—a lone male sophomore who claimed to be Billy's buddy. He always lurked nearby, grinning, never with a girl of his own. His cab-driver father was my father's friend. I never confronted him. But I stayed away from the area behind the chapel.

By early spring, my attention was on the upcoming ROTC ball. I was so positive Bruce would ask me that I practiced cancelling my original date with an upper classman. But Bruce was taking too long. Finally I said, "Are you taking me to the ROTC ball or not?"

He shrugged his shoulders and laughed sheepishly. "I'm broke."

Since Bruce grew up in an orphanage, I cut him some slack.

"Your ball date asked me if I wanted to take you, since we're seeing each other. He's met someone, too. I told him no."

That sealed it; I was definitely keeping my date. I didn't care if Bruce was a New Yorker; I had new dance steps to perform at the ROTC ball with an up and coming "officer and a gentleman."

In spite of all the fun I was having, sometimes I got real homesick. If anyone with a car was headed home, I squeezed in, too. One time, Brenda, a sophomore from a rural area near my home, and I put our change together and hopped on Greyhound. That meant changing to Trailways in Portsmouth and a two hour wait. It was just getting boring when up walked three Italian men fresh from the old country. Language was a problem but the five of us decided to go outside, take some pictures, and stroll in the fresh spring air.

Neither cars nor people were present. We determined which way to stroll through sign language. Based on nothing, we turned right. All hell broke loose. Profanities, as threatening as a dragon's fire, flamed from in front of a bar across the street. With her hands on her hips, an unkempt white woman spewed, "Find yourselves some white women; don't mess with dem niggers!"

Her hatred was loud and clear. The five of us retreated to the station's waiting room.

Brenda and I were prisoners in our own country.

By the end of freshman year, Audrey, my roommate, and I pledged the same sorority. There were three on campus. Except for their colors, I didn't see any differences in them. Each required a good grade point average; gave the same parties; and not a one of them had a sorority house like I'd seen in movies about white colleges. Primarily, they were all good sources of free cigarettes donated by the tobacco companies. The cigarettes came in the cutest little, slim boxes, only four cigarettes to a box. I always took more than two boxes. It saved me money. The brand didn't matter; I was too new at smoking to care. By the end of my freshman year, I was lighting up Kents with my roommate who had smoked for years. I practiced holding mine like Susan Hayward, my favorite movie star. I was growing up fast.

In choosing a sorority, I picked the one whose colors I liked the best. May have been shallow but I did just that.

The first time my fellow pledges and I appeared as a group, I overheard someone in the dining hall remark, "That sorority has a darker line this year; last year's was high yellow."

Back home in Rocky Mount that summer, my making the honor roll didn't amount to diddly squat. My work options remained the same as before: green tobacco on a farm or cured tobacco in the factory. Neither provided experience in speech correction, my major. Billy's two sisters who worked in that career field had told me, "Dorothy, you can always find work. And you can be hired by either a school district or a medical facility."

That was the very reason I chose speech correction. Theater promised nothing. Especially for a Negro. And I certainly didn't want my Tee and Sam's investment to go to waste nor did I want to starve. Probably more than any other reason, I never wanted to be a classroom teacher; they worked too hard.

That summer my mother solved the riddle of how to spend my time. She said, "Dot, Mae has lined up summer jobs for the three of us."

"Really? Doing what?" She was the one who had wanted me to clean her house.

"We're going to work up North, in New York."

"In New York City?"

"Not exactly. More like in the Catskills. Oh, it'll be fun, Dot. The two of us making money together in New York. Lots of people from Rocky Mount do it every summer. When we finish the season . . .."

"The season?"

"We'll stop off in the city on the way home. Do some shopping, see some sights."

That part sounded good. As we boarded Trailways a few days later, I asked, "What about June German?"

"Oh, Dot, it isn't anything like it used to be. No really big bands. Just a lot of new, young singers. They don't play any of the tunes Sam and I used to dance to. Songs like 'Marie' . . .."

My only reason, besides my parents, for returning home in the future blew away like smoke from my cigarette.

We were on our way to a Jewish resort. Before I realized it, we were in Washington, D.C. and switched to Greyhound. I grasped my charm bracelet from Billy. It played "Love Is a Many Splendored Thing." We had seen that movie together. We were still madly in love despite my college distraction, Bruce. Billy and I wrote letters all the time. He was stationed in California.

When the song became too emotionally disturbing, I turned on my transistor radio. Luckily, it was the size of a soft workbook only thicker. I could easily carry it on my arm with the antenna down. Local disc jockeys along Greyhound's route played "Tears on My Pillow," "Silhouettes on the Shade." By the time we reached the Catskills, I was an emotional wreck.

As soon as we registered at the employment agency, Tee's friend was wrenched from us and placed on a local bus. Tearfully, we waved goodbye to her. It reminded me of slavery when white slave owners separated my ancestors. I couldn't dwell on her predicament; I faced that same treatment.

Tee stepped up to that white woman and said, "This is my daughter, we have to be placed together."

Shortly, we boarded a bus headed for our assignment. In broad daylight, the Catskills was one desolate place, deprived of people. Stores, houses, and hotels were many miles apart. Street signs and street lights were absent. Beyond a shadow of a doubt, the Catskills would be one pitch black place at night.

Before evening, the bus deposited us at a three story, white with green trim, quaint hotel, on a narrow, two-lane road. They fed us, told us what time to report to work the next day, and showed us to our attic bedroom. I was exhausted. It was nice snuggling up close to Tee under tons of quilts. Although it was late May, it was freezing cold. I suspected we were at the end of the world.

In two weeks, three floors of guest rooms were ready. We had worked ourselves out of our attic room. It, like its neighbors, was destined for guests. The manager said, "Get your things. You're moving across the road. Take linens and blankets with you. Stay to the left side of the building and follow the footpath."

It sounded like an adventure; one I didn't care to take in the back roads of the Catskills.

She continued, "You'll see a staircase. Go down to a small porch near the bottom. Take your pick of the two bedrooms."

As we descended, a tinkling, hidden brook, probably the result of melting snow off the mountains, accented our footsteps. Soon we were close to the floor of the forest and there was the porch. Two doors opened onto it; we took the end one. As pretty and quaint as everything was, the thought of just the two of us isolated from the hotel staff was downright scary.

Two days later, Jimmy, a white ex-sailor assigned to the kitchen, moved in next door. On his heels, the male Chinese wait staff and a cocktail waitress arrived. I was surprised Negroes weren't hired for the dining room, like at home. With everyone in place, the hotel opened for business.

By the end of the week, our porch population totaled four; Jimmy had a roommate, the waitress. Things were different up North. All kinds of people got together. Down South, none of us females would be that close to a white man. A white man and a Chinese girl together was a first for me, too. As a matter of fact, I only saw Chinese people in Norfolk, Baltimore, New York, or the movies.

Free time didn't occur for us until mid-afternoon. With no television and poor reception on my transistor radio, Tee and I played many hands of gin rummy and tons of games of Scrabble.

It was a month before she discovered a movie theater—an hour's bus ride away. I could hardly wait to lose myself in someone else's happiness. As we got off the bus, the marquee featured *The Bridge on the River Kwai*. Those prisoners of war were as hopeless as I was.

We used the same movie entrance as the white people and purchased our tickets under the marquee, from a white woman. Without giving it a thought or feeling the stares from white people, we bought popcorn, and found two seats downstairs near the screen. I reckoned without lesser provisions for Negroes, white people behaved. Especially since they knew we were only in that godforsaken place to serve them.

After seven weeks, I verged on insanity. On cue, my daddy's letter arrived. Tee said, "Sam wants us to come home. My girlfriend only lasted three weeks in this desolation. We'll ride back with her brother, Walter."

Five days later we waved goodbye to the Catskills and headed straight to New York City.

Our adventure began on 34th Street in Manhattan. Saks, Orbach's, Macy's—stores I'd seen advertised in the Sunday *New York Times* stood there in front of me. We popped into Macy's for a short time, promising to return the next day. Walter, Tee, and I were exhausted from winding down out of the Catskills. He dropped us at the apartment of Mama's baby sister, Tee's Aunt Pearl.

The next morning, he picked us up. We returned to 34th Street where I bought new outfits for college—a slim tomato-red knit dress with a slight cowl collar, a green felt hat to pick up the tiny flecks of green in the dress, a stunning pair of green leather heels in my narrow width, and a green leather purse with a slender brass handle. Other purchases complimented something I already owned.

Then we went to Harlem to the Apollo. The gorgeous marquee held me captive. Tee said, "Dot, stop gazing at those lights, the show is about to start."

And what a show it was. Jackie Wilson live on stage, as sharp as a tack. His black processed hair gleamed. His black suit, white shirt, and red tie were perfect. When he sang "Lonely Teardrops," he sank to his knees, came face to face with the ladies on the front row. The theater went wild. He tossed his jacket to who knows where, his tie landed down front in the audience, and his shirt was unbuttoned to his navel. I loved it.

That fall, I returned to Hampton and moved into the sophomore dorm, Kelsey Hall. Its large lobby windows faced the waterfront. The sunken floor was perfect for its modern furniture. My second-floor room was above it. Audrey, my freshman roommate, didn't return for the sophomore year.

Pat, my new roommate, also from the South, was a nursing major. We hit it off fine. We each had our separate friends and classmates from our departments. She wasn't pledging a sorority at all. It promised to be a good year.

Bruce and I picked up where we'd left off in the spring. Thanks to his tutoring, I got a B in math. That horror was over for the rest of my college career. Bruce now owned a small maroon convertible. Things were really looking up for me . . . a smart college man from New York with a car. What more could I ask?

For a different major, speech correction was not my thing. However, my mother's saying plagued me, "Don't change horses midstream." I obeyed. She raised me on that stuff. "When a task is once begun, never leave it 'til it's done. Be the labor great or small, do it well or not at all." It flowed through my veins.

So, I stuck with speech correction. I firmly believed the good part was right around the corner. One day in audiology, an overly zealous classmate raised her hand. When the teacher called on her, she said, "It seems to me that we, as future speech pathologists, could benefit from a course in physics."

I thrust my fist against my mouth in panic.

Our instructor said, "That's a good idea. Why don't you enroll on your own."

As grateful as I was to our instructor that day, I still couldn't bring myself to take my fellow sorority pledge's advice. "Dot B. (my new nickname), you'd be amazed at what a difference a little thing like a cup of coffee with your instructor can make in your college success."

"I'll have to rely on my grades. I hate coffee. And I'm not that crazy about the instructor. So why should I drop by her office if I don't have to?"

"Just a suggestion."

Coffee with her was convenient since I worked in the audio-visual aids office next door. But not one sip of coffee passed my lips.

-When I was growing up, adults said, "People with limited vocabularies curse."

I never argued with them.

They added, "White people who ridicule you based on your color are ignorant."

Those two adages coupled with my mother's multitude of sayings weighed heavily on my young mind.

At the fall meeting for my college sophomore class, the floor was open for nominations for the attendant to ride on the float in the homecoming parade with Miss Hampton. Bruce popped up. "I nominate Dorothy Burston."

I was still in shock when a bright skinned guy sprang from his seat. "Dorothy Burston is too black to ride on the float."

I wanted to run from the room. He wasn't white; he had more than a few ounces of black blood.

On his heels, Bruce rose and argued the point. I gently touched his hand to guide him back into his seat. He refused, spoke his piece.

I learned something else that year involving my sorority-to-be. Often when visiting big sisters, we would have to sing. One big sister always got right in my mouth to listen to my voice. My high school suspicions about my vocal ability were confirmed by her rollicking laughter. At dinner one evening, Bruce said, "I quit the fraternity. One of the big brothers destroyed my convertible and refused to pay me for it."

So much for our plan to be sorority and fraternity sister and brother. Neither of us gave it a second thought except to regret the loss of his car.

As a theater minor, I had little free time. I was cast in Miss Rosenberg's production of *Right You Are* by Pirandello. It was okay but preferred her small choral speaking group. For the first time in my life, I was exposed to A.A. Milne's Christopher Robin. Found him delightful. We performed works by Langston Hughes, the Negro poet of the Harlem Renaissance. Placed him on a pedestal next to Nat King Cole. And appreciated the poetic logic of Robert Frost.

I kept my original promise to see everything cultural that hit the campus. I was front row center for Bambi Linn and Rod Alexander's ballet performance. I was as thirsty as a dry sponge.

Just before my Christmas vacation that year, Sam called, "Baby, your mother and I have a surprise for you. She didn't want to tell you until you got here. But I can't wait. We bought a brand-new house."

I was both thrilled and shocked. How could they afford it and send me to college? When I arrived home, Tee said, "Our new house is almost completed."

It seemed fast but I didn't say anything. We were finally leaving that ugly rental at the end of the street. My parents were like newlyweds. The next morning, we drove across town to see it. Sam said, "It's a Jim Walter's manufactured house. They assembled it when it got here."

"Sam picked the best lot. Burrell bought one, too. Just down the street from us. Little Alice will be closer to Booker T."

"What about Mama? Won't she be lonely on Happy Hill with no family left?"

"You know Mama. She'll love the long drive over for visits and the chance to brag."

When we arrived at the housing development, Sam drove to the last street which was one very long block. Tee said, "The green house on the left is Burrell's."

"That's nice," I said.

Sam slowed down in front of a cute, little white cottage with small green shutters on either side of its three front windows. He shut off the car, turned, and flashed that smile of his.

Sam and Tee at front door of their cute, little white cottage

Loving my freshman year
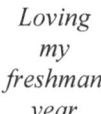

Steel Band at Hampton. (Hamptonian Yearbook 1960)

[11]Apollo Theater at Night

Mama's baby sister, Pearl

Scene from **Right You Are**

---

[11]Brooklyn4083, CC BY-SA 4.0 <https://creativecommons.org/licenses/by-sa/4.0>, via Wikimedia Commons, "Apollo Theater at Night," 2009, https://commons.wikimedia.org/wiki/File:Apollo_Theater_at_Night.jpg, (accessed April 17, 2023)

Betterment

On a bitterly cold March evening, Pat and I pulled into New York City aboard Greyhound. I was there for my first job interview. Pat came along for the ride and the sleepover at her aunt's apartment. The interview was at Irvington House, a Westchester County hospital for children with heart disease and an interim placement center for orphans. A white nurse at my daddy's job suggested I apply for summer employment there. He called me in late January, "Hop on it, baby."

My dream of living in New York, of escaping the South, was close at hand. Bruce grew up in Dobbs Ferry, a few towns over from where my job prospect was located. He said, "It's the suburbs, about an hour out of the city."

The evening we arrived, Pat expertly hailed a cab, gave the driver her aunt's address, and said, "I know how to get there."

There would be no roaming around the city running up the fare.

Next morning, we descended into the depths of the subway system—my first encounter. As we waited on the long concrete platform, I studied how things were done up North. Being underground would take getting used to, not to mention accepting a distinct air of indifference, an impoliteness, in my fellow passengers.

I turned to Pat to comment on my observations—she displayed the same aloofness. I copied her but only for a second. I was drawn to a small light far out into the darkness of a track. It grew larger and came with a terrible grinding and screeching of brakes. At the same time, a train roared in on the opposite side of the platform. Was this what I'd craved all my young life?

My anticipated joy of working at Irvington House dimmed as trains ruptured the station. I watched passengers gush through briefly opened doors at the same time new ones fought to enter. At least the subway wasn't prejudiced—some Negroes sat while whites stood.

Pat nudged me, "Dot B., here comes our train."

We boarded. The train took off, plunging us into momentary darkness. When the lights came back, I was propped up against a human back. I tried not to breathe into my other neighbor's face. It was unavoidable; I didn't make eye contact. I tried to find something to focus on. That's when I discovered Pat was missing.

Again, the lights went out. It was pitch-black inside and out. Nobody reacted. I muffled my scream with my scarf. The train snapped us around like in the game of "Whip." The lights returned. I saw the front and the tail of the train at the same time. Above the pounding of my heart, Pat yelled, "Dot B., over here."

My guardian roommate was three people away, clinging to an overhead strap. I shoved my hand across a neighbor and latched onto a shiny, vertical pole.

After many station stops, Pat squeezed past some human obstacles to me. "Our stop is coming up."

She steered me to the door. Grand Central Station lived up to its name. While I stared in amazement, Pat found our Irvington-on-Hudson train and pulled me to the gate.

The commuter train was clean and orderly. I relaxed, let the train's rumbling soothe me. Fewer passengers traveled with us. A uniformed conductor strolled by and punched our tickets. We coasted along above ground. Every now and then he called out stations. It was a sunshiny, clear day on the Hudson River.

Shortly, he announced, "Irvington-on-Hudson."

Our stop was named for Washington Irving, the creator of Rip Van Winkle. The trip had taken an hour, more or less. We grabbed one of the waiting taxis and climbed uphill to Broadway. A few minutes later, we turned right, up a narrow, steep, driveway. A stone building stood at the crest. Our driver stopped under the covered entry, "Irvington House."

The place was surrounded by trees and untamed shrubs. Pausing outside a pair of huge double doors, I mentally prepared myself for my first interview ever. The tobacco factory bosses just pointed to me when they hired me those two times.

With minutes to spare, we entered the office, just off a long, wide hallway. My interview was in a smaller office. Thirty minutes later, I landed my first job in New York. The supervisor took me on a tour of the interim care division. There would be no green or cured tobacco, no tables to wait, and absolutely no Catskills in my coming summer. Education was releasing me from such servitude.

By spring, the Greeks were in full swing on campus. In my sorority, we wrote and rehearsed our performances for the upperclassmen's dining hall and graduation circle. I loved marching in formation; took me back to high school band days.

I grew uncomfortable with the prospect of my upcoming sisterhood as the end of probation approached. I imagined a loss of self-identity, of freedom. I didn't want appendages. My fellow pledges seemed okay with the idea. What was wrong with me? Why couldn't I be like them?

After hell week, big sisters and little sisters were one big happy family. Elections were held for the incoming school year; I was elected secretary. I kept waiting to feel altered, reborn. Instead, disappointment greeted me. It was like the final curtain of a play but worse. The melancholy wouldn't go away. Even the presents from our big sisters for crossing over the burning sands failed to cheer me up.

I received one beautifully wrapped gift from Bruce: a pale-blue pair of soft, baby doll pajamas. A very un-southern like thing to give. Although I really liked him, his gift was embarrassing, especially when I innocently opened it in front of my roommate.

Besides, my true love, Billy, was still in California. His picture greeted me each morning. Bruce was flesh and blood and very persuasive. Neither of them knew of the other's existence. Even if I had considered canceling my relationship with Bruce—the possessor of a brilliant mind, exquisite speech, and a treasure trove of experiences like camping—I wouldn't have been able to do it. He was too unique.

However, I never shared my New York dream with him. Not even when he mentioned his, of meeting a southern girl at Hampton. What a disappointment I was for him. But all he said was, "You are so beautiful!"

No guy, not even Billy, had ever told me that before. In fact, the only time I'd heard it from someone other than my parents was from Little Alice, my adopted cousin. Bruce was speaking from his heart. Oh, yes, as the saying on campus went, "I had his nose; but he had mine, too."

During my first Irvington House summer, New York's magic came true. To begin with, my two roommates, an older girl from Formosa and a young, white girl, Susan, from Rocky Mount, and I were assigned to a large bedroom with its own connecting bath. The Formosa roommate was engaged to be married. Susan and I were connected by our hometown and by the same nurse my daddy knew, who years earlier, had introduced Susan's big sister to Irvington House.

At first, I thought Susan was a long way from home at her age; she was a brand-new high school graduate. Then I remembered—southern white girls matured much earlier than southern Negro girls. Our mothers, unlike theirs, tried to stunt our growth as a form of protection—a chastity belt. White girls could get abortions any time they wanted. Pimp, the teenager with the sex advice, had told me that years earlier.

For Susan and me, life was instantly simpler up North. We never talked about home where the stigma of segregation draped over everybody like southern moss. She was curious about me but not intrusive and she didn't assume she knew all there was to know about me. Her older sister treated us to my very first pizza, in Dobbs Ferry. In New York, we were free to focus on what really mattered: our new job, earning a good salary, and having fun.

At Irvington House, most of the counseling staff lived on site. A lot of them were Negroes. They treated me like a little sister, let me play their albums on their hi-fis, even while they were working; it was heaven.

My job assignment was in a dormitory of a dozen six to eight-year-olds. I didn't even have babysitting experience. In addition to taking care of children, I would write reports based on my observations of a new set of twin girls, Diane and Delores, and plan activities with four other counselors. Thanks to Tee's kindergarten, I knew lots of children's games and stuff.

Not by intent, my co-workers challenged me one day. They sent me shopping with the twins for clothes, shoes, and stuffed animals. It necessitated riding on two or more buses to White Plains, a nearby city. I had never been there or anywhere on my own, except the Greyhound bus to my new job.

On shopping day, with a little five-year-old hand in each of mine, I got us down the hill to Broadway. The bus to Tarrytown came too promptly; I needed time to savor my accomplishment. Our next bus closed its doors as we boarded. On our way to White Plains, I worried about finding the right store.

We were dropped off in front of it. I was shopping before I could see straight. By the time we found their favorite stuffed animals, they were hungry. While they ate, our return route played over and over in my head. I was never at ease until we were walking back up the hill to Irvington House. The rest of the summer, I rode over to White Plains, got my hair done, shopped on my own—I was into New York, at least the suburbs.

One of our field trips that summer, the Bronx Zoo, was a first for me. After a lifetime of no zoo, I went twice in one week. On the first trip, I lost a kid. Seeing my despair, a stranger suggested I try the monkey area. Sure enough, there she was.

Irvington House met all my needs including three meals a day and medical attention. I'd seen a doctor only three times in my life: when I was born, when I almost bit off my tongue, and at age twelve when I contracted an eye redness. That last time Sam arranged to have a doctor look at me in the driveway outside the hospital where he worked. That first summer at Irvington House, I came down with strep throat. I received a penicillin shot on the third-floor medical which also housed the laboratory each afternoon.

Working at that facility, I had a close-up view of children coping with life. In the interim care department where I worked, they ranged in age from babies to eight years of age. Often, they arrived late at night dirty and confused, usually as a result of domestic violence. Some had been abused or abandoned. They were all basically neglected. The hospital division was composed of younger children and teenagers recuperating from heart disease. Some were too ill to survive. Occasionally, under the cloak of night, the undertaker whisked a young, lifeless body away.

The facility was also a refuge from all that was occurring in the city that first summer. In certain boroughs, either reporters, police, potential or actual victims coined names such as, "the umbrella man" and "the cape man" who were assaulting people on the streets. We either read about it, or heard it on the radio or saw it on television.

As a first-time counselor, my effect on the children, aside from daily care, rarely entered my mind; but I knew they affected me. A six-year-old boy taught me the worst swear words I had ever heard in my life. From all of them, I gained another vital lesson.

One afternoon at nap time, two counselors and I prepared my twins for leaving as the other children rested. They were being adopted. Just as we finished packing and dressing the girls, noises came from the sleeping area. Until then all had been quiet. Charlie, the lead counselor, said, "I'll sneak out there. I betcha it's Michael."

Sure enough it was. He was our six-year-old albino mischief maker. That afternoon, he knelt at the foot of his bed, without his glasses, and sang off key through two missing front teeth, "Goodbye Diane."

The other children crawled to the foot of their beds and joined in the singing.

Diane and Delores, the twins, rushed to the sleeping area and stood quietly to be serenaded in turn.

We three counselors cried.

The ceremony ended with the children, including Michael, crawling back to their pillows. Delores and Diane came and took my hands in each of theirs. Another counselor picked up their few belongings—the things I'd purchased for them. As the girls clutched their stuffed animals, we walked the long hallway to the big front doors. They looked so small on the brown leather back seat of that black limo. Then slowly the driver drove away, heading for Broadway and the girls' new future.

Irvington House was such a great place to work. I encouraged Bruce to apply. Working there beat the heck out of washing dishes at Howard Johnson's in Tarrytown. He was hired on the spot and moved in later that day.

Before the first month ended, everybody was partying in Joe's Blue Light Café; his small, narrow, private room was decked out for partying. Counselors were off duty by nine at night. Joe's, across the hall and two doors away from me and my roommate, was a college student's dream come true. There was alcohol, music, romantic lighting, smoking, dancing, snacks, and no curfew.

Away from Irvington House, my summer was filled with excitement. Miss Rosenberg, my college theater professor, invited me to see Jason Robards in *Job* on Broadway. I could hardly contain myself. Once Bruce learned of the plan, he rushed me to *Two for the Seesaw* starring Anne Bancroft and Dana Andrews. We sat very close to the stage.

The next day, back at Irvington House, we made love—without the cute baby doll pajamas. He was everything I imagined a West Indian lover should be—exotic, like Harry Belafonte's album cover. Bruce's body was firm, thanks to the swim team. It was very exciting seeing all that beautiful, brown skin in the light of day. I was touching him shyly when I discovered a scar on his right side. He said, "I had my appendix removed."

When I knew him better, I would kiss it. At the moment, I was aroused at the idea of everyone else being either at work or away for their two days off. Who would rush to save me when I screamed?

A week later, I met Miss Rosenberg at Grand Central Station. Back at her apartment, she served a delicious beef noodle casserole. After two years of college, I ate anything. Before drifting off to sleep, I reviewed the two plays. *Two for the Seesaw* won; *Job,* based on the Bible had too many trials and tribulations.

Since I was off the next day, Miss Rosenberg suggested lunch at Rockefeller Plaza. First, we'd take the ferry to Staten Island, see the Statue of Liberty. I knew she meant well so I was polite. However, none of my ancestors were ever greeted by that torch bearing lady. In many ways, my professor reminded me of my mother in her kindness and naiveté. Not that I knew a whole bunch but, in their presence, I felt like the adult.

After the ferry, we ate lunch right in the middle of the winter ice skating rink, in the summer sunshine. All those years I'd been totally right about New York. It was where I belonged. I was still musing when she said, "The waiter thinks you're a model. Look at the way he's treating you."

"Really?" I hadn't noticed him. I was too much in love at the moment to be aware of any other man. However, I did smile when he refilled our water glasses.

She laughed and leaned into me. "Well, just look at you. Every bit a model. Plus you have that hatbox looking piece of luggage."

I laughed. The luggage belonged to my white home girl.

Interesting things always happened that summer. One day, Bruce took me to New Rochelle to meet some of his family. Nervous and shy about the prospect, I talked myself into going. I met four of his eight siblings, a cousin, and Aunt Lil. The latter was bent on finding a nice, fair skinned West Indian girl for each of the boys, including Bruce. Before each parade of girls, she was known to say, "It's the least I can do for your poor mother who died delivering her last baby."

Bruce, his siblings, and I hung out on Aunt Lil's large front porch. Her house reminded me of the South with its three stories. A green chest high hedge grew near the sidewalk. The neighborhood didn't resemble New York City in any respect unless you heard the residents speak. Jocile, a teenager and the only sister, said, "Let's take Dot to get a White Castle."

My confusion must have showed. Bruce laughed, squeezed my shoulders, and said, "You look so cute. Dorothy doesn't know what a White Castle is."

After their amusement, the seven of us took off for the White Castle. I was still in the dark. One brother, Johnny, smiled back at me as I walked next to Bruce. For the second time in my life, I had the delightful prospect of siblings in my life. I wanted that so much, I pretended to love that tiny burger with tidbits of onions sprinkled on it—a White Castle.

As the latest member of the "family," I hung out with Bruce, his older married brother, Don, who was working in New York for the summer, and his tall, handsome nineteen-year-old cousin, Thomas. Don decided the summer should be spent exploring New York's beaches and boardwalks. A few days later, we hopped on the subway and headed for our opener, Jones Beach on Long Island. On the trip to the island, Bruce's cousin was fidgety.

Bruce said, "Okay, Thomas, tell us what has you all charged up."

"No. You guys will tease me too much. What the heck. This week, I met this beautiful girl. Her name is Monica. She promised to meet us at the beach and bring her girlfriend along."

Bruce said, "Dorothy, Thomas always dresses GQ. You would think he was a model himself."

Thomas said, "Do you think she'll show up?"

Don offered the benefit of his twenty-three years of living. "Thomas, it's always this way. You make yourself vulnerable then you sweat out the waiting period."

Thomas said, "She seemed like she'd come. Dang. I'll feel pretty stupid if she doesn't show up. Oh, well, it's just you guys."

"We have long memories, Thomas," Bruce said.

"Oh, I forgot, did I mention she's bringing her girlfriend? What if the friend and I hit it off?"

Bruce said, "Relax, Thomas. Nobody's here yet."

After what seemed like a long time, we arrived at one of the entrances to Jones Beach. "Do you see her, I mean them?"

"Man, we've never laid eyes on her even once. But there are a couple of cuties over to the left of the gate."

Two, tall striking, model-looking girls in shorts stood there.

Thomas grinned. "Aw, man. Can you believe my good luck?"

After brief introductions, our party plowed towards the beach. The warm sand filled my sandals so much, I shed them. Once Don, the elder, declared the spot, we all spread our towels and plopped down for a much-needed rest. All that is, except the models, they sauntered over to the water and dipped in their toes.

I guess beaches have a lot in common once the prerequisites are met because I could just as easily have been at Sea Breeze Beach in Norfolk. But two major things made them different: the rampant Northern accent and the enormous amount of white people in attendance.

The day passed pleasantly with nothing more than laughing, sitting in the sand, and occasionally dipping our feet in the water. Although we removed our shorts and shirts, none of us wanted to get our swim suits wet. As girls, we had no intention of messing up our hairdos. Since everyone was short on funds, we pretended disinterest in the rides on the boardwalk and ate sparingly.

Next week, we did Rockaway without the girls. Thomas was a little down at first but he perked up when he saw new girls and the roller coaster. Bruce said, "Thomas, before you go chasing them, come on the roller coaster with us. After all, you were the one who selected Rockaway because of Playland."

Shortly we arrived at the Atom Smasher. Although I didn't mention it, I'd never seen a scarier thing than that monstrous ride. Nothing at our county fair measured up to the beast which loomed in front of me. I had to crank my head way back to see the top. The racket was horrendous. Every few seconds, ear piercing screams pricked the air like the first sounds of corn kernels before they exploded into popcorn.

Suddenly I was backing up, away from it, trying to melt into the crowd passing by behind me. At one point, the cars whizzed and whipped around bends, then slowly climbed to the very top. I could almost see the riders catching their breaths, putting their hearts back into their bodies.

Bruce said, "Watch this part, Dorothy. Watch! Don't close your eyes."

I gaped as they tumbled forward, picked up tremendous speed, flew away, and looped for what seemed like forever. I feared they'd never stop until rescue workers untangled their mangled bodies and laid them out for identification.

Thomas yelled, "Come on, I got the tickets. It's coming back. We can grab the first car!"

Bruce grabbed my hand and dragged me to the entrance. He climbed in first. The middle seat was mine. Good. They'd crush me before I flew out of the car. Just about then, the operator shifted a large lever. I was a goner. At last, my wish to be in New York City had finally come true but I wouldn't die happy.

Our flimsy, rattling car, grudgingly locked into each chain link of the climb to the top. I finally offered up a real prayer; no fooling around with a nursery rhyme. This was the real THING!!!

We plunged down like water gushing full force from a hose. I wished I could see the world for the last time but my eyelids refused to part. "Look, sweetheart, you're missing the good parts!"

Thomas laughed, "Best coaster ever. Let's do it AGAIN!!!!"

I fell heavily against Bruce for a moment only to be jerked back against Thomas. If the Lord spared me . . .!!!!!!

Pretty soon I was numb to the action. The Atom Smasher extracted more energy than any orgasm I'd ever experienced. Thomas offered me his hand to guide me out of the car. Weakly, I clung to it. Almost gently but firmly, he said, "Be right back with the tickets. We're doing this again!"

In August, Bruce and I headed to the annual Hampton alumni boat ride at the 125th Street pier in Harlem. As we walked the famous street, I felt the pulse of Langston Hughes. His poem, "I've Known Rivers," didn't mention the Hudson on which we would be cruising that evening. Instead, he spoke of the Nile, Euphrates, and Mississippi. There were the tenements painted by that Negro artist whose works hung in Hampton's museum. His painting features windows populated by dark brown almost black, light chocolate, or vanilla people watching the staccato, deep-red uniformed marching band below. It was led by a rared-back, strutting, white-suited drum major wielding his extended baton.

The inspiration for the Harlem Renaissance photographers pulsated in the faces of my people, reeling in dance, swaying to the beat, finger popping with the shoeshine man, going about their business with an occasional hello. And the barbershop's red and white stripes synchronized with the nearby beauty shop's shampoo scents and straightening pomades. I saw the black and white photographs of the local photographer posted at eye level on the street. I was consumed by the experience. It was what our across town section in Rocky Mount aspired to be.

Aboard the boat, we ran into alumni from our first year at Hampton. Already they bore that look of experience the world places on you once you've graduated. I didn't begrudge them their new status. Food and drinks flowed freely. Music filled the air causing us to yell in conversations. Dancing while desirable was limited to body swaying, shoulder twisting, and finger popping. Meanwhile, our makeup became sticky, our lipstick faded, our throats begged for quenchers. But we partied hardy.

Finally, the boat docked back at the 125th Street Pier. Slowly and wearily, we disembarked, swearing it was the best ever. For Bruce and me, it was our first. We made that return trek to the subway stop which meant a steep climb; the track ran above the streets along there. As we trudged, the sounds from a nearby club enticed us to enter. It was my first nightclub. I marveled at a torch dancer and struggled to remain nonchalant.

In one of our classier moments, Bruce discovered a free concert in Lewisohn Stadium. Wooden folding chairs awaited us. We sat and listened to the symphony. Daily, I was falling more exclusively in love with him. In such a stupor, I appreciated those elementary school assemblies in which Mrs. Neville played classical music for our entrances and exits to and from the multi-use room. My brief stint in the high school band had included such works when we performed as an orchestra. And I loved my daddy to death.

If I hadn't been so happy, so wide-eyed with wonder, I probably would have cursed the day my mother denied me all I was finally seeing.

By the end of my summer at the Irvington House, Susan, my one remaining roommate (the Formosa girl barely made it through two weeks) and I said our goodbyes. Neither of us mentioned meeting up in Rocky Mount.

Irvington House summer job in New York— me and my kids

Singing sorority pledges I'm 3rd from right, front row

Two for the Seesaw *on Broadway starring Anne Bancroft and Dana Andrews*

I Confront Life

That September, my junior year began without Pat. She was off to nursing school in Richmond for the next three years. Leticia, my new roommate and sorority sister, was from Norfolk. Her major was history. She said, "Dot B., my dad's a plumber. They make all the money. He's a Hampton grad from the trade school. That's what I should be studying."

There was a problem with her proposal; the trade school no longer existed and even if it had, the new dean of women would never allow a Hampton young lady to enroll. I was convinced about the plumbing career when I saw her family home—a modern tri-level on a Virginia Beach inlet. We arrived in Leticia's birthday present, a new blue Chevrolet Corvair.

My contribution to her? Shortening the hemlines on some of her dresses. She pouted, "You're ruining my clothes." I ignored her, continued cutting off material. Finally, I said, "There. The style is just below the knees, Leticia, I want you to be chic."

That was the year I began purging myself of annoying things. First, I quit the sorority. It had great value in the South which was not in my plans. The next thing was my minor, speech and drama. The department chairman returned from a two-year sabbatical and reclaimed her title. Miss Rosenberg remained on staff. The returnee picked out a few students upon whom to bestow her disdain. I was one of them.

Drama was my minor; she cast me in her production of *The House of Bernardo Alba*. The lead role was played by a statuesque, flamboyant, dark-skinned girl. I was the servant under the housekeeper. The rest of the cast was high to medium yellow in complexion. So was the director. I dreaded rehearsals. On performance night, I wanted to die in my limited stage appearances.

The experience proved invaluable. Beyond a shadow of a doubt, if I had to play a servant, I wanted no part of the theatrical world. The year was 1959.

After the show, Miss Rosenberg said, "Dorothy, you gave a most distasteful performance. Your voice was just awful."

At first, I almost explained how difficult it was to conceal my innermost feelings. Then I started to say my parents didn't train me to be a maid in either reality or on the stage. I even considered sharing growing up as a Negro; a dark Negro. And finally, I started to share my cousin's, Little Alice's, compliment, "Dot, you may be black but you sure are pretty."

Instead, I said nothing. I listened and left. Miss Rosenberg only knew theater—the lie about there being no small roles. I neither forgave her nor forgot her.

For the first time, I was glad to be a speech therapy major. To satisfy my craving for the creative arts, I turned to the radio part of the department, to Dr. Clancy. I liked him; he reminded me of Sam. I began writing adaptations of plays or stories for in class broadcasts and loved it.

By now, Bruce and I were a couple on campus. I had not seen my high school sweetheart, Billy, for almost three years. Time and distance were working against us. On the other hand, Bruce and I ate together each evening after his swim practice. One week close to Christmas break, I poked along trying to have something left on my plate when he arrived. Suddenly, I heard a familiar voice call my name—one I hadn't heard for a long time.

I looked up. Billy smiled at me. I almost swallowed my fork. He never told me he'd be back from California for Christmas. Yet, there he stood—in my college dining hall. I murmured a greeting, nodded to his smirking friend, the very one I'd secretly accused of writing the anonymous handwritten letters. I almost pushed my chair over in my haste to return my dinner tray. I had to get Billy out of there fast. Bruce was on his way for sure. Somehow, I managed it. We sped off campus in Billy's black Oldsmobile.

For that first block or so, I couldn't speak. This was the worst situation ever. Only one big problem remained—how to tell Billy about Bruce's upcoming Christmas visit to my parents' home. As awful as it was, I had to. "Gosh, I'm really glad you're back."

"You sure aren't acting like it. I have yet to kiss you. And that's all I could think about for those three thousand miles from California to North Carolina. And then for the three hour drive up here."

We found a place to park in the nearby small town of Phoebus. I slid across the seat towards him and offered my lips for his kiss. Immediately, I was shaken by that old familiar excitement he aroused in me by his mere touch. Prior to that moment of intimacy, I was certain of who I was and what I wanted—that New York, West Indian man. Now I wasn't so sure. If just the touching of our lips brought back such memories of longing, what would lovemaking do? *Dorothy, don't be ridiculous. Why complicate a bad situation even more?*

"So, why the big rush? Why couldn't you finish your dinner? I could have waited for you. I've waited all these years. A few minutes more . . ."

"You know darn well why I couldn't. I'm sure your friend explained everything to you."

"He just said you'd probably be in the dining hall. And sure enough, there you were."

"Why that son of a gun."

"Forget about him. He doesn't matter."

Billy knew about Bruce. I refused to believe otherwise. As I sat there quietly, I imagined Bruce's clean-shaven face, showered body, New York accent greeting me at the end of the day. *Stop it, Dorothy. You have to fix this. Nobody else can do it.*

"Talk to me, Dorothy." Billy said.

"I can't. You're going to hate me."

"Try me."

"I invited this guy I've been seeing on campus home for Christmas. There, now you see how impossible all of this is? Why didn't you tell me you were coming?"

"That wouldn't have changed anything."

For almost an hour, we sat in his car and talked about nothing and everything. He asked, "So, when do you suppose you planned to tell me?"

My insides ached as never before. "Never. You were three thousand miles away."

"Oh. I guess you'd come to that bridge when you had to cross it."

We both laughed. He sobered up first. "I'm not letting you off that easily."

"Okay. He is fun and convenient." I shed a few tears for emphasis. Then quietly I said, "Billy, I have to get back to the dorm. Curfew."

After we parted that evening, I wondered about Bruce. Did anyone tell him why I wasn't there waiting for him as usual? I fell asleep in turmoil with nothing solved except the spoiling of Billy's surprise arrival and his assumption that he would drive me home for Christmas.

The next day, he was gone. Our winter break didn't begin for four more days. I was given a reprieve of a sort. I could work on solving my dilemma.

I'd been home for two days before Billy stopped by. He found me alone; Bruce wouldn't arrive until Christmas eve, his last day of work on campus. That afternoon, before either of us realized it, we were clinging to each other for dear life. I was crying, the thing I do best. The closeness of him was so familiar. I longed to share those lost moments again, to feel him inside me.

Billy said, "No, we can't. Not with all of this hanging over us. You have to make up your mind. You can't have it all."

I wouldn't be denied something I'd spent long nights missing. I'd grown up; I knew what this new level of intimacy could feel like. I almost had him convinced when my dad parked in the driveway and I heard my mother's voice. Hastily, we pulled ourselves together and greeted them in the living room. After a few minutes, he left.

Frustrated, I went to my room only to be greeted by the eighteen-inch square box Bruce insisted I carry home with me. It was beautifully wrapped which reminded me I needed to shop for his gift. What could be wrapped in a box that size anyway? A stuffed animal? Although curious, I decided not to peek.

For the next two days, Christmas shopping, decorating, and visiting consumed my time. One morning, my dad carried me around with him and ended up at the doctor's house where he still did handyman jobs. Entering through the kitchen, I greeted the lady of the house whom I still didn't like; not that it mattered. I still had to be polite.

I Confront Life 199

She said, "Dorothy Leigh, I can't understand a word you're saying. You have gotten so proper—just like a Yankee."

Later that day, Billy and I spent time together, talking. I visited in his family's home briefly. After a while, he took me shopping at my favorite store, The Youth Shop. To my delight, I found a lovely tailored dress. "Billy, do you mind having a seat, I have to try on this dress."

This was a totally new experience for us. I appreciated his patience. I modeled it in the three-way mirror outside of the dressing room. Aloud I said, "I love it."

He murmured, "It looks good on you."

I was taken aback by such a lackluster remark. Bruce would have practically done cartwheels. I could imagine him saying, "Fantastic! You do wonders for that dress." To put Bruce out of my mind, I tried to change my mood. I turned to the saleslady, "May I use your phone to check with my mother about it?"

"Why of course. You can lay it away for a few dollars, if she agrees." And she handed the phone to me. Five minutes later, I gave the saleslady a small deposit to lay away my beautiful green dress with a red-checkered, cape-like top which had four large buttons. On each sleeve, a three-inch zipper closed it to the wrist. The dress was lined from the neckline to the hemline and both sleeves. A long zipper extended from the neck to just beyond the hips. Beautiful. I smiled all the way home where Billy gave me a small kiss before leaving.

It was slightly after lunch time the next day, Christmas Eve, when Bruce and Jason from campus arrived. He was continuing to Durham, his hometown. I was surprised at how much I'd missed Bruce. He was eating lunch when Sam arrived.

"Hi, Bruce, so how is school going? That was nice of you to show Dorothy around New York last summer."

"School is just fine, Mr. Burston. It was my pleasure showing her around."

"Oh, you can call me Sam, everybody else does. Dorothy Leigh, do you two have any plans for the evening?"

"Yes, we do. Jocile is having everybody over for a party at her house. Bruce, she goes to Howard."

"Why don't the two of you use my car this evening?" And he handed his keys to Bruce.

What exactly did that mean? He only met him once before in September when they drove me back to school. Certainly, I hadn't talked about Bruce to him. Oh, well, probably Tee shared my summer activities with Sam. Yeah, that's why he was being so nice.

Jocile's party could have been a heck of a lot more fun if Billy had not been there. In addition to showing off my New York boyfriend, it was the first time I got to reveal my new college achievement, my dancing skills. All the other holidays the previous years, there were no opportunities to dance. My parents' home was too small to accommodate that type of party. I had to marvel at how smoothly Billy and Bruce handled the moment. Maybe because Bruce knew only that he was someone I dated in high school. That night Billy was Jocile's date.

Bruce and I returned to my folks' house in a very good mood. When we entered, Tee was behaving rather strangely, pulling me into the den, peeking behind her to make sure Bruce had gone into my bedroom turned guest room for the night. I wondered what was wrong with her. I looked for my dad then heard him snoring in their bedroom.

"Here," Tee said and placed a beautifully wrapped box on my lap. It was rectangular, flat, the type clothing was usually wrapped in. "Open it."

From my seat on the daybed, my accommodations, I stared up at her questioningly. She always made me wait until Christmas morning to open any gift no matter how hard I begged. I continued to stare from her to the box. "It's from Billy."

"I didn't get him anything."

"Open it."

I did, probably slower than she wanted. Once I removed the white tissue paper, my olive-green dress appeared tucked into the red-checkered, cape top. "This is the dress."

She smiled down at me. Without a word, she joined my daddy in their room. I was now in a new quandary. Maybe some people didn't talk about their intentions, just did them. I closed the box, folded the wrapping paper on top, and slid it all under the day bed. Christmas day was only hours away.

In the morning, the floor furnace kicked in. Bruce appeared at the door to my bedroom as if on cue. I said, "Hi sleepyhead, it's Christmas. Time to unwrap presents."

We hugged each other briefly before he escaped to the bathroom which opened into the den where I had spent the night. I joined Tee in the kitchen. She was preparing breakfast. For as long as I could remember, Sam always slept through Christmas morning. I never knew why or even bothered to ask. Maybe it had something to do with growing up in his grandfather's house. He was a preacher. Nobody ever talked about it. Sam always bought tons of presents for both Tee and me, so he did observe the holiday.

Bruce returned to the living room, Tee and I joined him. "Time to open presents." And I reached under the tree for my gift to Bruce.

"How nice. This is a good-looking pair of leather gloves. I like the tan color. Thanks, Dorothy." And he gave me a kiss. "Would you mind opening my gift to you next?"

I didn't answer, just picked it up and shook it. No sound came from it. I laughed. "It's too beautifully wrapped to undo. How did you pick out this paper at the store's gift wrapping service? They usually offer too many choices."

"I wrapped it myself."

Tee said. "Well, it certainly is pretty. I've never seen such lovely paper—all purple and that deep-red accented with the touches of gold."

At first, I played with the gold ribbon bow, then decided to just pull it off. Luckily, it didn't come apart. "Bruce, it almost seems a shame to open it; but I will." Sliding my hand beneath a few of the tape pieces, I had the wrapping paper practically removed and began opening the flaps of the box. Tissue paper cushioned whatever was inside.

"Just toss all of that stuff aside," Bruce said.

I gladly did—only to reveal a smaller, beautifully wrapped new box. "What?"

Bruce laughed.

I sped up. I wasn't interested in the snow scene paper. This one had to be it. I became apprehensive. Bruce's face was no longer light, festive. It had turned serious. I really didn't want to go any further when I recalled the embarrassment his baby doll pajamas had caused me. Would this gift be something I couldn't handle?

Although Bruce was sweet and thoughtful and generous, he lacked those social graces for which the South was notorious. I often scorned and tried fervently to ignore them. However, I was finding Bruce's ignorance of those things caused me consternation. *Stop it, Dorothy, you are being such a prude. Here you have this charming, unique, handsome man, and you have the audacity to find fault with him.*

I returned in earnest to the moment and tore into the last wrapping paper. At that point, I stared into his face, searching for answers. "Go on, Dorothy, open your present," he said.

This had better be it. I'm not playing this guessing game anymore. By now the box was petite, a square. Reluctantly, I opened it. The final box was unwrapped. It simply bore the name of a jewelry store in Virginia. Suddenly, my hands were no longer so adept at unwrapping or easily lifting lids, especially tiny lids. But I managed. A lovely, small, solitaire diamond ring in a platinum setting greeted me.

Initially, I was puzzled. I didn't recall hearing a question at any time whose answer was this. I looked up at Bruce. His eyes sparkled. I was speechless. Not Tee, "What about Billy?"

What an embarrassment she was. Ignoring her, I extended the dainty case and my right hand to Bruce, then rose to hold this treasure of a man in my arms for all eternity.

Changes

Bruce and I got happily through the remainder of his visit including meeting Mama. Before I could introduce him, Mama squinted her eyes, "Billy, is that you?"

"No, Mama, this is Bruce Williams."

"That's not Billy's last name. He's from that family who live over on . . . .." I refused to play whatever game she was concocting. I said nothing more. Still, I hugged her and planted a kiss on her cheek before leaving. I could have sworn she winked at me.

A few days later, two guys from my high school class stopped by. I introduced Bruce. The three of them hit it off. In a few days, Bruce returned to Hampton. A week remained before I returned.

While professing to be in love with Bruce, I spent some more time with Billy. Two days later, Bruce surprised me. "Hi, I'm back. Work was dribbling down to nothing. I'd had so much fun here and I missed you—so here I am."

I was dumbfounded. I didn't realize just how much I was enjoying my freedom from any real physical attachment to anybody. That was when I made a startling discovery: I loved Bruce more—away. Maybe I had no business getting married any time in the near or distant future. After two days, I said, "Bruce, I'm sorry but I don't think I'm ready for marriage. Please forgive me. Here is your ring."

His eyes became snake eyes. Before that moment, I'd never noticed how small and piercing they could be. I averted my eyes.

"So, you are still in love with Billy?"

"No, to tell you the truth, I'm really not in love with anyone. I just need to be me for now."

"Well, let me give you your space. I'll stay over at your home boys' for a few days before going back to campus."

"Okay. And I am truly sorry."

Two days passed before he stopped by. "I'm returning to Hampton. We'll talk when you get back."

"Okay, Bruce. However, I doubt I'll change my mind. Marriage is a huge step."

Once he left, I felt terrible. Everybody on campus would know what had happened. Billy was returning to California knowing we were no longer sweethearts. I was sick to my stomach. I found a place to lay the blame—on Bruce's shoulders.

I tried to recall where all of this had started. I had never asked for a ring. Sure, we'd looked at them once. But a ring for me? True, he was cute and brilliant. In reality, I was crazy about him and he was from New York. Could I pass up all of that? By the end of the first week back on campus for Spring semester, we were re-engaged. Everything felt so right.

In February, at the popular George Washington Day sale, Bruce bought a 1953 light-blue Studebaker for $25. It ran; he gave it to me. I had always loved the car's unique shape. However, I didn't have a license; I didn't even know how to drive. That didn't stop him, he began instructing me immediately. As my teacher, he was relentless. That's how I had made it through math but I absolutely hated him as a driving instructor. Daily, I'd stopped the car in the middle of the street, get out, and walk away. In the end, his method worked; I got my driver's license.

Spring semester flew by. I was returning to Irvington House for the summer without Bruce; he needed a full-time job. His private foundation grant was not renewed due to poor grades and class attendance as he had joined me in my classes instead. This also meant he would be spending the fall semester in New York.

My assignment that summer was unchanged: same dormitory, same co-workers, and same roommate, Susan. Before the end of week one, our supervisor met with the two of us. "Welcome back. We've been pleased with your work and glad you returned." A big smile crossed her face, "I'm giving each of you your own room this summer."

I turned sharply to Susan; her dubious expression stared back at me.

The supervisor's voice sliced through the moment. "Here are your keys."

We thanked her in unison. The symbols of separatism scorched our hands. Wordlessly, we rode the elevator to our old room to pack. In the prevailing silence of the expanded space, tears flowed uncontrollably from each of us. We rushed to embrace each other because we, in our youth, knew the South's ugly prejudice had found us in Westchester County, New York. All last summer, we had escaped its ugliness; it would not allow us to pretend any longer.

A week later, neither Susan nor I commented when a trio of new female counselors moved into our former accommodations. The South had so corrupted our psyche, we could not even accept truth.

That summer, Bruce and I explored Greenwich Village. I couldn't believe I was actually there. The occasion was a chance to see the jazz pianist and singer, Nina Simone. I tried to contain my excitement, but then giggled when we walked into the VILLAGE GATE. The music emanating from the room talked of jazz whose aroma reeked of its presence. Photographs at the entry proclaimed its gods and goddesses. I was so hip; I was occupying the same space with them. In my mind, I was raised far above the mere level of audience.

Bruce found our seats not too far from the stage; his first experience, too. We held hands for a moment in anticipation of what we were about to hear. The opening act, a male singer, primed us for her appearance. I was too much of a novice to know he was there to warm us up. Soon, Nina appeared and claimed her position at the piano. She commanded it like it had been waiting idly just for her touch to come alive. And she went to work on such numbers as "This Is a Man's World," "I Put a Spell on You." What an amazing performance. I was grateful to Bruce for exposing me to live jazz.

In the fall, I returned to campus without him. I felt a new lightness, an unobligated existence. I liked it. I attended classes, had free time, and for the first time in four years, I had a single room. I didn't mind that I was a senior living in the junior dorm. Single rooms were limited on campus.

What if it was extremely narrow. In my imaginary world, it was a studio in the city.

On my birthday, a medium-sized, heavy box, marked fragile, arrived from New York, from Bruce. Inside was a four-piece place service for four, in a soft, aqua with a platinum rim. It was the "Silver Pine" pattern by the Franciscan China Company which screamed modern. Bruce and I had found it during the summer. I displayed the squatty, delicate, cream and sugar pieces on my metal desk.

Our engagement took on a new status having become undeniably real. Bruce was preparing a nest. Our commitment was growing. I loved him so much.

That Christmas was spent apart but I joined him in New York for New Year's Eve. He met me at the bus station. Early the next morning, we went to Orbach's. Three cocktail length dresses, pre-selected by him, were presented for my approval. As I followed the saleslady to a dressing room, I thought I was in a movie.

Once inside, I selected the first dress, waited to be fastened in, and waltzed out to meet Bruce's adoring eyes. "You are absolutely, beyond a shadow of a doubt, the most beautiful woman I've ever seen."

Although each of the remaining dresses was pretty, he chose the white, strapless dress with the gorgeous red, satin band attached just below the bodice. Afterwards we walked on 34th Street. Bruce sang the Ray Conniff Singers' "Make Her My Bride for Christmas."

He was full of surprises. We had reservations at a nightclub directly across the street from the El Morocco that evening. It wouldn't have surprised me at all if Nat King Cole sat at a piano bar when we arrived. We left the large spacious apartment which overlooked Central Park that he and Thomas were subletting. I floated downstairs in my new gown on Bruce's arm. He was attired in a dark suit, red striped tie, gold cuff links, the works. Outside, he expertly hailed a cab.

I was still euphoric when we arrived at the door of the club. As I laid my hand in Bruce's to exit the cab, I pouted my lips in a kiss to him. We walked arm in arm to the large wooden door. It opened on a dour scene of elderly white couples muddling around a currently silent piano. We were shown to a small round cocktail table. Sometimes reality can be so harsh, so disappointing. Nonetheless, Bruce insisted we have one drink before leaving. To tell the truth, as in love as we were, we could have stood on the sidewalk all night in each other's arms.

Another day, we explored the portion of Central Park near the Tavern on the Green, a first for me. Thanks to the thick blanket of snow, everything looked like a fairyland. The sight almost made me forget how bitterly cold it was until Bruce spoke, "Is my baby freezing?"

I nodded.

"We'll buy some chestnuts from that vendor over there."

I told myself I must be dreaming. I waited until Bruce made his purchase and turned to me. "Here, Dorothy, let me help you."

Looking at him, I almost cried with happiness but I didn't dare. My tears might turn to ice on my face; it was that cold to do so. I kissed his cheek instead. "Oh, Bruce, you have made this the best New Year's ever."

Finishing up the stuffing of my gloves with chestnuts, he said, "That's because I love you so much, I'm always thinking of ways to please you."

When he said that, I didn't need chestnuts or even gloves, I was cherished in a way I never even dreamed of. Snow lightly fell on my face as I kissed my wonderful man. On cue, Nat King Cole sang out "Chestnuts roasting on an open fire, Jack Frost nipping at your nose . . .."

At the start of the spring semester, Bruce returned to campus. I would finish in May. I grew more anxious day by day. I began to doubt I was ready for the job market. I wanted to learn more. Weeks later, I accepted the fact—my carefree life was ending. With Bruce's help, I applied for real jobs in speech therapy.

On campus, job interviews were beginning. The dean of education, my philosophy professor, called my dorm one day and urged me to interview in a nearby Virginia town. I said, "Thank you so much but I'm not interested in working in Virginia."

He didn't take "no" for my answer and firmly suggested I at least go for the interview. I agreed, just to get him off my back. There was nothing the South could offer me; I wanted out. After much persuasion, I allowed Bruce to deliver me to the dean's job choice. I knew one thing and one thing only: should an offer be presented, I knew how to say no.

We arrived that Saturday morning at the appointed school site for the interviews. There were Hamptonians from other disciplines waiting to be seen. After that part, we were loaded on a school bus for a tour of the school district followed by lunch. At the end of the forty-five-minute tour, I thanked my escort, found Bruce in the parking lot, and returned to campus.

I barely crossed the threshold before the head mistress assailed me. "Call the dean at once." He was furious. I waited for my turn to speak and said, "I have no intention of working in the South."

Days later, the Baltimore City School District asked me to interview. Bruce and I hit the road. My Studebaker behaved admirably on the trip. We sang songs and laughed all the way to my Cousin Olivia's apartment. The next day, I accepted the job.

Not too many weeks after, on a beautiful spring day in May, I wore a cap and gown with gold cords denoting honor status. As my daddy had projected years earlier, I was headed for the circle. My eyes swept across the visitors on my side of it. There stood Mama beaming with pride. The good Lord had spared her. She was surrounded by Aunt Burrell, Aunt Sister Hattie, Cousin Marie, Little Alice and our Norfolk relatives.

Although happy, I was growing apprehensive about my new role as a beginning therapist. Had I prepared myself well enough? Maybe I needed a master's degree instead of a position.

As I climbed the broad steps of Ogden Hall, I imagined the pride Sam had to be feeling. He and Tee sat in their assigned seats inside. This graduation, he had a daughter walking in cap and gown. He had dreamed this wondrous dream twelve years earlier. *Grateful he wanted it for me.*

My Graduation Walk

Tee & Sam at my Graduation

My Hampton graduate friends

My 1953 Studebaker Champion

Adulthood

It was September of 1961, my Studebaker was packed, my room key returned, and my goodbyes said. I was leaving Irvington House for the last time. In a way, I regretted not seeking permanent employment there. It was only an hour away from my target city, New York. But I had to try my wings down in Baltimore. Was I actually worth a whopping $4,500 a year?

As I drove down the hill to Broadway, a light rain began to fall on my first solo road trip. No worry, Baltimore wasn't that far. Besides, I had no choice. I was a woman on my own. In August, Bruce enlisted in the United States Air Force, foregoing completing degree requirements. "I think I need the discipline of the military." They sent him to San Antonio, Texas.

On the morning he reported, we drove into the city to the Whitehall Street induction center. Bruce double parked, kissed me goodbye. "Can you handle the car?"

"I have to, Bruce," I slid beneath the steering wheel. He stood on the curb while I pulled the heavy bench seat forward, adjusted my mirrors, and inched out into traffic. Instantly, a cab driver hit his horn and held it down. At the first traffic light, a brash New Yorker pounded on my car hood. I was in his crosswalk. Impatient drivers gave me the finger as they swung around me. I pressed down on the Studebaker's accelerator as soon as possible, shifted into second, and headed back to the bucolic safety of Irvington. There, the most that ever happened to me was a rash from poison ivy while hiking down to Washington Irving's estate.

A month later, I drove down to my first speech job in Baltimore. I was moving in with Cousin Olivia, her husband, and their toddler in their first three-bedroom home. Bruce was almost finished with basic training and would be off to OTC (officer training) in Waco, Texas. He had signed me up to receive a government check each month. I was surprised; I thought only wives received that. Aunt Burrell would have appreciated the arrangement. "Uncle Sam's money is the best."

Unlike back in World War II or the Korean Conflict, it was peace time money. Bruce was doing standard military stuff, preparation.

Meanwhile, I was having a pretty good time in Baltimore. There was just enough excitement to keep me busy and ample Hamptonians to make it pleasant; the district hired four speech therapists from my class. My work assignment included four elementary schools to be serviced weekly. At the end of each month, I received five hundred dollars. What more could I ask?

To make things really nice, my new girlfriend, Carol, a fellow speech therapist from Hampton, and I discovered a calypso music club. The very first night, I behaved like a school girl—stared intensely at the conga player, Harry Belafonte's twin. He strolled his tall, cute self over to our table at intermission. Talk about roots—I knew how to work them.

My soft-spoken drummer lived with his sister. We frequented the movies and also live shows at a theater on Pennsylvania Avenue where The Shirelles, a girls' group, sang "Please, Please, Mr. Postman." We heard Jerry Butler's rich, deep, velvety voice croon "He Don't Love You, Like I Love You," and many other performers. Jerry Butler was running a close second to my all-time favorite, Nat King Cole.

The city of Baltimore showed me what "team spirit" and "let's hear it for the home team" was all about. The locals were crazy about the Colts' quarterback, Johnny Unitas. His picture was all over the city on billboards and stores. My cousin's husband was a season ticket holder. I wasn't into football.

At Christmas, Bruce got leave and flew to Baltimore. We drove to my parents' home for the holidays. During that time, we also made wedding plans for early August after his OTC graduation. It was great having him back even for just a short time. A few weeks after he left, Carol and I moved into a furnished third floor Victorian walk-up apartment, located two blocks off North Avenue, convenient for both of us.

She claimed the kitchen. No argument from me; I couldn't cook. Decorating was my forte, and our narrow, long living room screamed my name. I loved modern art and furniture. Since we had neither, I hand sewed chocolate and aqua coverings for the loose cushions on our western motif sofa. Drapery for our one tall, skinny window was next. But I postponed making them to spend my Easter break with Bruce.

Boldly, I walked into a travel agency and booked a round trip plane ticket on United Airlines. I had never flown before and here I was going all the way to Waco. As I paid, I heard Mama, "If the Lord meant for us to fly, he would have gave us wings."

Contrary to Mama, Cousin Willie Mae said, "There's nothing like flying, Dot. The way they treat me up there in the sky is way better than down here on earth. They serve me just like I'm a white person. And here I am on my way to work for a Jewish woman in her Florida vacation house."

Maybe that was the heaven they sang about each Sunday. On a spring evening in 1962 with my curiosity aroused, I strode in pointed toed, high heels from the United Airlines terminal, right onto the black tarmac—and froze. Fellow passengers detoured around me. I stared at that ominous, glistening mass of metal. It bore the number 707. The same type of airplane had crashed over a New York City neighborhood just months earlier.

I backed up to turn around but the crowd behind me had become an avalanche. It propelled me forward, urged me up the staircase, and channeled me into the jet's belly. In no time, I was strapped into my assigned seat, beside a white person. I watched and listened to the stewardess' safety instructions; I was doomed.

Later that night, I arrived unscathed, in Dallas. My connecting flight to Waco was long gone. I didn't care; I needed a break from flying. As Willie Mae had predicted, I was treated equally from start to finish; United Airlines even put me up in a motel.

The next morning, back at the airport, I boarded a toy plane whose tail sat on the ground. I had to walk up hill to my seat. Unlike in the 707, the landscape moseyed by. At last, our tiny plane lifted its wheels. We stayed up all the way to Waco.

To me, the base there didn't compare favorably to Langley Field in Hampton. Bruce and I often drove out there to look at the planes on special days. My favorite was the Voodoo, the F-101, a fighter. Aside from the base, I saw very little of Waco. The chance to spend time with Bruce was worth every penny.

When I returned to Baltimore, time flew. I resigned from my job and returned home to spend my last unmarried summer with my parents. They were in the midst of adding on to their cottage. Sam said, "Dorothy Leigh, everything will be finished in time for your wedding."

"Punjab, we're adding on a large master bedroom and a bigger kitchen to fit our big, new refrigerator."

"I wanted Christine to have a service porch for her automatic washing machine."

One afternoon, I paid a visit to my favorite high school teacher, Mrs. Armstrong. She was still beautiful. I brought her up to date on my life.

She said, "You were always such a unique person."

As usual, whenever I sensed kindness, tears pooled in my eyes. A compliment from her was always special. I listened.

"When I cast you in the Christmas play your freshman year, someone told me 'You don't want her. You can find someone better. Don't put her in the play.'"

"Who said that?"

"Let's just say it was an adult."

As Mama frequently said, "My mind didn't fool me." It always urged me to get out of my hometown. It was definitely more than a hunch. What manner of evil lurked in the South that an adult should stoop to hinder a child's development?

The remainder of the summer I played Scrabble with Tee and her new friends. Just when I was too bored to move, one of my bridesmaids, Rosemary, arrived for a visit; she needed to escape her mother's very late life pregnancy. With three years of marriage behind her, my friend counseled me on that institution: "Charge anything you want. Bruce will pay for it."

Though terse, it was better than my mother's: "Always take a towel to bed with you."

Bruce arrived three days before the wedding. What a fine specimen he was—all tailored and handsome. He was a commissioned Second Lieutenant in the US Air Force, assigned to Mather Air Force Base in California. I was so proud of him.

His second day back, we went to the local Volkswagen dealership to pick up the new red convertible he had ordered. The dealer said, "Sorry, it has not arrived, yet. I've been told not to expect it until at least 10 days from now."

Bruce said, "That will be too late. We're getting married Saturday and leaving on Monday for New York. My family has some legal affairs to finalize. After that we're heading to California, my new base."

"Real sorry about that. But sometimes things work out this way. Could I interest you in a white sunroof? Naturally, the quality is the same. All brand new. Why don't you and your bride-to-be test drive it? Then make up your minds."

We took it for a spin. I said, "Bruce, do you really have to be in New York? We can't hang around here and wait just a few days to see if it comes in?"

"Sorry, Dorothy. My brothers have it all arranged with the lawyer. Leon, the oldest of us died a few years back and Monday is the distribution of his will. It won't be huge but some of them have very little. I don't want to be the hold up. What do you think? Do you mind terribly not owning a red convertible?"

"As long as I have you, nothing else matters. Matter of fact, I like the sunroof."

The day before the wedding, our attendants arrived from Virginia, New York, and West Virginia ready to fulfill their roles: Bruce's older brother, Don, as best man; a younger brother, Johnny, as an usher; sorority sister, Rosemary, as maid of honor; her husband, Chester, as second usher; my first-year roommate, Audrey, and my high school friend, Jocile (whose party we'd attended during Bruce's first visit), as bridesmaids.

The afternoon of our wedding, Sam and I waited in the vestibule of Mount Zion First Baptist Church for Miss Mary's organ cue to enter the sanctuary. We were joined by the white photographer who had photographed my Shirley Temple curls. He took a few candid shots of my dad and me, then entered the sanctuary.

Sam squeezed my hand and said, "Dorothy Leigh, are you sure you want to do this?"

"Yes. Besides, everybody's here. Some of them came from so far away."

Miss Mary's organ bang came. We locked arms for our journey down the aisle.

Before I knew it, the wedding and the reception were done. The only disappointed person was my daddy when he learned we had to leave two days later for New York. He said, "I wanted to take the four of us on a fishing trip."

He couldn't hide his disappointment. He held onto me. I hugged and kissed the best father in the world.

That Monday morning after breakfast, we climbed into our new car after loading up our stuff including a few presents and headed for New York. The bulk of the gifts would be handled by a moving service hired by the government. Although Bruce and I were alone in our Volkswagen, his older brother, Don, followed us in his faded, gray Morris Minor. The relatives would have been complete if Johnny could have joined us. Unfortunately, he was in the Air Force, too, and stationed in North Carolina.

Our honeymoon trip was without incident until two hours later just near the Virginia border, Don signaled he needed to pull over. He had to leave his Morris Minor at a local gas station for repairs. The front seat of our car became his. I crumpled up in the back seat with our gifts and luggage and romance flew out of the open sunroof.

The rest of the way, I daydreamed about California. We were scheduled to live there for the next eight months while Bruce received navigator training in the B-52 airplane, a bomber. We had no idea where we'd go when he graduated. In other words, it appeared New York would not be a part of our future for at least four years, if we decided to return. At the moment, Bruce was assigned to strategic air command (SAC) just like June Allyson and James Stewart in the movie of the same name. Thank goodness, we were not in a war.

We arrived in New Rochelle, New York about six hours or less after Don joined us in our new car. He, Bruce and their sister left early the next morning for the city. The rest of the family would meet them there. Three hours later, they returned with checks in hand. After a quick lunch, we all watched Don board Greyhound back to Virginia to pick up his car and return to his family in West Virginia.

In less than an hour, we, too, waved goodbye. With our AAA triptik in hand, we officially began our honeymoon. Bruce said, "Dorothy, look up some points of interest along the way to California."

"Okay. By the way, have you noticed that other VW drivers toot at us?"

"Yeah. Some even wave, too."

"Guess we belong to a club. Let's do it, too."

Our first big stop was Chicago. From that point, we explored the vastness of America. Bruce and I became unconditional citizens of our great country—slept in hotels on Main Street; dined in fancy restaurants. We were served by waiters in tuxedos, ate cowboy dinners in a covered wagon by a campfire; and bought movie tickets before white people, who politely waited their turn under the marquee displaying "The Music Man." We were in Omaha.

Heading west on the northern route across the United States was a wise choice. Segregation rarely, if ever, reared its ugly head. For the first time in my life, I actually felt I was in the land of the free. My negative thoughts and apprehensions vanished. I relaxed, enjoyed myself—until Wyoming.

We stopped for lunch at a diner in wide open land. No conversations halted in mid-air when we entered. The white waitress maintained her smile as she seated us at a window and presented the menus. I accepted mine as my due. I was living in the lap of freedom, enjoying all the goodies when segregation smacked me in the face. And I wasn't even its target.

Without the window seat, I might have missed them. There they were walking in the heat of the day on that steaming hot, black asphalt road. I stared; I'd only seen Indians in cowboy movies. I waited for them to come inside; they didn't. The man led his wife and two children to a shaded area. He settled them down on the ground and approached the diner alone, by-passing the front door, then veering to the side of the building.

My apple pie ala mode arrived. I concentrated on it. As I spooned up the last delicious bits, the Indian man returned, cradling two large brown paper bags. Apparently from our diner; no other buildings existed. I quit the melting dessert.

I recalled being ten years old in my home town, waiting for my daddy outside a white-owned barbeque restaurant. He had gone to the back door to order. Only whites entered the front door, sat down, ordered from the printed menu, and were served. Sam's cost was the same as theirs.

The memory and the similarity in Wyoming suffocated me.

"Bruce, are you done?"

"Let me get the check."

By the time the bill was paid, the Indian family was gone. Back in the car I said, "I need to scrub away the stench I acquired from just being in there."

Bruce listened, hugged me. "Don't worry. I'm sorry it all happened. But cheer up, we're headed for California, the golden state. Things will be better there. You'll see."

Our trip planner at AAA was right. The northern entrance into California was breath taking. We came from the whiteness of Salt Lake City into the desolation of Nevada, and landed in the lush eden of Lake Tahoe, California.

Bruce was moved. "Dorothy, we still have four days before I report for duty and we're only a few hours out of Sacramento. Would you like to spend two days in this romantic lodge?"

"Oh, could we, honey?"

The desk clerk said, "It's still early in the day. Your room has to be prepared."

Bruce said, "No problem. We'll explore the facility while we wait."

Hand in hand, we strolled down to the end of a small pier and stared at the majestic Sierra Mountains reflected in the pristine lake. It was breathtaking.

As time passed with no word on our room, I said, "It seems to be taking an extraordinary amount of time."

Bruce was quiet.

"Do you think they have any intention whatsoever of renting to us, to Negroes?"

"Hell, no."

We resumed our travel never knowing whether we were right or wrong. We only knew how bad discrimination felt, even worse, the suspicion lingered with us like a stubborn cough.

Bruce and I trekked up the Sierra Nevada Mountains in our heavily packed German Beetle. We were probably just a bit faster than those pioneers' covered wagons. One wagon train, known as The Donner Party, suffered heavy human losses in their extremely harsh 1846-1847 winter migration from the Midwest. There was a plaque dedicated to them. We were grateful for summer.

Late afternoon that same day, we wound down the mountains into the Sacramento valley—a sizzling hell. Lush greenery was replaced by brown, dried out fields leading up to Mather Air Force Base. We found guest quarters, piled in, and stirred only long enough to find food.

After a few days of hibernation, we looked up Brit, my cousin, a master sergeant, stationed at Mather. He and his wife, Dorothy, from North Carolina, too, lived on base. I felt lucky to be near him again. They invited us over.

Things were going so well, Brit said, "Cookie (his pet name for me), why don't you guys save some money; move in with us while you look for a place."

I loved the idea.

Back at guest housing, a barracks, Bruce said, "We can't accept their offer."

"Why not? It'll be fun. Besides, their place is so much nicer than this."

"The Air Force has rules. Brit's a non-commissioned officer; I'm a second lieutenant. Trust me." I declined their invitation.

A few more days passed; we were on the verge of being kicked out of guest housing. There was no vacancy in officer housing. Off base was our only alternative.

I said, "Bruce, it's no problem. Other couples in our squadron have furnished apartments as close as 15 minutes from the base. I'll take care of it while you're in class."

My search began at the first desirable complex outside the gates. A vacancy sign was in the window. Inside, the white manager said, "We're filled up."

I drove down to the big boulevard, turned right, and pulled into a nice-looking apartment complex. We knew a couple who lived there. When I approached the manager, he said, "Somebody on the other shift forgot to take down the vacancy sign."

It didn't matter that Bruce was training to guide a bomber to destroy enemies of the country, people who had never done him any harm. Racial hatred was alive and well in the Golden State.

Back on base, we were acquiring enough vacate notices to wallpaper a room. Then the base chaplain, a black man, came to our rescue. He drove us to Sacramento's Oak Park neighborhood, a good thirty minutes from the base. As he pulled up in front of a spanking, brand-new apartment building, I touched Bruce's shoulder and said, "Bruce, honey, let's not bother looking. I'll go back home, wait for your graduation, and your new assignment."

"Just a minute, Dorothy."

"Without me, you can move into bachelor's quarters."

Getting out of the car, the chaplain said, "Let me do the worrying."

He was greeted by a young white couple who stood near the building. They walked over and invited us to inspect a ground floor, unfurnished apartment. We moved in the next day with only suitcases and the few wedding gifts we'd brought in the VW.

*Sam relaxing
in the living room*

*Me in front of
Olivia's house
in Baltimore*

Sam waiting to walk me down the aisle

On the Pennsylvania Turnpike headed to California; beginning of honeymoon

Cousin Brit

[12] B-52 bomber

[13] F-101 - Voodoo

[14] Boeing 707

[12] US Air Force http://www.af.mil/, Public domain, via Wikimedia Commons, "Boeing B-52 Stratofortress," photograph, 2012, commons.wikimedia.org, https://commons.wikimedia.org/wiki/File:Usaf.Boeing_B-52.jpg, (accessed April 17, 2023)

[13] USAF, Public domain, via Wikimedia Commons, "F-101B New York ANG in flight 1978," photograph, 2010, commons.wikimedia.org, https://commons.wikimedia.org/wiki/File:F-101B_New_York_ANG_in_flight_1978.jpeg, (accessed April 17, 2023)

[14] United States Air Force, Public domain, via Wikimedia Commons, "116th_ACW_E-8C_Joint_STARS_96-0042," photograph, 2012, commons.wikimedia.org, https://commons.wikimedia.org/wiki/File:116th_ACW_E-8C_Joint_STARS_96-0042.jpg, (accessed April 17, 2023)

Coping

A month later, Bruce and I no longer slept on the floor or ate standing at the kitchen counter in our new apartment; we had a Sears account. By some miracle, we survived the torrid heat of our first Sacramento summer but questioned its replacement, the fog. Little did we know the real test, the rainy season, was yet to come. With no job, I often rode out to the base with Bruce, that way I had the car all day.

On weekends, when money allowed, we escaped to San Francisco; Sacramento was dead. In the city, we stayed out late, engaged with people, inhaled the city's fumes. We frequented jazz clubs in Little Italy. Ones like the La Strata where we listened to pianist Horace Silver. The area reminded us of New York's Greenwich Village. Ethnic foods stimulated our palates and neon lights captivated us. It was exhilarating.

To escape the boredom of the weekdays and to add funds to our coffers, my cousin's wife, Dorothy, and I applied for jobs at the telephone company. Neither of us could have done that back home. We filled out applications, interviewed, and left jobless in no time. That could have been attributed to any number of things—including bias towards race, or bias towards military wives. With no job prospect and a limited time to spend at this particular base, I relaxed and yielded to an invitation to the officers' wives' world from the wife of Bruce's squadron leader. They latched onto me and two other brides like flypaper.

In no time, we were introduced to military decorum, drilled in the importance of gloves, encouraged to play bridge, and presented with the guaranteed steps for ensuring a husband's military success. Final advice given was to "always bake extra for the base commander's wife."

I drew the line on the last edict; I could barely cook. My best friend was Betty Crocker. Besides on a second lieutenant's salary, we had food only for us. It was a real stretch to put away ten dollars a month for a rainy day. I leveled with the major's wife, "Bruce's success will have to depend on him."

As was typical of the early 1960s, he was the only black in his squadron. For Negroes, financial or professional success in most careers had a byproduct of loneliness. Luckily, other squadrons had some black officers. We got to know them in a hurry. It was comforting. That's not to say the majority of the military families, regardless of color, were not warm, generous people. It's just that having some black members made it so much better.

We had white friends, too, from our squadron as well as others. And we had Patrick, a white guy. He and Bruce had been together since the Whitehall Street induction center in New York. For some strange reason, Bruce admired him; I tolerated him and his snide, southern like compliments. "I knew that was you, Dorothy, walking towards the Officers' Club, you always wear that style of jacket."

My mode of dress was very chic; stylish like Jacqueline Kennedy's.

Maybe his wife and I could have gotten along but Bruce ruined that—he worshipped the very ground on which she trod. Couldn't get enough of her blond hair and flat behind. Whether or not she returned his obvious interest was beside the point; she enjoyed it. Although I resolved to bear the six remaining months of social functions, our next assignment couldn't come soon enough for me.

Prior to the guys' graduation, they elected and received assignments to remain at Mather for the next four years! I wept. The thought of moving into base housing cheered me up until I learned our houses were less than a block apart. They got pregnant first and we came along two months later. When their baby girl was born, anyone would have thought Bruce was a proud uncle the way he went on about it. When Patrick and his wife ran short on money and showed up at our door begging, my husband said, "Of course, we're glad to help."

I said, "Bruce, we need to discuss this first."

"Sure, sweetheart. How soon can we let them know?"

"Now, the answer is no. They should manage better. I have no respect for white people borrowing from black people."

"Dorothy, why are you acting like that?"

"They have too much, too many opportunities compared to us."

"Can't you just think of him as a friend in need?"

"I will consent on one condition: they pay us interest."

Old good Samaritan Bruce persuaded me to lend it interest free.

In July, almost a month later, Paul, our son was born. He arrived two days before Bruce's birthday, a lovely present for him. I happily set about learning how to care for an infant. Prior to his arrival, I'd only looked at them. On my own, away from family and close friends, Dr. Spock and I became bosom pals.

About the same time I was training to be a mom, I grew suspicious of my husband and his blackness. He had spent his childhood and teenage years growing up surrounded by white people. And, he was an orphan. This was probably his first opportunity to cultivate a relationship with white people on a semi-equal basis. Therein, I concluded, lay his fascination with all things Patrick.

I had another opportunity to study Bruce. He had a seven-day duty assignment in Nevada. I was home alone in base housing with Paul. On Bruce's third night away, a knock came on our ugly gray, metal front door. I peeked out its round porthole. Standing there was a white hood with cut out eye holes!

Shocked and frightened, I rushed from the living room to get my baby. To protect him against all evil—"both foreign and domestic." As I hurried to his room, someone called out "Dorothy." It came from outside. I peeked from a corner of the hallway to see who was at our front door. There was Robert's white face in the porthole. He was a southern bachelor in the men's choir Bruce had formed. Storming to the door, I yanked it open. "How dare you!"

"Gosh, I was just joking. I thought it would get a laugh out of you."

"If you ever come to my house again, I'll be notifying the Military Police that you are a klansman."

In my mind, Bruce had the type of relationship with his white associates which permitted them to take liberties. Liberties we as black people could neither afford nor tolerate.

Adding fuel to my belief was the rampage which was enveloping the South. There, blacks were speaking out, no longer turning the other cheek. If I were still living there, I'd have a choice of violence or non-violence.

Unfortunately, I could partake of neither. I was a runaway in California. In college, I had only participated in one sit-in. I needed to go home, needed to be fire-hosed, chased by police dogs, beaten with billy clubs, thrown into jail. But I couldn't; I had the welfare of my newborn son to consider.

Then came November 22, 1963. President John F. Kennedy was shot to death in Dallas, Texas. It scared the daylights out of me. What chance did my black son have in a country where they strike down the President—a white man?

All morning, throughout that day, and into the darkness of the night, I pondered how to save myself and Paul. Finally, I wrote, new for me. But my brain, my soul, didn't know that. I had never written so profoundly as I did that night huddled in the small confines of our cinder block bathroom, my "bomb shelter."

I wrote of all those years of insults to my parents. I wrote of the constant struggle of my people to carve out a decent existence. I wrote of the hope and promise with which our black young men entered the military only to return home after their term of duty to be treated as if they had made no contribution worthy of consideration in these United States.

I knew my infant son was in for an almost sub-human existence in a land which demanded allegiance and offered unequal rights in return. The irony of it all involved my own compliance in bringing him into these United States. Now I was responsible for not only his livelihood but his utter wellbeing. I had to teach him how to live a guarded existence.

There in our two-bedroom house with floors of dark-chocolate speckled linoleum squares and 1950s modern crank-out windows, I wrote. As my husband and my son, a victim-in-development, slept, I wrote. I wrote on into the night and at dawn, flushed my notes down the toilet. It was all so pointless.

Soon after the assassination, a place I never heard of erupted. The French were wiping their hands of it, Vietnam. We, the United States, the champion of the downtrodden, took up the gauntlet. I didn't know just how bad it was until I heard the thundering roar of our B-52 bombers taking off. That meant the KC-135 refueling planes were leaving, too. I ran outside. There they were climbing into the clouds. Their usual shiny aluminum bodies were camouflaged in war dress. This was not supposed to happen. This wasn't a movie; I wasn't June Allyson.

They disappeared. The mass exodus was unreal. Usually, they lazed on the tarmac in the California sun unless on a mission from which they always returned. Their area was deserted. With them went our friends, people we passed in the housing development, in the base exchange, at the base nursery. I cried. I cried even though Bruce was safe at home.

In December, Tee arrived via Greyhound, to see her very first grandchild. My father, in the true spirit of people on the East coast, chose to wait for me to come home for a visit rather than make the trek with her. Life on base after Kennedy's death was very subdued; all merriment was curtailed. The Officers' Club usually a scene of celebration was content to only serve meals as needed, no parties, no bingo, no celebrations, no ladies' luncheons. We were in mourning.

Consequently, we sought entertainment for my mother off base and she was delightful. On a visit to San Francisco, we stopped for brunch at The Nut Tree, a charming restaurant enroute with a landing strip for small aircraft, a miniature train which toured the facility, and a charming gift shop. Afterwards, as we approached San Francisco, Tee remarked, "Oh, my, it looks just like popcorn."

In the sunlight of the crisp December morning, it did indeed. Throughout her visit, Tee was most gracious, helpful, and loving. Three weeks later she boarded Greyhound to return home. I felt she was deserting me. I didn't want to let her go. I stood helplessly by as the bus driver backed up. Suddenly I found myself charging back through the waiting room, exiting the building on the street just as the bus appeared at the corner of the building and turned right into traffic. Running parallel to it on the sidewalk and jostling Paul in my arms, tears streamed down my face.

A month later what I thought was a bad case of the flu turned out to be morning sickness. My first experience using a contraceptive, the diaphragm, had failed or I had. It promised to be another long, hot summer. Hopefully, the end would be a girl.

This new conflict in Vietnam, termed a police action, was forcing service men to make decisions about their lives. It had already claimed huge numbers of black young men with no means of escaping those body bags. Unlike their white counterparts who could evade the draft with help from their friends in high places or flee to Canada, they were placed on the front lines of combat. Bruce, thanks to the air force, would not be on the ground. However, planes were being shot out of the air, too. With almost two years remaining to be served, we worried that the war would escalate and prevent his quitting the service. Unfortunately, there was nothing to do but bide our time.

At nine months of age, Paul, who appeared to be a combination of my husband and my dad, stood up and walked. It was on Mother's Day, the prelude to the extreme heat. I grew more uncomfortable as the weeks progressed. Boy or girl didn't matter; just arrive on time. Two weeks before my due date, Tee called, "Mama died in the hospital last night."

"I'm sorry to hear that but at least you can get a rest after all these years. Of course, I won't be able to fly back now."

"I know. Funny. One of the last things she did was to make Rhone sign a deed giving me half of the house."

"That's good on her part but don't forget all those promises she made to her family when she wanted them to do something for her. They might want to claim it or at least what they deem their share."

"Nothing to worry about. They all knew Mama's promises were of the moment."

The last week of August, the nurse placed a beautiful, petite baby girl with black button eyes and smooth chocolate skin reminiscent of an Almond Joy candy bar in my arms. Suzanne.

Although Bruce's service time crawled along, the war kicked up its pace. Pilots and navigators around us were leaving for extended periods of time. The conflict was the evening news every day. Bruce's vacation leave time was approaching. We decided to combine a trip back East with camping along the way. Again, we chose the northern route. Only this time, we'd go farther north to Yellowstone Park and all the sights along the way. But we needed a larger car.

A white, used 1964 Volvo two-door sedan caught our eyes and our funds. Bigger than our Volkswagen, it offered a similar economy of operation, with more space, and a safety feature, seatbelts. We snapped it up. In less than two hours, we were headed home in it to plan our vacation.

First of all, Bruce was concerned about the welfare of our babies. He researched and found seatbelts which could be welded to the floor and their straps wrapped around the back of the back seat. Via the means of a strap harness, Paul and Suzanne could either sit or stand. Bruce ordered two sets and installed them at the base shop. "Honey, you are the smartest daddy in the world. Thank you so much." And I showered him with kisses.

The rest of the winter and spring, we busied ourselves with locating a one-wheel trailer and creating a waterproof canvas to cover our belongings. Our tent would be rented from the base. Through Bruce's cleverness, our sky-blue canoe would ride on top of our Volvo.

"I'm sure we can pull it off. After Yellowstone, we'll head for the East coast and New York. It's been three years since we were last there."

"It'll be great seeing my brothers and my sister, too."

"Can you believe my dad has never seen either of our children?"

"Well, he'll have five whole days with them."

For some reason, Bruce and I always worked well together. We weren't afraid to tackle anything. No job was too great that he couldn't figure it out.

What a monumental undertaking that vacation was. Even with our meticulous planning, the most efficient and comfortable automobile, and the world's best babies—the stress and strain of the physical demands found us aborting the New York portion two days after Yellowstone. The park itself was spectacular. Then came the Badlands, the monuments, and the scenery along the way; none of that could blot out the enormity of our initial plans. A few days later, we arrived in West Virginia where Don and his wife Columbia, welcomed us with open arms.

It was amazing to see the similarity in the little cousins. They had two boys and one girl a few months older than Suzanne. All of them could have been siblings. After three days, we loaded up and headed for North Carolina. I could hardly wait to see my daddy, to have him and my mother hold their two grandchildren.

After three days of doing nothing there and visiting family and friends, we were ready to hit the long road back to California. The idea of it hung over our heads like an ominous ordeal. There were no shortcuts and no camping planned. Once we got home, Bruce would have to return to work. On our fifth day, we headed back.

In California, new decisions had to be made. The big one was Bruce's. He said, "I've decided. So has Patrick. I'm out of the Air Force. Contrary to popular belief, I'm positive we can live a good life as civilians."

"I'm sure we can, Bruce. I'll go back to work. By the time you resign, I bet we'll have found a house and everything."

He said, "Frankly, I don't see any value in returning to the east coast, do you?"

"No. We're grown now. What about completing your degree?"

"I'll have to. Also planning on part-time employment in real estate. I'll start as soon as I pass the test and go full-time when I get out. What do you think?"

"Sounds like a plan. I'll apply for a teaching credential. It shouldn't be a problem. After all, I worked for one year in Baltimore."

With our plans laid, we grew even more optimistic. Our military friends asked, "How can you make it without the government?"

True, we were leaving free housing, utilities, and cheap food. We bought gas for peanuts and babysitters were inexpensive. For entertainment, there were dirt cheap movies, first rate performers and dining at the officers' club, and any number of facilities for hobbies like photography which Bruce was fond of doing. On the other hand, we were gaining the opportunity for Bruce to live. My two kids would have a daddy.

In no time, Bruce got his license and my credentials arrived: speech therapy or teaching at the junior high level. I crossed my fingers for speech and filled out applications with local school districts. Almost instantly, I had an interview for a part-time therapist position. The personnel director also offered me an additional part-time position, writing articles for the district bulletin. I accepted them both.

We needed all the funds we could get. Although I put up a good front, I wasn't positive life outside the military was all that friendly.

Just as our plans were coming together, I collapsed in excruciating stomach pains on our living room rug. It was the end of a Sunday spent with friends at a picnic in the park. I couldn't move. Helplessly, I watched Bruce bundle up the kids and take them out to the car. In seconds, he was back for me. Together, we managed to get me in the front seat and he drove as rapidly as possible to the base hospital less than fifteen minutes away.

Immediately, they placed me in a wheelchair while Bruce provided the necessary information. Although, I believe it was fast, I thought I would pass out before they checked me in. I glanced at my two babies wide-eyed expressions; I could offer them no solace. I felt like I would die at any moment. That's probably when I passed out. I never saw them leave.

The next thing I knew, I awakened to soft, dim lighting. Some apparatus was touching my upper lip from my nose. A hose of some sort. A black lady clad only in white appeared at my bedside. "Are you an angel?" I asked.

She smiled, "No."

I was confined for two weeks while they pumped out my stomach and calmed my body. Gall bladder surgery was scheduled in a month. I was too weak for the procedure at that time. They released me with a restricted diet curtailing seasonings and fried foods. In no time, my figure dwindled from a size nine to a three. When I regained some strength, I shopped for fabric and created outfits in preparation for my new job search; the earlier positions had been relinquished. I had so looked forward to the writing and reporting one.

Bruce and I continued our brazen plans to leave the military. As Tee often said, "Where there's a will, there's a way."

In 1966 gall bladder surgery was invasive. It necessitated hospital recuperation. I was placed in a private room in the base hospital. During my infrequent awake times, I noticed a female patient in a blue robe who paused at my doorway, gravely shook her head, and limped away. I thought she was part of my delusions. With all my tubes, frequent oxygen masks, and weakness from surgery, she became a constant figment of my condition—always with the same demeanor.

Finally, one day she spoke and came into my room. I stared at her. She said, "We thought you weren't going to make it."

I was told it was the second week of recovery when Bruce brought my babies to see me. It took an effort but I managed to say, "Hi, Paul, how is my big boy?"

"Hi, Mommy." He came to me for a hug and kiss and remained next to my wheelchair. Suzanne, now 18 months old, clung to Bruce and refused to either approach or speak to me. I wasn't surprised, just disappointed. I so wanted to hold her and reassure her I was still her mommy.

After that, I worked hard to return home before she forgot me completely. I was finally released. Bruce left me alone at the house while he went to pick up the kids. Exhausted, I tried to relax on the living room couch. Then, as if in a dream, Billy, my old high school sweetheart, appeared at our screen door.

He said, "Hello, Dorothy. I'm sorry to just show up like this but I didn't have your phone number. I wanted to see you. I'm over in Stockton."

"Billy. How nice. Sorry I can't get up. They just released me from the hospital. Come in. Come in."

"I hope you don't mind; I have a buddy with me. Harry, this is my friend, Dorothy."

"Nice to meet you. Why don't you guys have a seat. I can't believe you're here. I've wondered about you, Billy."

"I've wondered about you, too. Even visited your parents when I was home. Your mom fixed dinner for me."

I said, "So. Are you married?"

"Nope. But I have two sons and a daughter."

"You beat me. We just have a son and a daughter. If your mom is like mine, I know she looks forward to seeing your kids every chance she gets."

Just then Bruce drove up. When he came in through the kitchen, I said, "Bruce, I'm not sure whether or not you recall, but this is Billy from my home town and his friend, Harry."

In his cordial fashion, Bruce said, "Hello. I think we met about three years ago in your home town." He extended his hand to Billy.

"Yes, we did."

"Bruce, Billy's stationed over in Stockton or is it Merced?"

Billy said, "It's neither. I'm out of the military but I'm employed over at McClellan. Sorry to drop in like this but I was visiting friends and remembered Dorothy's mother saying you guys were stationed here. Since I didn't have your phone number, I got your address from the MPs at the gate."

"Paul, Suzanne, come to Mommy." No one spoke as the little ones left Bruce and came to me. Suzanne was still shy but came slightly behind Paul. Oh, how I longed to grab them and never let them go. I started to reach for Suzanne but Bruce stepped in.

"Here, kids, let Daddy lift you up on the seat beside your Mommy. Remember, sweetheart, you shouldn't lift either one of them for a while; give yourself time to heal."

"Of course, you're right. It's just been so long."

Billy said, "Dorothy, I'm so sorry I picked today of all days. You must be exhausted. It's great seeing you. I just wondered about an old friend."

Bruce said, "Sure."

"Thanks for thinking of me, Billy. Imagine that, both of us out here now, far, far away from Rocky Mount."

He nodded in agreement. "Goodbye, Cookie." And he closed the screen door gently behind him without looking back.

But he left me a message of a sort. "Cookie." He rarely called me that; only when he was being extra sweet. I was glad in a way that he left. Hmm. Wonder why he suddenly looked me up after all these years? It was then I noticed the children had slipped away.

Suzanne said, "Play with Mommy, Paul?"

Paul said, "Yes, bring your doll for Mommy."

My two precious toddlers came from their room bearing "gifts"—Paul with a small car in each hand and Suzanne clutching a yellow Playskool bead in one hand and dragging her baby doll by one leg in the other. They set up play at my feet.

I was at peace.

A few weeks later, civilian life preparation began in earnest. We needed shelter, a house in Sacramento. My illness had robbed us of some precious days, only six months remained. Since neither of us had a job, I couldn't get too excited. And not just any job, we needed one with health coverage, for sure. We quickly found a ranch styled house near a golf course with my longed-for curved driveway. It had three bedrooms, two baths, a large living/dining room, a breakfast room, and a kitchen, on a block long street. A fireplace was in the living room at the back of the house. From the outside, our new home looked like a cottage. A curved, rustic, rose vine covered fence swept from the other edge of the attached garage down to the sidewalk and arched around a swirl of green grass. I loved it.

The purchase price of $16,500 was most desirable. Bruce had picked up a part-time job at AEROJET, a major link to the space program, and worked part-time for a black realtor. He just needed to make that first sale. Unfortunately, only residential properties in certain areas of town were available to black real estate salesmen. As usual, this was not a written law but a practice which was strictly adhered to.

Still, we never doubted our decision to leave the military. It was fully solidified for us when the conflict claimed a dear friend of ours, Marshall, a veteran black warrior, and a Tuskegee airman. As a World War II pilot, he flew a small fighter, the P-51. He named it "La Petite Mado," for his French wife, Madeline. His latest plane, the KC-135, a refueler, was shot down over Laos.

About a month before we moved into our home, I was hired as the therapist for a nearby school district's HEAD START program (under President Johnson). My primary function was in language development with emphasis on parental involvement. The site was only twenty minutes from our new home. The best part of all was health coverage. In addition, my hours were ideal, 9 a.m. to 2 p.m. I needed a babysitter or childcare. Suzanne was not quite two and refused, in the midst of our life style changes, to be potty trained. That was a major criterion for the nursery school. Until I could hire a babysitter, I had to keep the one we had on base.

My ad in the local newspaper for a combination babysitter and housekeeper yielded prompt results. The best candidate was a middle-aged white woman, Nora, recently from Newport Beach in southern California. Her rich husband had dumped her . . . a la the mid-sixties. She began right away and was ideal. Sometimes I arrived home to find freshly made jam from our backyard apricot tree. She even tried to do Suzanne's curly, fine, long hair; it was cute. One morning she called, "I won't be able to come to work today."

I panicked. I had to arrange child care at 6:30 a.m. My only hope was the base babysitter, the hour-long delivery, and the return to work. Bruce had early appointments. I was so disappointed in Nora. She probably got tired of pretending to like the job; probably resented having to work in the first place. And to work for a black person was the worst. Later that day I called, "I won't be needing your services any longer. You're not reliable."

My search began anew. This time, I hired a young black lady who fell in love with my children, even volunteered to take them to her house for weekends. I declined that latter offer.

Life was acquiring a nice rhythm. Our decision to quit the Air Force and to settle in Sacramento was wise. We had just finished patting ourselves on the back one spring evening when Patrick called. Bruce said, "How terrific is this. Sure, come on over."

He was in our home for less than an hour before, "Bruce, my wife and I used to laugh at you. About the crush you had on her." He laughed alone.

I was appalled. How could he say that in another man's home, in front of his wife? I waited for Bruce to deny it, to toss him out, even lie. He merely shrugged his shoulders. Bruce was despicable. Curtly I said, "I need to leave." And went to the nearby shopping center. I had no respect for Bruce. When I returned an hour later, Patrick was gone.

In three months, so was my job. The speech therapy component was written out. In fact, the district itself contracted speech therapy services from the county office. My supervisor added my name to their list. I interviewed and was hired at a better pay rate. Our new health coverage resembled that of the military. I hastened to use it. Ever since my surgery, I hated the scars that remained. I wanted them removed.

Highly optimistic, I reported for my internal medicine appointment. The female doctor ignored my surgery request and instead, focused on my blood pressure. She insisted I see a gynecologist. Even though her recommendation puzzled me, I kept the appointment.

In his office, a raspy-voiced, boisterous male gynecologist asked, "Are you a dancer?"

"Sure I dance. It's fun. Why are you asking me that?"

He leaned across his desk, "Do you get paid to dance in clubs?"

If I had been closer, I would have slapped his face. The nerve of him.

"Are you aware you have high blood pressure?"

My reading was 200/98. Like the light bulb in comic strips, I recalled the military nurse expressing concern about my blood pressure when I was recuperating from surgery. That doctor had brushed off her concern, "She runs a slightly high reading."

This one choked his pen, dug it into the appointment pad, slammed the pen to the blotter, and pushed the paper across to me. "Bring along your husband. I'll have your internist here, too."

A week later, the three of them spoke as if I wasn't there. Hysterectomy was thrown around. Tubal ligation (foreign to me) was played like a ping pong ball. Soon, Bruce became an onlooker, too. Neither professional wanted the final say so. At last, the gynecologist declared, "She could die in a pregnancy. At least, she must have the tubal."

I turned to Bruce. He shrugged his shoulders. Right then, I realized just how much I disliked him. I bet he'd never wanted children. I suspected the tubal thing suited him to a "t." I looked at the doctors, it could all be a conspiracy. The two medical people cited tragedies they'd heard of or been involved in. In the end, I consented to the tubal. I thought Bruce smiled.

After the surgery and a brief recuperation, I returned to my speech pathology job and our new life in Sacramento. Though I thought I disliked school or classes, I enrolled in a technical writing course at the local college. It surprised me to discover I might have a knack for writing. I wrote about everything. One article, "Creative Dramatics for Speech Therapy" was sold to a national education magazine for the sum of thirty-five dollars. The professor announced my sale in class.

I was on a roll. My next big article was on Stokely Carmichael, whose approach to equal rights for blacks was in opposition to Reverend King's. My professor suggested I try writing for the local paper. I pursued the idea to no avail but I continued to write.

In April of 1968, Dr. Martin Luther King, Jr. was shot to death in Memphis by a white man. Not an unusual finish for a black man in the South where such atrocities were commonplace. Only this black man was a world figure, a proponent of peace. Global outpourings of sympathy and disbelief poured in. Although I never embraced his non-violent attitude, preferring the thunder of an H. Rapp Brown, a Stokely Carmichael, or the Black Panthers, I respected and admired Dr. King.

As Aunt Burrell often said, "There's more than one way to skin a cat."

On the evening of Dr. King's murder, Bruce and I were in a quandary. An abyss threatened to envelop us. We drove out to Fulton Avenue to its flashing neon lights, car dealerships, restaurants, shopping centers, and purchased a used mahogany Hammond M-3 organ. Neither of us played an instrument or went to church but somehow that organ soothed us in a way we couldn't articulate.

As usual, life moved on. Bruce graduated and found employment as a salesman for Xerox. We gave a house party and invited everyone we knew, white and black. It was going swell, people were dancing, eating. I went to our bedroom. When I opened the door, I found this white woman, a friend of our neighbors, languishing on my side of the bed. I recalled Bruce had added the couple to the list.

I said, "Are you not feeling well?" Before she could answer, "I'll get your husband. He needs to take you home." Earlier, I'd seen her being a mite too cozy with Bruce in the kitchen. In minutes, I was bidding the couple good night at my orange front door.

It's hard to pinpoint when the major tears in our marriage were no longer repairable. Almost daily, Bruce seemed to be growing up or growing out of love with me. He said things like "I wish other women paid more attention to me."

He introduced me to his new friends and associates. One evening in a white couple's expensive, modern home, marijuana was offered after dinner. I declined. I was loaded up on high blood pressure medication and valium. The latter was taken only an hour prior to Bruce's arrival. In spite of my medications, I was unable to work a full day without running to the doctor's office.

At a New Year's Eve party I'd been reluctant to attend (hosted by the same couple I'd dismissed from mine), the evening had been uneventful, almost pleasant. We were minutes away from the end of the year. Bruce and I were dancing. Drawing me closer, he whispered, "Our hostess, Janet, wants us to switch partners once everyone else leaves."

My dance posture collapsed. My feet turned to lead. He braced me up, kept me moving. When the record ended, he settled me in a chair. "I'd better get our champagne."

His mood upon returning with our drinks was high. It rivaled the bubbles tickling my nose when the stemware touched my mouth. Someone yelled out, "Happy New Year!" The cacophonous metallic, noise makers, whinny coiling and uncoiling paper snakes, and the loud off-key singing of

"Auld Lang Syne" rang in 1968. I don't know when it happened but I was standing and being kissed by Bruce.

All that exuberance drained the party goers; they began their good-byes. With each bundling on of coats, my concern grew but I was unable to take any action. In no time, the room was cleared. Only Janet and Ronald, our hosts, and Bruce and me stood amidst the now trite confetti. Janet's red paper party dress (a new fad), crinkled as she drifted closer to Bruce. For a brief moment, I watched a drama unfold on stage; one I knew but was compelled to see performed. She sprang into action gathering up Bruce's Christmas gift to me, my silver evening coat. Her husband, Ronald, entered the scene in his overcoat, and helped me into it. I was unaware he had ever left the room. The "new couple" ushered him and me to the front door. I glanced back at a smiling Bruce.

The drive to my house was conducted in complete silence. I was in shock; I didn't know his reason. I heard myself give him one direction, otherwise he seemed to know the way. A few minutes later, "The babysitter needs to be paid; she lives next door."

"I'll take care of that."

At my front door, I rang the bell and Kelly, the teenage babysitter answered. I felt it necessary to say, "Bruce is driving over in a minute. Didn't want both of them to get lost...his wife I mean."

Ronald paid her and saw her to her front door on the right of my house. He was back in no time. I hadn't moved; I still stood in the small entry with my Christmas coat on and belted. His only obvious discomfort of the evening was a slight sigh as he unbuttoned his jacket.

What more can I possibly lose? It's just a matter of a few minutes and it's done. Besides you'd look pretty stupid crying now. I reached for his hand and led him on tiptoe down our narrow hallway to the bedroom which the master had vacated.

From that point on, I tried to imagine myself someplace else, far, far away. If my own husband no longer wanted me, why would he? That thought inspired me to shed my thin strapped slip of a dress which Bruce, himself, had marked for hemming above my knees. At his further suggestion, I wore no bra or panties.

I watched my partner-to-be shed his clothing. His body was fuller than Bruce's but not fat. They were probably very close in height. With no remorse, I peeled off my seamless black mist panty hose and met him on the side of the bed. Wordlessly, we lay together on cool white sheets in black and white skins. At least he was aroused, I wasn't but I forced myself to fake interest and caressed his penis. We attempted lovemaking motions as though being directed by someone off stage.

I cried, "I'm so sorry but I can't do this. Do you mind leaving and going home? I really need to be alone for a while."

"I understand." He dressed quickly and found his own way out of my house.

I picked up the phone and dialed information. "Stockton, California. (pause) May I have the listing for Billy . . ."

"*My mode of dress was very chic; as stylish as Jackie Kennedy's*"

Decorating front door of first apartment in Sacramento, CA (brand-new Oak Park)

[15] *KC-135 Refueler*

[16] *P-51-Mustang*

[15] United States Air Force, Public domain, via Wikimedia Commons, "106th Air Refueling Squadron KC-135 Stratotanker -2" photograph, 2012, commons.wikimedia.org, https://commons.wikimedia.org/wiki/File:106th_Air_Refueling_Squadron_KC-135_Stratotanker_-2.jpg, (accessed April 17,2023)

[16] Arpingstone, Public domain, via Wikimedia Commons, "P51-d mustang 472216 arp," photograph, 2007, commons.wikimedia.org,. https://commons.wikimedia.org/wiki/File:P51-d_mustang_472216_arp.jpg, (accessed April 17,2023}

Tee's first visit to California – Mather AFB in January 1964

Second Christmas at Mather AFB — I'm holding Paul and Suzanne

First published article with a payment of thirty dollars

Special Education

Creative dramatics for speech therapy

DOROTHY B. WILSON

ALL public school speech therapists labor over problems of scheduling. Inevitably, there is one primary stutterer plus a sea of articulatory cases. Ten minutes of individual therapy for the stutterer is not very ample, and what about the others? It is really best to include such a child with other articulatory problems for the entire thirty minutes.

But having done this, what activities should be tried? Sound drills and games may fail to service each child's needs. The directions prove too complex for them to grasp. The stutterer may refuse to talk. Often such problems can be solved through creative dramatics.

Creative dramatics is ideal for either mixed therapy grouping or primary stutterers. In such a group experience, every child is guided to express himself. The drama is improvised, and as he works and plays with others to create it, he experiences his own fulfillment. The speech therapist is able to treat each child's problems as unique entities.

Many therapists have a case load which includes both kindergarteners and preschoolers. With their large imaginations and love of impersonation, they are ideal subjects for creative activity. No scripts are used and there is no necessity for preparing written material. Children simply utilize their own vocabularies, with occasional new words and ideas suggested by the therapist. Sound drills are incorporated in the creative dramatic production as the need presents itself.

Therapists typically load themselves down like the traditional door-to-door salesman. Of any five persons entering a school, the one most heavily laden is likely to be the speech therapist. Props, especially large or dramatic ones, often help set the action rolling.

Yet creative dramatics requires no technical aids. No costumes, lights, scenery, stage, or makeup are necessary to motivate or heighten a mood. This is all created by the child's imagination. He can be a knight rescuing a damsel in distress while riding a folding chair.

Unnumbered therapy goals are realized with creative dramatics. First, the child can become someone else. Children possess an uncanny ability to lose themselves in make-believe and rarely stutter during such sessions. Words flow easily and the actor is swept away in being Jack the Giant Killer. Tensions give way to pure pleasure. Again, the therapist identifies some of the apprehensions which normally the child cannot or will not express to others.

What are the creative dramatics requirements for speech therapy? Initially, a group of children and enough space are all that are necessary. The major gripe of speech therapists is lack of space. Well, if your room is small, imagination doesn't always require a big area. Think of how little children nestled in the arms of an adult pretend, talking out loud to themselves. Charles Van Riper, a noted speech-therapy author, encourages the idea of self-talk, with the child pretending vocally wherever he may be.

The last requirement is the easiest to obtain and the most reliable— an idea from which to create. In a relaxed atmosphere, children seem to create ideas constantly. On occasion, they amaze adults for imagining in such minute detail. Nothing their eyes encounter remains the same. While seated on a stool, they are upon a bucking horse, piloting a jet fighter, or riding a motorcycle, all in the scant time of ten minutes—and accompanying each activity is a group of appropriate sounds and vocabulary.

Aside from being immeasurably revealing to the therapist, creative dramatics is of great value to the individual child. It develops confidence and creative expression. Social attitudes and relationships result from working in a group, and children grow in poise, in self image, and in emotional stability. Body coordination, which precedes the finer motor coordination necessary for speech, develops through creative dramatics.

Speech therapy cannot exist day in and day out on a meager diet of drills, games, and impromptu conversation, and thanks to creative dramatics there is no reason why it needs to. To yield the utmost gains, new ideas must constantly be used when dealing with ever changing children. They must be allowed to bring ideas into the therapy sessions and express them in a free fashion.

Creative dramatics provides for spontaneous expression, free from most tensions. At last, the child finds an adult willing to enter his world of pretend, understand his conflicts through play, and provide channels of expression to help him. The speech therapist is no longer a giant correcting his every word. Instead, he becomes a participant whose ideas can be accepted and hopefully utilized.

MRS. WILSON is a speech and language development specialist in Sacramento County Schools, California.

Where Do We Go From Here?

It was the week after New Year's. "Bruce, Billy and I are having dinner together Saturday night. You will be babysitting." He looked surprised but said nothing. Instead, he nursed a wart which lived on his right thumb.

I said nothing more; some things require no discussion. They just are.

The morning of my date began. I was anxious. All day, I prayed for something, anything, to intercede and wreck my plans. Maybe Billy should not have been contacted; I had tried not to. *Heck, I chickened out of calling him on New Year's, fearful of two rejections in one 24-hour period.* It took me two more days to work up the nerve to talk to him. Usually, when I postpone an action, I never go back to it. *But this, this business of Bruce's was too much. I had been too devastated on New Year's Eve. He deserved a comeuppance and I was ready to deliver. There. I felt so much better.*

Somehow, I got through the day. Then came time to dress for my date. I showered trying not to mix in tears with the pulsating water. In no time, I was dried and pulling on a slippery, blue fitted dress with a mandarin collar—man-catching bait. Since my hair was in an Afro, practically no time was spent on that. Next came makeup: turquoise eyeshadow, liner, mascara, rouge, eyebrow pencil, a light touch of liquid eyeliner on my highly placed beauty mark near the outer edge of my left eye, and red lipstick. In a matter of minutes, I slipped my long legs into black pantyhose and tucked my feet into black pumps. I was ready.

Paul and Suzanne were already in pajamas. I went to each room to say good night. In spite of myself, my hugs were tighter than usual. Although my goodnight kiss to Paul was normal, I couldn't let go of Suzanne. She let me hold on longer, as if she suspected I needed it. I sneaked in an extra kiss, too. Afterwards, it was hard holding back the tears. I managed by hurrying to the front door. Once inside our new Lincoln, which he drove all the time, I backed out and headed for my prearranged meeting spot. If these rendezvouses became regular, a more romantic place had to be found. A grocery store parking lot reeked of domesticity.

I pulled in. Sure enough, there he was waiting under the neon sign in a light-blue Oldsmobile Cutlass. I parked next to it; our sedan slid into the category of station wagon. Maybe neither Bruce nor I was cut out for cheating. We hadn't the slightest idea about the aura it required.

Billy opened his car door, came to my driver's side, and assisted me from my Lincoln. "Hello. I'm glad you called me." And he gave me a quick kiss.

"What a beautiful car, Billy. I love the lines of it."

"Would you like to drive it, Cookie?"

With that one last word, I knew I'd done the right thing by coming to meet him for dinner. "Oh, may I, Billy?"

"Whatever you want, I'll try to deliver." And he tucked me in behind the wheel of that sharp machine. I was thrilled. "So, where are we eating tonight?"

"I thought you might like a steak. I know I would."

"Your wish is my command."

Starting up his powerful engine brought everything into focus. The enormity of what was about to happen really jarred me. What was I doing? Quitting early would have been outlandish. Forcing myself to continue, I backed up, put it in drive, and chirped, "What do you say to running up to Lake Tahoe? I bet this beauty is great on winding roads."

"You better believe it."

I steered his gorgeous car onto the nearest freeway entrance. It was marvelous. "Are you hungry? Should we eat before heading up there?"

"Whatever you want, Dorothy."

Would I ever grow out of loving to hear him say my name? Would a day come when I didn't tremble inside? "There's something you should know. I don't really want dinner."

"You don't? But that's what you suggested, that's why I'm here, to eat with you."

"I lied."

"Not you, not my Cookie."

We both laughed, almost like back in high school. "I want you to make love to me again."

"I'd love to."

"There's a string of motels just a few miles up ahead; quicker than driving all the way to the lake. I pulled over to let him drive.

In a few miles but still in town, we pulled into a motel. I waited in the car while he registered. Then we drove to one of the nearby units. As we undressed by lamplight, I reflected on this stage of our lives. "You do remember we rarely made love in a bed."

"We had no choice; there were no motels for colored people."

"It's exciting just lying next to you." Neither of us mentioned our one and only lovemaking experience in a bed, that of his parents.

He still had that fresh scent I remembered. I wanted to crawl into his skin and never come out. I felt so at home with him. His kisses were still warm, sweet. Soon our snuggling became more urgent, more focused. He meant so much to me that I began to feel guilty. "Billy, I lied about everything tonight. I wanted you to want me because of what happened between me and Bruce. On New Year's Eve, he wanted to switch partners with another couple."

"Really?"

"I need to know that I am still a viable woman, desirable to a man."

"You are, believe me."

"Maybe I didn't lie at all. Maybe I seized this opportunity to be with you, to make love to you. Oh god, I've missed you so much in spite of myself."

Later, I returned home, to my children.

In a vain effort to save what was already spent, Bruce and I resorted to marriage counseling. A few months later, the counselor said, "Dorothy, let it go; the marriage is over." Bruce had quit immediately. My mother taught me to never leave a task undone. For another month, I worked on my marriage alone. We continued to live together and sleep in the same bed—separately.

I was disintegrating, existing on tranquilizers. I resigned my job. Bruce revealed years of relationships with other women. From somewhere,

I managed to continue writing a weekly column for a small black newspaper. The pay was minimal but I liked doing it. Bruce had found it for me a year earlier. He had also arranged a television audition for me which was promising. But later, the show was postponed.

On an early Saturday morning in March, the resolution to our marriage dilemma was revealed. Paul and Suzanne gave it away; they stopped playing. I couldn't ignore their abrupt silence. I rounded the corner from the kitchen into the entryway, and almost fell into the living room. There they were, safely nestled in between their Playskool toys. I started back to the kitchen but noticed they were staring intently towards the bedrooms.

Following their gaze, I found nothing out of place. Still, they stared, peeked around me. To what? That's when I saw it; our largest piece of Samsonite luggage standing outside the master bedroom doorway. Oh, he could be so cold, so final. He never mentioned it the night before. Everything was so like him. I recalled what he'd told me about his father's grave side service. "All my brothers took turns shoveling dirt onto his casket. I refused. I didn't want to ruin my new suit."

Now eight years and two children later, Bruce was leaving.

Needing to be closer to our children, I sank to the floor, grabbed the nearest small wooden block, struggled to build something—anything to distract them from what was about to happen.

No. I wanted to distract me.

My children focused on the hallway. They knew it wasn't a business trip.

I continued to stack blocks. From the bedroom area, came the sound of closet doors sliding and bouncing together. I quit building.

Suzanne edged closer to Paul who made room for her. I shielded their eyes, blocked out the suitcase. There were no doors. The three of us formed a tableau.

His shoes clicked on the hardwood floors. I didn't want him to catch me staring. I scurried back to the kitchen to hide. But where? I paused, listened. Nothing. An idea surfaced—close the pocket door between the kitchen and the entry. Yes! It was so simple, I almost laughed out loud. I extended my finger for the small metal pull, but stopped in mid-air. The kids might come looking for me.

Turning, I gripped the edge of the kitchen sink. I wished I could wash myself down the drain. I wanted to grind up everything that was about to happen into teeny, tiny bits in the disposal. I turned my back on the sink and came face to face with the range top. There was the exhaust. I wanted to be swooped up and drawn out of the house, dispersed like so many odors.

Bruce's heels came closer, louder. The clatter of toys interspersed with the sound of his shoe heels. I covered my ears.

Suzanne yelled, "I'll hide, Paul, Paul, okay, okay?"

Paul was silent.

I was too. Those nights alone hadn't prepared me for the hurt. My imagination had not done it justice. I was relieved, but at the same time, scared, scared of being on my own, scared my children would know I was scared.

I didn't hear Bruce for a while. He might be at the entry into the living room or near it.

"What are you doing, baby girl?"

He was near them.

"How's my big boy?"

Toys clattered on the hardwood floor.

I moved deeper into the safety and obscurity of the kitchen. Ready to pounce at the first cry from the children. They remained quiet. I was chilled to the bone. My orange kitchen ceiling provided no warmth.

Bruce said, "Put the blue block on top, Paul. I'll help you, Suzanne."

I scorned his helpfulness and turned to gaze out the window. There was my longed-for curved driveway.

Footsteps approached. I swung around. Bruce stood at the entry, heavier than when we had first met. His hair was as curt as his speech. Together they represented his "Northern attitude" with a hint of Jamaican spice thrown in.

I started to go to him out of habit but caught myself. Distance—I had to learn distance. I leaned my right hand heavily on the cold, brown and beige tiled counter. My eyes went there, too. I was so ashamed in the face of our failure. I stared down at the speckled green linoleum floor. Wished to plant myself there, cover up, and only emerge when the misery ended. I looked beyond the threshold, to the entryway floor, to the single piece of gray luggage. Like us—a broken set.

My blurred vision coincided with the arrival of two pairs of small hands. They came from behind me from the dining room. Earlier I forgot they could reach me from there. They caressed me. How did they know my pain? I should have been comforting them. "Aren't you going to say goodbye to the children?"

Tears rolled down my cheeks. I couldn't move. Paul and Suzanne wouldn't release me. Their little faces turned up to him; they said nothing.

"I'm going away," he said.

They did not offer him a kiss.

He looked up, "Maybe you'll get better . . . ."

He seemed not to mind our quietness, our inability to talk to him. He said to the children, "I'll be back and we'll do some fun things together."

They didn't buy it. They were so wise. From them I gained not only strength but self-respect. My tears stopped. I recognized him, too. "Goodbye."

I never realized the children had left me. I was alone with him.

Bruce added a "sorry" to his goodbye, then shrugged his shoulders, picked up his piece of Samsonite, and opened the door. He barely cleared the threshold before I closed and locked my orange front door.

"... life loved the person who dared to live it."
The Heart of a Woman, p. 3
By Maya Angelou

Learning My Way

It was early May when a call came from Anita, a college friend of Bruce's. She and her husband owned the local country and western radio station. I still had difficulty connecting them, Jewish people, with that kind of music. A year earlier, Bruce had a summer marketing internship at their station. The four of us had become friends. She said, "Dorothy, Sacramento State College is having Summer Stock Theater. You have to enroll."

How could I come up with the money? My only funds from Bruce came sporadically. It was a silly idea anyway after my dismal experience at Hampton. "Thanks, Anita, I will." Hanging up, I recalled having dinner with her and two out-of-town businessmen. Throughout that evening, she constantly referred to me as an actress. At least somebody thought so.

I hadn't worked since January. Depending on Bruce for money was not only embarrassing but insufficient. I'd resolved to only ask my parents for help if and when everything else was exhausted. Like a flash in the dark, I recalled Bruce saying he was getting food stamps. His sales weren't good so his commission was down to almost nothing. If he qualified for food stamps, surely I could with two children to feed. I hurried to the welfare office.

"You don't qualify."

"Why not?"

"You own a house."

"Can you help me in any way at all?"

"No."

"Can you ask Bruce's job to garnish his wages?"

"We don't want to jeopardize his employment by making him look bad."

"Can you lend me some money until I get a job?"

"We don't work that way."

Leaving the building, my Aunt Burrell's wisdom prevailed. "Dot, you have to do what you have to do."

I called my old supervisor, not to reinstate me because he couldn't. I had resigned instead of taking a leave of absence. He offered me a summer speech position which I accepted. Next, he informed me of two full-time speech therapy positions and one part-time in three different school districts. I profusely thanked him and arranged an interview for the part-time job. I was still on valium and couldn't handle full-time work. At the interview a week later, I was hired on the spot for the incoming school year.

Next, I swallowed a huge gulp of pride and borrowed $35 from a friend. I was out of options if I planned to enroll in Summer Stock Theater. And I needed that as much, if not more, than the valium. When I showed up at the Theater Arts Department, it was a homecoming among strangers. I smelled the grease paint, felt the energy; I auditioned.

In the midst of my misery, I was finding my way. My tranquilizer usage lessened. I was on stage, rehearsing, dancing. The show was no dreary drama. I belonged and my children were with me. They went to my summer job, too; I couldn't afford a sitter so it was natural to go to college together after lunch.

I wanted Summer Stock Theater to last forever. I even did modeling for a photographer on campus before rehearsals. Things were looking up. I was finding myself. I vowed to never set art aside again in my life. Some of my summer earnings would go for fall classes. My part-time job would allow plenty of time.

A problem arose—a new restriction on enrollment at the college. It appeared I might not be able to pursue theater arts there. At the same time, there was a rash of divorces involving people I knew. One couple from the business department had split. Bruce and I had gone out with them a few times, visited in each other's homes. The husband invited me out once he learned Bruce and I were separated. I accepted. A good thing, too. When I explained my enrollment dilemma, he said, "Don't worry about it. A newly created department is opening. My friend is chairing it."

"Oh, but Dwayne, I know nothing about business and absolutely hate numbers."

"This should be right up your alley. The department's called 'international affairs.'"

"It does sound interesting, different. Maybe I'll need to take some political science classes first."

"Leave everything to me. I'll invite him, his girlfriend, and you over for dinner."

"What can I bring?"

"Avocadoes for the salad."

I arrived early with two of the firmest specimens from the grocery display. Dwayne laughed, "Is this the first time you've bought avocadoes?"

"Yes. I was very careful not to get the ones with all the mushiness and the black skin."

"Have a seat, I'll fix you a Black Russian. You do drink vodka, if I recall."

When his other guests arrived, I greeted them warmly. I was enrolled in international affairs before dessert.

Journalism became my minor. I was venturing away from theater. Early on, the professor, impressed with my writing skills, suggested I teach a workshop for my fellow classmates. "Thanks, but I'm not sure I can teach it. I just write."

"Judging by your samples and the way you interact with the other students, you'll be ideal. We'll get together at my place once or twice a week to work out plans."

My concern must have registered on my face which has always been notorious for expressing exactly what I feel.

"If you prefer, we can meet at your home. I forgot you have two small children."

Aside from the opportunity he was affording me, I did not wish to get involved with him alone. His girlfriend and I had become new friends. Occasionally, Paul, Suzanne, and I spent the night at her place with her two older elementary school-aged children. I knew for a fact just how crazy she was about him. Plus, he had a wife back home in India.

Frankly, I didn't need any more drama in my life. I resolved to discontinue that major when the semester ended. After all, it had been a means to an end in the first place. At fall registration, I entered the theater arts graduate program. Audition announcements were posted right away, and

I landed a role in a drama. Next thing I knew the drama had been dropped in favor of an adaptation of a Shakespearian comedy, *Do Your Own Thing*, with music. I had a leading role. This wasn't like Hampton at all. An even greater shock came at the first reading—two solos, for me. After rehearsal, I spoke to the director privately. "I can't sing."

"Don't worry about it, our music director will work with you."

At each practice, I anticipated a music rehearsal in a private room but all I did was sing out loud to piano accompaniment. I tried to recall how real singers looked, their demeanor, even though I couldn't emulate their musical talent. Still in my naiveté, I clung to the belief of private lessons. Finally, the realization hit me the afternoon I arrived at the theater to find the technical crew finishing up the apron projections which thrust out into the audience.

I watched the crew clear away their stuff. On their heels came the orchestra. Things were moving along at a frenetic pace. Where were my private singing lessons? From somewhere in the darkness of the theater, my director projected, "Dorothy, let's see how you feel out on the thrust. Sing a couple of notes while you're at it." I wanted to evaporate.

Luckily, I didn't; I would have missed a truly special part—publicity. The local McClatchy newspaper, The Sacramento Bee, was sending out a photographer and the theater arts department wanted me to be the featured actress. I had the choice of either 1) writing an article on the "middle years" based on one of my solos (in reality, I was thirty-one) or 2) posing for a full-page picture of me. Naturally, I chose to write and to pose in my costumes. I was in heaven.

Opening night I strutted out on that projected ramp into the audience's lap—singing. Admittedly, staying on key was a bit of a problem but I looked beautiful trying in three spectacular outfits.

A week after the show closed, I had a routine appointment with my doctor, the one I saw almost daily while married. That particular day he said, "My wife and I enjoyed your performance last week."

I was shocked. Probably, my blood pressure reading reflected it. But I couldn't help myself. This man had seen me through some awfully scary times. After that visit, I regarded myself as a healthy person, one with a future. I no longer dropped in asking to be seen.

In the spring, I auditioned again. This time for the black students' production, *Whose Got His Own.* No singing but on opening night, I forgot my lines. I was petrified. It had never happened to me before. None of the actors on stage realized it or were too inexperienced to cue me. It seemed like hours before I could retrieve the lines, but I did.

That summer I appeared on the summer stock stage again with the newly formed black theater group, The Zebra Company. The production was LeRoi Jones' *The Dutchman.* I played Lulu and wore a blond wig. For the first time in a very long time, I was performing with blacks. There was no doubt about it, this was my new June German.

After rehearsals, I was included in the parties. At least as much as I could afford to; I had a babysitter to pay. On closing night, we all went to a fellow actor's apartment. This time there was no dancing. No one sat on the sofa or in a chair; we all settled in a circle on the floor. Conversation was modulated, soft, almost a whisper. There seemed to be an expectation, an anticipation of someone or something. I assumed the mood with little to no effort. It was relaxed, pleasant. Max, on my left, presented me with what appeared to be a cigarette butt. I thought to myself, "Oh, my goodness. I'll get my Winston's from my purse and share."

I almost rose to retrieve my own pack of cigarettes from a nearby chair. But the "roots" were working hard, trying to get me to not embarrass myself. I responded to my neighbor's gentle nudge and accepted my very first marijuana blunt. I took a drag or whatever they called it. Hmmm. It was pleasant enough. It lacked that harshness I associated with a cigarette. This thing almost made me swoon. I took another drag and held on to it. I let it consume me as I talked and laughed. Then suddenly I sensed my turn had ended when I finally noticed the polite but hungry eyes focused on me. No words were said; no gestures made. It was probably the most courteous experience I'd ever had in my life. I passed it on to my neighbor on my right.

During my return to college experience, I was riding high. Things I didn't even touch, turned to gold. A local small theatrical company invited me to audition for *Cabaret.* I couldn't pursue it; my part-time job had turned into full-time. I barely had enough time for my classes in playwriting and puppetry. But I kept them.

Sometimes I wondered who listened to my cries. Who presented the answers that took me to the next step? Who, if not a root worker?

I made another discovery. Instead of being a pariah, my divorced status was fashionable, an asset even. One day while shopping downtown and waiting for the light to change, an average looking black male in a suit crossed, headed in the opposite direction. I stared straight at him, made eye contact. Without missing a beat, he made a U-turn and invited me to dinner.

Another time, I was studying a window display in a downtown shop before entering when a young man walked past, backed up and said, "You're kinda cute."

Taken aback yet delighted, I said, "Why thank you." And laughed. He had just supplied a missing ingredient in California, that uncanny ability of a New York man to make my day. And judging by his speech, he wasn't even a New Yorker.

I needed tires. A friend of mine, Carlos, sent me to an automobile tire shop with his card. A good-looking Italian man, dark hair and all in a white sweater, sat across from me as I waited for my tires to be installed. After conversing for some time and sharing our similar tastes in jazz, we exchanged telephone numbers. He called a few days later offering a dinner trip to San Francisco which I declined. Too much could go wrong.

This newfound freedom was so intoxicating, I had to remind myself I was a single parent. The children had seen their father only once since early January when he kept them while I had gone to Lake Tahoe. After that visit, Suzanne chattered about him; Paul said little to nothing. Then Suzanne went silent about her father as well.

A week later, my son embarrassed me to death. Carlos and the three of us were in his light-blue, cream-topped, long Ford convertible when Paul called out, "Dad." I was denied the luxury of dying in my seat.

A short time later, I overheard my son rehearsing Suzanne who out and out told him, "I just can't get it, Paul. I can't say 'daddy' to him."

That brought me to a new realization. I was the grown up. Too late for playing. There were a number of things I'd never known about before, like a father/daughter club at the YMCA, flag football. Bruce was neither interested nor willing.

It was a Saturday evening, Easter break, when Geri called. "Dorothy, get dressed. Let's go out and have some fun."

She surprised me. We weren't really friends; she was white and from Arkansas. Her black boyfriend and Bruce knew each other. I never would have sought her out; white women and black men were getting together. I never argued with human nature, but as a black woman, it was the principle of the matter. Even on the evenings when we formed a foursome, I kept a respectful distance from her. Not Bruce, he recommended her for a job where he worked.

Was she calling me out of gratitude to him or pity for me? "Gee, I'd love to but I don't have a sitter."

"We'll share mine. How soon can you be ready?"

"Well . . ."

"Get dressed. Bundle up the kids and come over. I'll have an appetizer and a glass of Cabernet waiting. Then we'll hit the clubs."

I arrived with the kids. After the food and wine, my spirits were up. I hadn't had a big night out since Bruce left months earlier.

Geri backed out of her driveway. "Brown's Paradise, here we come." In less than fifteen minutes, she pulled into a dimly lit, industrial parking lot. Loose gravel pelted the steel bottom of her pale-green Volkswagen. She sang out, "We're here."

Not one human being was in sight. I envisioned my children as wards of the state. I turned to my mentor. She was cocking her head from side to side and primping in her small compact mirror.

Wanting to check behind us, I twisted her rearview mirror towards me and patted my Afro. The faint interior car light accented the wariness creeping over me. Meanwhile Geri pouted and puckered her red lips and tamed a stray strand of red hair. When she batted her extra pair of eye lashes, I almost declared, "Enough. You're irresistible."

She beat me to it, "Let's go."

We crunched along, in heels, towards a small unattached glittering building, Brown's Paradise. I was upbeat until I noticed the scarcity of parked cars. At first, it concerned me but I figured the other party people traveled in pairs, too. Besides, Geri had said, "If things are slow, we'll leave."

Closer to the building, I could distinguish the swaying green and brown palm trees wiggling around the roof's perimeter. Not wanting to be a drag, I forced myself to perk up—snapped my fingers above my shoulders, twisted my hips from side to side, and sang "You know the neon lights are bright on Broadway."

Geri joined in.

On firm asphalt, we laughed and pranced like majorettes. Suddenly, my spirit was squelched. Bruce's words played in my head, "You're a poor talker and a lousy dancer."

I wanted to turn around, drive back to Geri's place, pick up my kids, I couldn't. My white 1964 Volvo was parked in her driveway. That was followed by a pang—Bruce had driven off that last day in our brand-new Lincoln. Not that I wanted it; it came with car payments.

Just at that moment, Geri cracked open the wooden door. A plume of acrid cigarette smoke peppered with cigar fumes rushed out. We forged ahead.

Being an actress, I had practiced the art of the powerful entrance; but Geri raised the standard. The Christmas tree lights surrounding the bar on our right bounced off her skintight, purple mini dress. My outfit—a candy-apple red, long-sleeve, crepe shirt, under a long white-and-blue-checkered wool vest, over a sleek pair of navy blue slacks, and shiny, red boots—absorbed whatever leftover light there was.

Except for the boots, my outfit was Bruce's last Christmas gift to me. One of his favorite things to do was dress me. And darn it, he knew what looked good on me. Nothing was ever too expensive, within reason, of course. However, one day in the latter stage of our marriage, I purchased an outfit from a Joseph Magnin department store on my own. It was a black and white, herringbone two-piece skirt and vest combination. I paired it with a black, long-sleeve, heavy silk, tailored shirt with covered buttons. It was topped off with an exquisite black and white pearl pin at the neck. I rushed home to model for Bruce.

I found him in our bedroom. "I have a surprise for you."

I changed and presented myself.

"I don't like it. At all."

"What don't you like about it?"

"Everything."

"Come on, Bruce, what is it exactly?"

"I'm never going to like anything you buy without me."

I shook my head to clear that memory, recalled where I was and managed a weak smile in Geri's direction. I was glad to be out with her. She charged forth as if her throne was in the adjoining room. All I saw was an empty dance floor. As we skirted its perimeter, a glitter ball darted lights on us. Choosing a small round table near the dance floor, she said, "This one affords the best exposure."

We crossed our legs and awaited our prey. Wilson Pickett sang "Funky Broadway." The cocktail waitress appeared. "What's your pleasure?"

I was so startled by her blond-streaked black hair, dark Egyptian eye makeup, and erupting breasts, words wouldn't come.

Geri said "I'll have a rum and coke."

"Ditto."

The too-prompt waitress threatened my limited funds. We had barely been in our seats a minute before she showed up; money was a precious thing for me. I watched her clip clop across the empty dance floor. "We need sugar daddies in a hurry."

"Don't worry about the minimum drink requirement. Later, we'll drop the rum."

The waitress was back, balancing two tall, dark, chilling glasses on a small round tray like a juggler. She set them, with expertise, on palm tree motif, paper coasters and placed matching napkins nearby.

Glass in hand, I turned to Geri, "To our first—"

She didn't respond; she was placing money on the waitress' extended tray. I scrambled for mine and the tip, my contribution to the evening.

The waitress thanked us and swished away to Stevie Wonder's "Yester-Me, Yester-You, Yesterday."

After my mistake, I took a big gulp of my drink. Returning it to the coaster, I noticed Geri sipping hers through a red straw identical to the one I'd shoved aside. Marvin Gaye's "Ain't That Peculiar" filled the room. We chatted about nothing but in an animated fashion, followed by a merry little laugh. Our glasses continued to empty, no men in sight. Geri crossed and recrossed her legs three times, then said abruptly, "This place is dead."

Since I didn't know any clubs, I pretended to have a good time and watched for guys. Our waitress was making her rounds again. "Geri, she's—"

Just then, two lone men interrupted her advance. The heavier, muscular one wore a dark suit, light shirt, and a tie. He was bright skinned with a broad grin, outgoing. His partner, casually dressed, same height, slimmer and darker, was more conservative. They sat directly across the dance floor from us.

Geri's antennae shot up; my confidence plummeted.

More customers arrived. Good . . . no bad. The first two guys would never notice me. I hadn't dated in eight years, was older and my wardrobe needed updating. I had no small talk. Probably the first words out of my mouth would be, "Hi, my husband just left me."

The waitress appeared again at our table, "Do you two ladies want repeats?"

Geri laughed, "Very definitely."

I nodded to her. She left. I whispered, "Geri, when do we eliminate the rum?"

"Never." She jumped up and adjusted her dress. Her smile was huge. Since I wore slacks, I remained seated. "Expressway to Your Heart" was the new record. I closed my eyes to capture the essence of it; such a great beat. When I opened them, the two guys across the dance floor from us were out of their seats and heading straight for our table.

I panicked. Turned to my mentor; she was totally enraptured with the music, performing back up for the singer. Still, I tried to ask her what to do. What to say. They would reach us in no time.

Geri writhed; they picked up speed. It was too late for advice—they stood in front of us. The muscular one extended his hand to me. I stared up at his Cassius Clay face and rose to join him. As my red boots took to the dance floor to boogaloo, Geri's laughter welcomed his friend.

When the music ended, I hadn't missed a beat. I glanced up at him. He was taller than my ex-husband. Good. I'd had my fill of short men. On the way back to my table, he told me his name, William. I hardly heard him. I was concentrating so hard on what my new name would be. "Dottie,"

"Dot," or "Dorothy." Since "Dorothy" was the last and I was more mature, I chose it. He thanked me for the dance and returned to his table. I sat down on my hard chair as if it were down filled.

That's when I noticed Geri and her date still on the floor for the next song. Oh, no, I failed "second dance." My condemnation was curtailed by the arrival of our second drinks. I was certain the waitress noticed my stamped forehead: "The woman who wasn't asked to dance twice."

I wanted to check on my athlete. I bet he had a better dancer. Eyes were on me. I searched in my purse for my pack of Winston cigarettes, glanced up occasionally, but still couldn't see him. Thanks to my lighter and the smoke, I boldly stared across the room. There he sat alone at their table. I took a puff, placed the lighter on the table, and sipped through my straw in the sexiest way I could. William, Sweet William, the same name as Mama's flowers.

After Geri's second dance with Ed, the guys asked to join us at our table. We danced all night, pausing only when thirsty. At closing. Sweet William said, "What about some breakfast?"

Geri didn't hesitate, "Great idea."

He turned to me. "Dorothy, will you ride with me? Geri and Ed can follow us to Mom's breakfast place on Fruitridge for some down-home cooking. Plus, she gives you a lot."

We walked together to his car, a powder-blue Ford Torino two door. I liked the sporty look of it. Actually, it suited him. He opened the door for me and I directed him to Geri's VW around the front of the building. To think I had almost stayed at home and missed this hunk of a man.

After breakfast, the others left and we talked until 4 a.m. When he dropped me at Geri's, I drove away knowing two things: I'd pick up the kids around noon and I'd see Sweet William Saturday night for a movie. I was crazy about the idea of a football player looking man.

Within two weeks, aside from daily phone calls, I stopped by his place on the way home from work and he dropped by mine when he got off at midnight. I always greeted him in a silky entertaining outfit.

One day, Geri said. "Dorothy, I think you have something in him. He's masterful, gentlemanly, caring, with a heart of gold. Besides, he'll be a good, firm father for Paul. When does your divorce become final?"

"I still need to talk to a lawyer; I don't have any money."

"Say no more. My sister works for Attorney Debnam, the best lawyer in town. I'll get you seen."

Sure enough, Veronica called me with an appointment. I arrived on time and presented my case. With no hesitation, he said, "I'll represent you. And don't worry about the retainer fee."

I thanked him.

He led me to his office door but before opening it, he placed his left hand on one of the upper panels, and said, "Would you like to kiss me before you go?"

I was stunned. By accepting his offer, I had incurred a greater debt. Not only was he physically stronger than me, he was a highly placed political figure. In trying to extricate myself from Bruce, I had created an obligation. My concern must have been evident, he said, "We'll wait a bit 'til you get to know me better."

Temporarily relieved, I exited to his outer office. His words followed me, "It'll be a pleasure to take your case, Dorothy."

Turning back to him, I murmured, "Thanks." I waved to Veronica and hurried to my Volvo.

Weeks later he and I appeared in court for the interlocutory decree which granted each party the right to resume the relationship before the final divorce. That day, my neighbor from across the street, testified on my behalf. Bruce did not show up for the proceedings.

Afterwards when my attorney and I were alone, he said, "By the way, Dorothy, I'm having my annual cattle round up at my ranch next weekend. Why don't you come out with Geri? It's casual fun and lots of interesting people always show up."

"Thank you for the invitation, I'll check with her." This divorce was becoming expensive.

Geri and I showed up. I was actually enjoying the day until our host walked over to us. Geri politely left. Up close, he said, "Everybody's watching the two of us. I think they suspect what's going on between us."

I wondered, was I back in high school? Is this the man who's helping me? He had already done what I needed; the court would send me a letter when the divorce became final. Good. I'd stay clear of him from now on.

I was free to concentrate on Sweet William. Almost on the eve of my decree, he announced, "I'm moving to the Bay Area to begin air traffic control training."

The stars were lining up against me. I doubted our newly formed relationship could sustain such an early separation. I tearfully said goodbye and wished him success the day he departed. Before driving off, he backed up, "Almost forgot. Can you mail these to me?" He handed me his laundry stub and money.

I kissed the stub.

When he received his laundry, he called to thank me and said, "Can you come and visit me this weekend?"

He sounded so sexy. I said yes.

That first visit began a new routine for us. Weekends when he didn't have to work were either spent in Fremont or in Sacramento. If it was the latter, Paul and Suzanne were always a part of picnics, site seeing, drive-in movies. Frequently, Bill, as I called him, invited their neighborhood playmates, Mark and Todd, to join us. When just the four of us were in his Torino, we looked like a real family. One weekend, he drove for hours to Willits so the kids and I could ride the Skunk Train. The trip included a fancy dinner and a sleep over in a motel.

At breakfast, Bill said, "Well, how are you doing, Brother Paul?"

Everywhere black men regularly referred to each other as "brother." From Suzanne's and my seats directly across from them, we saw a slight frown form on my son's seven-year-old brow. Paul did not hesitate to respond. Making no eye contact with Bill but instead looking straight across at me, he said "I don't like it when you call me 'Brother Paul.'"

Bill instantly replied, "I'm sorry, Paul. I won't say that ever again."

On one of my solo visits to Bill's place, he parked in front of the Fremont Chamber of Commerce. We were welcomed by a quaint, little white lady who worked there. She said, "Only two black families live here."

Bill took my hand, thanked the lady and we left. In the car, he said, "We don't want Paul and Suzanne in a situation like that."

I didn't even know or suspect we were considering "situations."

He drove two cities away to San Jose where we explored open houses. It was apparent there were more than two black families in residence. We saw them in shopping centers, in neighborhoods. Paul and Suzanne were invited for the next visit.

Bill had told us to bring swimsuits and dress up clothes. His surprise was a full day at Santa Cruz beach which was loads of fun. Afterwards, we rushed back to his apartment in Fremont to change for an evening cocktail party aboard the brand-new 747 jet in San Francisco. It was a whale of a plane which thrilled the kids. They explored it thoroughly. I was really into Bill. Like Geri said, he had possibilities.

We had been dating a little over a year when he asked, "What would you say if I asked you to marry me?"

"I'd probably say yes. I really don't want to marry again. I'm not good at it. Could we just live together?"

"No. I want you for my wife."

"But I'm so much older than you, seven whole years."

"I'm twenty-four but it seems older than that. If the age difference doesn't bother you, it doesn't bother me."

"Bill, I can't give you children. I've had a tubal ligation because I have high blood pressure. As a safety measure, my doctors projected a pregnancy could drive my pressure out of control and kill me."

"I'm very happy with Paul and Suzanne."

Six months later, Sweet William and I put the finishing touches on our small, intimate wedding plans. I had no misgivings and lots of good expectations. He had never mentioned anything other than love and caring for me, Paul, and Suzanne. Actually, it was fun preparing for it. I made my wedding outfit: a pea-green, sleeveless jumpsuit and a multi-colored, full-length, sleeveless vest. Suzanne's dress was also full length in a turquoise with a bodice in the same material as my vest.

Bill and Paul shopped in Fremont for their coordinated ties, a suit for Bill, and a sport jacket and pants for Paul. They also got their haircuts together. Later in the evening, they would polish their shoes and lay out their outfits.

Early that morning, Suzanne and I went to the beauty salon. Then drove out to Rancho Cordova to pick up my three-tiered wedding cake. As I drove back in the blistering afternoon heat, Suzanne rode with it on her five-year-old lap for 30 minutes; the car air conditioner was out. After leaving the cake at Sam's Ranch Wagon, we picked up the flowers at our nearby florist.

That evening, things were abuzz in my house. Babysitter Kelly, a high school junior, and some of her friends were selecting music to be played at the wedding. It was all very festive and exciting.

To celebrate and consecrate the coming union, Bill elected not to make love that night but held me close instead.

Aside from Paul and Suzanne, Bill had his best man and I, my matron of honor. From the moment my little daughter left me to join her brother, my betrothed, the best man, and the matron of honor in front of the massive stone fireplace, and with friends and business associates in attendance, tears began flowing from my eyes. Neither of our families could attend due to the distance, nevertheless, it was a most happy occasion on a beautiful day. After another party at our residence, Bill and I honeymooned in Lake Tahoe. Upon arrival, we consummated our marriage again and again.

We returned three days later to our respective jobs. Within three weeks, my honey left for two months of air traffic control training in Oklahoma. His belongings were already back in Sacramento. I overheard Paul informing their playmates, "You can't call him 'Bill' anymore; you have to say 'Mr. Brown,'"

Although, I didn't inquire, I knew why. Paul was the type of kid who liked things done the proper way. Plus, he referred to their fathers by their last names. Even his sister noticed his exacting attitude when he introduced his playmates to me. When Bruce first moved out, I had the kids with me while I shopped in an upscale department store. Paul strayed from me. I found him watching a fashion show from the rear of the store's third floor auditorium. "Why are you up here?"

He simply replied, "I thought I might find something you might like."

When Bill completed his training in Oklahoma, I met him in Las Vegas for a brief second honeymoon and the return drive to Sacramento.

Six weeks later, we were discussing a change of residence. Although he demurred, the four-hour drive and the eight-hour work shift was getting the better of him. In one last feeble dissent, he said, "I can't ask you to leave your friends, your job. What about the kids' school and their playmates?"

I sent out job applications. As happy as I was, I wondered, *would this marriage be another flash in the pan? Would he tire of me, too?*

Bill and me after our July 24th wedding, standing behind his car – I'm in my hand created wedding dress.

*"I wanted Summer Stock Theater to last forever.
I even did some modeling for a photographer
on campus before rehearsals."*

*Dottie Wilson
models three outfits
from the play
Your Own Thing
to show that a woman
in her "middle-years"
can still be sexy.
She will play the
part of Olivia
in the Sacramento
State College
production which
begins this Friday.
Bee Photos by
Ward Sharrer*

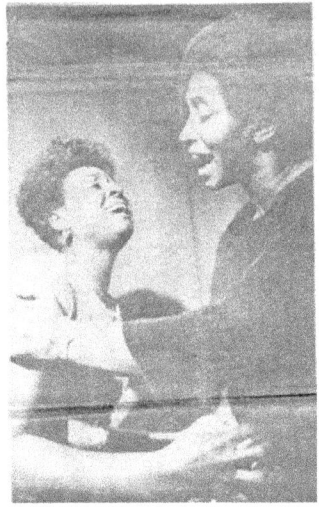

*"In the spring semester, I was cast in the black production, **Whose Got His Own**."*

*Newly formed black theater group The Zebra Company's production of **The Dutchman** by LeRoi Jones.*

Lucky Number

In January of 1971, a telegram arrived. My daddy was in a coma. Early the next day the kids and I boarded a plane home. Ruth, our old schoolteacher/roomer in the ugly rental, met us at the Raleigh-Durham airport. Many years after my summer of integration concern, her daughter had been a test kid for it. That night, Paul and Suzanne rode up front with Ruth and talked. I sat alone in the back seat.

When we arrived home, I embraced my emaciated mother. Worry and stress had replaced her spirit and laughter. She was a prime example of a caretaker carrying a heavy burden. Even I left her to go to my dad.

I pulled into his hospital parking lot at midnight. I sat there momentarily gaining strength. Looking up, the eerie familiarity of the towering building struck me. I almost dismissed it, almost opened the car door. But it came to me—this was my reoccurring nightmare. Only it was not a foreboding house across a street; it was a modern, huge block of architecture. Although I'd never seen the creature that dwelt within, I knew it.

The nightmare originated during an especially bad period in my first marriage. My psychiatrist attributed it to Bruce. He was wrong; it was my dad. As in my nightmare, I had no alternative, I had to enter. I trudged towards the hospital.

In Sam's room, Little Alice sat there guarding him. I clung to her. Finally unwrapped myself from her and moved closer to Sam. He appeared unchanged. I whispered his name.

No answer came. Tears ran down my face. After a while, I turned to Alice, "Can you be here for him tonight? I want to be with Tee."

Early the next morning, Martha Ann, the daughter of the white lady my mother used to work for, stopped by our house to drive Tee to the hospital. I was surprised to see her. Her mother, Mrs. Wilson, had been dead for at least five years. Now Tee was no one's maid; she directed the black YWCA. I watched them drive off to the hospital, then told the kids to dress and gave them breakfast. While they ate, I prepared to join Tee.

But Alice's three school aged children appeared. The oldest said, "We've come to take Paul and Suzanne to school."

"They're not enrolled. And we probably won't be here long enough for that."

Her younger brother said, "It's okay with the teachers."

With no other alternative, I let them go, and hurried to my parents.

I arrived in the midst of a flurry of activity. Ambulance attendants already had Sam strapped to a gurney. Passage into the room was blocked. Someone said, "They have a kidney machine available for him at Duke University Hospital. Hopefully, it'll stabilize him so they can diagnosis him."

The attendants pushed us aside with Sam and his gurney. They were down the hallway in no time. Tee was swept away in his wake. One glance at her and I spoke to the nearest nurse, "Please give my mother something for the journey to Duke."

"Certainly."

I should have said, "…the journey to Mecca."

Pilgrimages there were often the last stop before a cure or the end. I couldn't dwell on the outcome; at least it was different from comatose. With both parents secured in the ambulance, I felt lost until I remembered the money Bill had given me the night before we left. Just before the ambulance doors closed, I put it into Tee's hand. She smiled weakly. I forced myself to smile back.

On cue, the ambulance's siren shrilled in the winter air. I covered my ears. As it sped from the grounds charging for the nearby freeway entrance, I dropped my sunny face and indulged my petrified state of mind. The thought of my children halted my descent into self-pity. Driving off in Sam's brown Dodge, I thanked my new husband for the funds. In my mind, I made trip preparations for Duke later that day or early the next morning.

By late afternoon, Tee was back. Unbeknownst to me, Martha Ann beat the ambulance to Durham and waited for her. Now the two of them brought me the news—Sam was out of his coma, thanks to the kidney machine. Maybe now they could identify his problem and begin treatment. In spite of my joy and relief, I regretted not being at his side when he came out of the coma.

The next morning, Paul appeared to be coming down with something similar to pneumonia, which had necessitated his hospitalization a few years earlier. It didn't look good. Suzanne could stay with Aunt Burrell and her cousins. Paul would have to come with Tee and me. Once arrangements were made, we left for Durham. The freeway made the trip a swift one. In Durham, we found a reasonably priced motel near the hospital, next to a small café serving fried pork chops, eggs, grits (done the right way), with buttered toast and other local goodies. When we visited Sam, Tee went first. Paul and I waited in the lobby.

As soon as I saw her start back down the stairs, I stood up. She came and sat next to Paul. I hurried to my daddy. The trek included a very long corridor. At the end, there he was, sitting up in bed, his old self again. Even before his Clark Gable wink, I was at his side. For about thirty minutes, I sat by my daddy's bed and held his hand. Mentally, I added my name to the list of Duke believers. Sam pointed to the empty bed across from him and said, "He went home."

"Lucky for him."

"His permanent home," and he laughed.

I laughed, too. And so began our visit. We talked about everything. He led the conversation, "The number 13 is my lucky number."

"Really?"

"Oh, yes, Christine and me got married on the thirteenth of May."

I listed all the anniversary presents: the vacuum cleaner, the glistening chrome coffee maker, the Homer Laughlin china set, the wringer washing machine.

"You were born on the thirteenth. And we bought our house on the thirteenth."

We were going strong, laughing a lot, when his white, female doctor arrived. "Good morning, I'm his daughter, Dorothy. I'll get my mother from the lobby."

When we returned, the doctor excused herself from my dad and led Tee and me back down the hallway. We stopped in front of a wall mounted x-ray viewer. She inserted Sam's x-ray. It clicked into the channel at the bottom and lit up. To our two pairs of untrained eyes, the x-ray appeared normal. We stared like students determined to absorb as much of the new instruction as we possibly could—until she spoke. "It doesn't look good for Mr. Burston."

After a giant pause, she looked directly at us. We stared back in wide-eyed innocence.

"Do you see these large holes in his ribs and spinal column?" She touched them in a staccato fashion.

I wanted to squeeze my eyes shut. Pretend to be a mute. Instead, I nodded yes. Denying the quarter sized holes in his ribs would not have accomplished a thing. Tee nodded, too.

"Mr. Burston has multiple myeloma. Cancer."

Tee nor I said a word.

I was struck by the doctor's politeness, referring to my daddy as "Mister." I wanted to thank her. But I couldn't form the words.

"He has five months to live."

I opened my mouth, nothing came out. The x-ray was robbing me of my ability to speak.

Tee remained silent, too.

"Do you have any questions?"

We both shook our heads.

After a bit, the doctor took my mother's hand in hers and touched my shoulder with her other hand. Then taking our hope with her, she walked back up the hallway.

Tee returned to Sam. I to Paul. When she came down, we went to lunch but had little appetite for food. My son played with a bowl of chicken noodle soup which reminded me of a slogan he wrote and I submitted to the Campbell Soup Company: "How many Campbells does it take to Campbell up?" The company sent him two Kool-Aid mugs for his unsolicited effort.

At least somebody stood a chance of being cured. Paul's symptoms were subsiding. He could turn the corner any day. After dropping Tee back at the hospital, I took him to see a Disney movie; maybe I took me. It stirred memories of the Keystone Movie Projector Sam gave me one Christmas. I returned to the lobby to wait for it to end.

On the twelfth day of my visit, I received two job interview requests. Both were in neighboring towns, only minutes away from Bill's job.

Meanwhile, Duke was about to put my daddy on outpatient status. I could return to California. Come back in the spring, in the June German season.

The kids and I went home. I attended the interviews. At the first one, the main question was, "Do you know how to teach white children?"

That was the very same city with only two black families. They mailed me a letter of regret.

I accepted the second job, located in Milpitas. In February, Bill rented a house in San Jose. He was swayed by its orange kitchen (my Sacramento kitchen had an orange ceiling and an orange front door). There was a creek nearby, at the corner. When I saw it, I wanted to be a kid again.

The cost of housing in San Jose far exceeded Sacramento. My empty house back there was costing us money. That first weekend we went house hunting up the hill. Bill promised to put us in a bigger and better house than the one we had left.

His kindness made me cry. Until that moment I had not shared a very embarrassing tail end to my first marriage—bankruptcy. I said, "I didn't want you to know about it. It was such an awful time."

Bill held me in his arms while I released all those pent-up feelings. "At first, I felt so helpless. I'd failed not only my children but my parents, too. Thank god, they were three thousand miles away."

He said, "Judging by the conversations I've had with your dad and your mother, you could never embarrass them. They love you unconditionally."

"The moving van drove up one sunny afternoon while the kids played across the street. They backed part of the way into my driveway, blocking me from leaving. A heavy-set guy in a white t-shirt knocked on the door and said, 'We're here to repossess the items on this list.'"

Bill interrupted me. "You don't have to tell me anymore, Dorothy."

"No. I need to tell someone what it felt like. I've never spoken of that day." I walked away from Bill to the window. "At first, Paul and Suzanne continued their game with their friends. But they stopped when the men carried out our pine trestle dining table. By the time the bench and the two captain chairs reached the truck, they were calling me, 'Mommy. Mommy!'"

"I was in the kitchen near the front door. Placing a hand on each of their shoulders, I steered them into the room with me. 'Don't worry about the things they are taking.' At that very moment, our Hammond organ passed by the kitchen door. I had no words to explain the money had run out. I had no job. Their daddy had left us. There wasn't time for that anyway."

Bill said, "I get the idea. You don't have to go on."

Ignoring him, I continued. "I said to the kids, 'Let's go stand over there in the dining room while the men do what they have to do.' Thanks to me, they had an unobstructed view of the cord being pulled from the wall and the color television being wheeled from the living room. I said, 'Don't worry, we'll have a brand-new set one day. Until then, we'll see how things look in black and white on the old set from our old house.'"

Bill said, "Oh, Dorothy . . ."

I continued. "Meanwhile, the men were now emptying and unplugging my Whirlpool washer and dryer from the garage outlet. I said to the kids, 'Good. It's faster taking our dirty clothes to the laundromat. I prefer that anyway.' Both of them stared at me."

"You did what you had to do for the kids' sake." Bill said.

"I never suspected Bruce would come while we were away and take the black and white television set."

Bill said, "You'll never be in a situation like that again."

"You are so sweet." We kissed. As we snuggled, I said, "Back then I had to keep food in the house and gas in the car. So, one morning I drove downtown to a shop I'd found in the yellow pages. Wearing my best smile, I said, 'Good morning, I'd like to pawn my engagement ring and wedding band.' The owner examined them with his jeweler's loupe and said, 'Best I can do is $35.' Since it was more than I had when I entered, I took it and left."

Bill said, "I'm glad you chose me to share it with. Our life is going to be filled with love and the security you and the kids deserve. You can count on that."

In early May, Tee called, "Sam died."

I'd so hoped for June. It was not to be.

At the funeral, in the midst of my grief, I crumbled to the floor. It was May 13—their wedding anniversary.

*Tee in Reno, Nevada on vacation
with me, Bill and the kids
(two months after Sam's death)*

Little Alice's children

Tee on December 23, 1973

Second Time Around

Moving to San Jose was good right off the bat—better weather, closer proximity to San Francisco, and a split-level house on a hill. Across the road, wildlife, cattle, and horses roamed on rolling acreage. There were empty spaces for Paul and Suzanne to build club houses with their new friends. Their elementary school was a tri-level modern environment. Best of all, Bill and I had shorter commutes.

Our new neighborhood, formerly an orchard, grew everything well. Tee arrived for a visit in July bringing iris bulbs from home in her luggage. But that was not enough; she shopped locally for snapdragons, sweet peas, and trees: a magnolia, a dogwood, and a crab apple (all common to my hometown). She did exactly what I'd wanted Mama to do to our ugly rental back when.

In this new job, one of my three schools had a significant number of black teachers reminiscent of Baltimore. My recent job in California had employed less than ten blacks in the whole district. On my first day at that job, a second-grade teacher introduced me to her class as Miss Black. As she tried to undo her snafu, I smiled at her.

However, the speech therapy meeting was a different ball of wax. A fellow pathologist extoled her rights as she saw them by declaring "as long as I'm free, white and 21." I thought our white male supervisor would have a stroke trying to clean that one up. "Dorothy, you'll have to forgive us; we're apt to say anything."

I said, "I won't forgive you and I don't expect that kind of behavior."

In my Milpitas job, three days a week I worked on the same staff as Tommy Smith, the black Olympic gold medalist. His raised black glove fist and bowed head during the playing of our national anthem at the awards ceremony in Mexico City had caused a major disturbance at home. Frankly, he reminded me of Paul Robeson—casting aspersions on America like that. I was in awe of him. One day he said to me, "Are you from the islands?"

Aha. That's the "raised in another place" my mother's friends meant when I was little. Even as an adult, I was still thought to be from somewhere else. Natives from Africa even asked, "Where are you from?"

Before I could respond, they said, "Ghana."

On the one hand, the idea was exotic but on the other, I felt alien. Especially when one white teacher declared, "Your face is so big."

Another teacher, a charming southern black lady, approached me in a voice reeking of magnolias. "Dorothy, I'm about to ask you a favor."

I armed myself for the upcoming attack on my non-religious status.

"You wouldn't happen to be one of my sorority sisters, would you?" And she told me the name.

Relieved, I said, "Yes. But I haven't been active for years."

"I want you to join us; we need everybody to start a new chapter here in San Jose."

I couldn't fix my mouth to say no; I joined.

That action resurrected my theatrical skills. The sorority's founders' day program was approaching. My recent dramatic success at Sacramento State College inspired me to volunteer a program entry—choral speaking of black poetry by young children. With only two members, Suzanne and Paul, I set about recruiting four others, their three black classmates and our neighbor's daughter. Our name for the program entry was "The Young Blacks." A traveling, educational company of young actors was founded.

I was the playwright, director, producer and manager; the young players created dialog which connected the poetry. Rehearsals were conducted over my stove top which divided the kitchen from the dining area. On rehearsal afternoons, the actors shifted the dining table and chairs to a far corner. The large suspended light globe proved to be an interference, so the actors ducked or leaned to protect themselves. Our performances grew from fifteen minute tight, rhythmic, and well-paced presentations to thirty-five-minute productions in local and out-of-town schools and civic organizations.

In our second season, The California State Children's Theater president invited us to perform for their conference in San Jose. As a result of that performance, The Young Blacks appeared at the Capital building in Sacramento. We spent the night in a Holiday Inn. The next day after our performance, we met Mr. Nate Holden, a black legislator from Southern California. My young players were engaging, verbally polished, and self-assured.

The modest funds garnered from our performances covered operating costs, theater tickets to San Francisco play productions, and workshops in modeling and dance. They actually were natural singers. Our coffers grew with grants from The City of San Jose and the Hewlett-Packard Foundation. Our productions increased to an hour and thirty minutes.

For ten years, The Young Blacks of San Jose accomplished a great deal including appearances on a Bay Area black radio station, KBLX, and an audition for San Francisco's public broadcasting television station, KQED. In addition to the support and appreciation of the company's parents, I received an especially poignant thank you note from twelve-year-old Sheri's white mother and her black father:

"Thank you for all that you have done for our daughter. Before The Young Blacks, she was lost between two worlds at a vulnerable time in her life. Her inclusion in the company has resulted in a new found identity. She wears her 'The Young Blacks of San Jose' shirt proudly."

I remembered that "one-drop rule" (one-drop of black blood as social and legal principle of racial classification in U.S.).

Just as our two kids were on the verge of becoming teenagers, Bill examined his air traffic control job namely, the challenging shift changes and emotional strain in relation to the favorable financial rewards. The job lost; he returned to junior college for an AA degree. Upon completion, he transferred to the university's accounting school. I elected to complete my master's degree in theater arts. Our lifestyle changed immediately.

The GI bill, Bill's college tutoring salary, and my part-time therapy paycheck curtailed impromptu expensive dinners and trips. Cheap drive-in movies ($1 a carload) figured prominently in our new program of austerity. However, one movie, *Prime Cut* starring Lee Marvin, forced us to leave the speaker dangling on its post and charge for the exit. Over his shoulders, Bill yelled to the back seat, "Cover your eyes, kids."

We laughed all the way home at Paul's performance of what we had seen.

With careful planning, we avoided a repeat of that fiasco. Friday nights began with a swim at the YMCA, followed by Chinese food in our desolate downtown, and ended in a stroll across the university campus to fifty-cent movies in the Tower, an ivy covered building on San Jose State College's campus. They showed first run features in that old auditorium. Even though the wooden seats were uncomfortable, Suzanne and I would fall asleep after swimming at the "Y."

We weren't the only ones in our family chasing education. Tee was enrolled in a nurse's aide program thanks to the new junior college back home. Her action dissolved an earlier guilt I'd harbored—my existence. It was right up there with Mama's spending her college savings. Upon graduation, she was promptly hired. Bill and I were bragging about her success when she quit. Why? Like a lot of young dreams, her nurse's aide reality wasn't nearly as wonderful as she had imagined. She returned to the junior college, entered the teacher's aide program, and loved it.

As for Bill and me, in two and a half years, our austere living ended with degrees and salary increases. No theater teaching jobs were available in my district so I resumed full-time work in speech therapy. Bill acquired a defense contract auditing position with the government in Palo Alto, just across the bay but a busier commute. We became enthusiastic working members of the local NAACP chapter. Of course, Walter White was long gone from the national picture, but I remembered that long ago Sunday afternoon when he spoke in my hometown.

Bill could not do enough for us it seemed. He replaced the things repossessed before I married him with new ones, and included a visiting organ teacher for Suzanne. Preferring guitar, Paul took lessons three blocks away from home.

Like other families, we followed the children's interests. Paul continued with the Boy Scouts. His first project, the miniature downhill race car, was a father and son project. The two sanded and painted their entry. Once home from racing night, Bill said, "It was unbelievable. Some clever engineering fathers had created fast Indy 500 miniatures."

Paul said, "What do you think about the upcoming cake decorating contest, Dad?"

"We won't lose that one, son. My mother taught me how to make a melt in your mouth white coconut cake."

A month later, the cake night results were in. "One kid showed up with a huge castle including the moat."

Turned out that flag football was their calling. Paul ran the ball; Bill refereed.

Then Paul and Suzanne joined "The Soul Steppers," a precision black drill team. Their purple and pink outfits with plumed hats and banners waving could be seen for miles. Suzanne twirled the baton; Paul beat out the catchy cadence on his drum. From blocks away, The Soul Steppers set hearts beating and my feet stomping. They were the best and had trophies to prove it.

Suzanne's involvement with The Young Blacks and The Soul Steppers honed her sense of self-worth to razor edge sharpness. She tackled all semblances of racism in their high school in the late seventies and early eighties including the time the staff allowed the white kids to play their music over the speaker at lunch time and refused the same rights to the black student union. The affair ended up with no music at all. Suzanne was pleased. We were proud of her.

As San Jose State University alumni, Bill and I supported sports not only because we enjoyed them but also to give the young black players the benefit of our presence and concern. The two sports we followed were football and basketball. Bill played football in high school which led to him being awarded a Grambling State College scholarship. However, he joined the Air Force instead. Basketball was my favorite and rightly so, I had grown up in basketball heaven—North Carolina. I understood it but Bill taught me football. I learned when to cheer. In battles against Stanford, UC Berkeley, Fresno State, I rose to my feet in victory or stayed on the bench in defeat.

Before we realized it, Paul was off to Florida A&M University, a predominantly black college in Tallahassee. Suzanne followed him a year later. For the first time in their lives, they were the majority race. I felt good about that. They would experience that and the South in all its nuances. I wasn't prepared for Suzanne's discovery—she was too black for the sorority I had chosen in my college days. She was surprised but not incapacitated by the revelation.

Neither fraternity nor sorority membership was a sign of an individual's worth in our family. However, I was just disappointed to learn the South still worshipped fair to white skin for its females. Suzanne had another problem; she hailed from California. Her dormitory mistress said, "That explains your attitude."

Her college experience sounded like a rerun of mine.

On a beautiful Mother's Day afternoon in 1983, Bill and I ambled onto the Mercedes Benz car lot to kill time. It was safe, we had our wits about us—our funds went to Florida A&M for Suzanne and Paul.

We wove in and out among the shiny new cars until a hungry car salesman arrived. His appearance changed everything. Bill geared up to dicker with him about the price of one shiny, black car. A few minutes later, it came time for the game to end, "What do you think, Dorothy?"

"Nothing here appeals to me." I began strolling back to our black Oldsmobile at the curb.

The salesman said, "What's your favorite car?"

"The 190 SL."

"That's the way Dorothy is. Can't get her interested in anything else."

"Pardon me, Mrs. Brown. Can I show you something in the small showroom?"

"What?" I yelled over my shoulder.

"A 1960 190 SL."

I froze momentarily. Then close to a whimper, I said, "What color?"

"Red."

My sweetie said, "Honey, do you want to look at it?"

The salesman said, "Won't hurt to look. Doesn't cost a cent." He walked away occasionally glancing back over his shoulder.

Bill said, "Honey bunch . . ."

"No. I'll want it."

"Just take a peek at it, Bunchaboo."

"I'm not following that pied piper of a . . . .." I caught up just as we neared the rear showroom. There it was—a lipstick-red 190 SL coupe. In my youth, my affections strayed from it, embraced the Karman Ghia, flirted with the Triumph, the Citroen, the British Jaguar.

I rushed past the salesman. The hard top was on it. Drool threatened my lower lip. My eyes caressed the soft, curved contours of its rear and ended at its long vamp of a hood. The ecstasy of it all caused me to swoon.

My left hand grasped the door handle. I fell in love all over again. I sat down on the edge of the slick, cold, black, leather seat, turned my legs, and slid under the ivory white steering wheel. More black leather covered the dashboard. The metal was red. Chrome dials, pulls, and levers reminded me of a Tonka toy. My feet reached the pedals and I could see over the steering wheel at the same time.

"Well, what do you think, honey bunch?"

I said, "It costs $20,000."

He said, "It doesn't matter if you want it."

"I'll run and grab the key so we can get this baby off the floor." The salesman bounced from the showroom floor.

Sure enough, he returned quickly, licking his chops, and waving a license plate.

Bill whispered, "Honey, step out. He has to drive it off the showroom floor."

Reluctantly, I obeyed.

As if by magic, the glass wall of the showroom disappeared. The salesman slid under the steering wheel and started up my car.

Bill squeezed me like I'd won a prize for knocking down the most bowling pins. Hand in hand, Sweet William and I followed the 190 SL coupe out of the showroom, onto the black top.

As soon as possible, I was back at the wheel beginning my driver preparation. Darn. I had no kid leather gloves, no racing glasses, no dashing scarf to blow in the wind.

Joining me in the front seat, the salesman said, "Just turn the key and press this button to start her." And he rared back in his seat.

"You look cute, honey."

"Let's take 'er for a spin," the salesman said.

Did he smack his lips? I couldn't tell. No matter. I concentrated on my car; didn't want to stall out. I pressed the shiny starter button. The 190 SL sprang into action.

I shifted into first, gave it some gas. It was ready.

I pulled out onto the boulevard. The 190 SL rushed up to 30 rpms.

I went to second. It was a hungry beast.

I put it in third and settled into fourth. As I cruised the boulevard, I knew I was born to drive the 190 SL Mercedes.

When the kids returned home for summer break, the 190 SL shimmered in the garage. It proved to be a real flirt when I drove it—charming women, luring men, causing little two-year old boys to jabber and point. Famous people succumbed to it. Keena Turner, a San Francisco 49er football player, sat in it while it was being serviced at the dealership.

The coupe became my trademark. Friends saw it in mall parking lots and found me in nearby shops. Once, while backing out at a grocery store, a middle-aged man stuck his head in the passenger window, "I'll go with you anywhere and you don't have to sleep with me."

"Then of what use are you?" The 190 SL made me say it.

Bill and me at a
San Jose State University affair

"The Young Blacks"
A traveling
educational
company
of young
black actors

Me introducing
"The Young Blacks"
before their
performance at the
Montgomery Theater
in San Jose

Sweet William

*Me in my
1960 Mercedes Benz
190 SL coupe*

Me and Tee at my door during Tee's 1980 San Jose visit

Proud day for Tee as she graduates with a nurse's aide degree

Mother's Day Brunch with Tee in 1983

Consequences

The summer of 1983 brought one huge excitement. My play, *Pinch,* a graduate studies project, was selected for the Loraine Hansberry Theater's Play Reading Series in San Francisco. I had to "pinch" myself. My university playwriting professor had suggested I use *Pacific Overtures,* a current production playing in the city, as a model and add music. I followed his suggestion. *Pinch* became a musical documentary. Prior to it I'd only written lyrics for my young theater's productions. A co-worker who was a junior high school music teacher by day and a jazz singer/pianist by night, set those lyrics to music. I approached her with *Pinch.* Her creations were more than I had imagined. I was extremely excited.

Pinch dramatizes the turbulent reconstruction era in New Orleans which resulted in the first black governor of a state in 1868—Pinckney Benton Stuart Pinchback. I'd never heard of him until Bill told me his state's history. My research began in the annuals of the university library. Pinchback was an interesting character for any period.

In the play reading series, Paul had the male lead. Suzanne's summer job interfered with her also being in it. The other readers and the director were from San Francisco. I was nervous but thrilled. The leading lady was a jazz pianist studying in Boston during the school year. The director used her talent to include some of the songs in the production. After two weeks of Sunday rehearsals, Bill, Suzanne, and I sat in a real theater in San Francisco listening to my dialog being read out loud to a live audience. It was at once rewarding and revealing. There were kinks, rewrites, and condensations to be considered. I had no real objections. The director introduced me at the end of the performance. It was a struggle to stop grinning long enough to answer their questions.

```
                *** 1983 PLAYREADING SERIES ***



                              PINCH

                               by

                          Dorothy Brown


         Pinckney B. S. Pinchback.....Lester Jones
         Henry Warmoth......................Len Pera
         Caius Antoine; Reporter........Paul Brown
         C.A. Weed......................Bill Sabados
         Nina Pinchback.................Doris Rowe
         Cora Antoine...................Lynn White
         Frances..........................Kim Euell
         Senator Bovee; Reporter...Kenneth Addison
         Senator Ingraham;Reporter...Stanley B.Roy
         Senator Campbell;Reporter...Stephen Ramos
         Sen. MacMillan;Reporter...Marc McClelland

                   Gordon Pinkney, Director



                             * * *



                        SEW Productions
                   LORRAINE HANSBERRY THEATRE

         1115 Geary Street                     8:00 PM
         San Francisco                    June 15, 1983
```

Originally written as a play, **Pinch** *emerged as a musical documentary*

In the spring of 1986, Paul and Karen, his wife-to-be (Suzanne had introduced them) graduated from college. Their wedding was planned for August in Los Angeles, Karen's hometown. Due to internships, including one with the Bank of Boston, Paul was graduating a year late. Suzanne would finish in August, instead of with them. Her internship with a big accounting firm in New York, required the summer session to graduate. Regardless, Bill and I were delighted; our five-year investment was coming to a close. We didn't even object to the multiple airline tickets that spring and summer for ourselves and our graduates.

During those five years in Florida, Tee, still living in North Carolina, seized any and all opportunities to spend time with her grandchildren. One time, she took the bus down, rented a car, and took them and Suzanne's roommate to Disney World. Unlike us, she was no stranger to the campus when she arrived for graduation. The three of us would make the return trek for Suzanne's August ceremony and fly to Los Angeles the next day for Paul's wedding.

The coming nuptials posed a problem in logistics: Suzanne's graduation was Friday afternoon and the vows were to be said early Saturday afternoon. I had no intention of short-changing my daughter of her celebration rights. If we made it to the wedding, great. A friend of mine said, "Dorothy, if you miss Paul's wedding, you can always make his second one."

She caught me off guard momentarily but when I understood it, I laughed for a long time. Even though the idea of it all bothered me, her remark kept me going.

Then I heard from Karen, my daughter-in-law to be, "I've managed to get the wedding ceremony changed to two hours later."

Oh, how I wanted to tell her what my friend had said but I doubted she'd find the humor in it all. Instead, I said, "Gee, thanks."

I told Bill, "We've been granted a stay of execution. Your brother and his wife are flying in from Texas early. They will host the rehearsal dinner Friday evening."

We watched Suzanne receive her Bachelor's degree in accounting in August. I resented the fact that Paul was not there to witness it. Again, my friend's remark . . . . That evening the four of us went to dinner. Afterwards, Suzanne joined her friends for a final get-together.

The idea of only one Los Angeles flight hung over my head like a cloud. The next day we had a two-hour drive from Tallahassee to the Jacksonville airport.

On departure day, our prospects looked good. Tee and Suzanne were packed and the apartment was clean. Bill and I arrived on time to load

Suzanne's stuff into the car. We were ready to leave when Suzanne discovered her tediously acquired antique toy collection in a most unusual place. "Gram, what is my toy collection doing in the dumpster?"

A deep silence fell upon our small gathering. All eyes were on Tee. Finally, she said, "I took them out of your foot locker to make room for your plastic hangers."

Suzanne looked at me. I hardly knew what to say or do. Just then, Bill said, "Suzanne, honey, time is running out. The plane won't wait for us. I'm so sorry but we have to go."

She and I cried for a few miles, then quiet filled the car. Two hours later, we arrived in Jacksonville with one last quandary—an oversized framed picture.

A kind stewardess stuck it behind the very last row of seats. Once buckled in, Suzanne and I ignored my mother.

We checked into our hotel upon arrival in Los Angeles. As soon as Paul heard we'd arrived, he drove over to pick up Suzanne. Fingers were crossed that her dress would fit as she had mailed her measurements to Karen's seamstress from school.

Two hours later, I held the usher's arm as we walked down the aisle. Tee and Audrey followed me. Audrey had moved to Sacramento two years after we moved to San Jose. By some magic, I contained my tears all the way to my seat. But as soon as the two of them sat down next to me they flowed like a river and throughout the ceremony. Audrey cried with me. Tee, seated between us, supplied Kleenex. Neither of us knew why we were boohooing. Everything was beautiful including the bride and Suzanne's dress, which fit her better than any of the others' dresses fit.

I guess my emotional collapse was due to the stress of getting there. Anyway, I perked up at the reception. The champagne, the dancing, and our hometown friends helped a lot.

The next year the newlyweds completed their MBAs at their alma mater and were hired by Kodak in Rochester, New York. Suzanne returned home and began working for Westinghouse. In January, Duke University's school of business called. Bill took the message. "We'd like Suzanne to enroll in our MBA program."

We could hardly wait for her to get home from work. When she learned of the offer, we still had to convince her of its validity and her own ability. Took all of twenty minutes. The next day she accepted the opportunity to attend Duke in August.

In March, Martin, the chairman of my thirtieth high school reunion committee called. "Dorothy Alston had agreed to be our banquet speaker but she can't return from Germany in time. We wondered if you could step in and save us. We'd love to have you, Dot."

"I'd be delighted. How exciting. I can hardly wait to see everybody. What is the theme? How long should it be?"

With the particulars in hand, I told Bill. "I'll make your reservations, honey," he replied.

I did the same thing with Suzanne. "That's great, Mom. Maybe you can use a few of the 'ice breakers' some of the big executives used when they spoke at FAMU."

"Great." I chose the creative and financial rewards of entrepreneurship for my theme. Once the speech was written, I practiced and refined my work. As the reunion drew closer, I looked forward to going home.

I arrived there in late June, registered in the hotel, and went to the bar for a cocktail. In Rocky Mount? I was shocked. Herman, an old classmate who had moved to Canada, invited me to dance. It was fun. The next afternoon, my seventh grade first date, James, called my room. "Come to the hospitality room; someone wants to see you."

"Who?"

"You'll see."

I knocked. The door opened right away. Walking into the room, I recognized him instantly even with the extra weight. I walked over and embraced the love of my young life—Bunny. Neither James nor I could persuade him to come to the dinner or the alumni dance the next night. But he did consent to a picture. "Dorothy, come sit on my knee."

Bunny held me close. I kissed his cheek before rising.

The next evening at the dinner, I opened with Suzanne's ice breaker. My speech received more than polite applause. It felt good answering questions from the podium.

Later, my bubble burst in the hospitality room as three former girlfriends, Barbara, Helen, and Marsha lounged on the king size bed. Cutting through the merriment of the moment, Barbara seized a split-second gap, "Dot, where were you when we were growing up? We were having so much fun. You missed everything."

Up sprung my super sensitive shield: Beware criticism alert. No way could I interpret her remarks as not a "gee, we missed you." I was thrust into the familiar abyss of my past where I lay bare to ridicule. For a brief moment, I struggled internally to answer her. Should I say I was confined at home because my daddy wouldn't let me hang out? Which was true. Or should I confess that the times I was out, I spent them with Billy?

The moment lay bare awaiting my answer. I was stymied. Helen said, "Dot was busy with the theater but she always attended school functions. Don't you remember?"

Barbara continued to stare accusingly at me.

As soon as I could, I left with Marsha, a friend since first grade, a fellow "Easter Monday falls explorer" and bicycle riding adventurer, and we went to my room. There I burst into those tears of my youth.

I still didn't know how to deal with the southern ethos.

In August, Suzanne and I began our three-thousand-mile drive to Duke in her Toyota Corona. There is nothing like the confines of a small car and a five-day motor crossing of the United States to develop an everlasting bond. The night before, "the all-knowing one" Bill, had said, "You should be able to make it to Utah or at least to the other side of Elko, Nevada on your first day out."

The reality of the trip hit me on day one, shortly after an early afternoon departure; I was at the wheel. Less than an hour into our trip (before Stockton), an overwhelming desire to close my eyelids swept over me. I jerked back. "Suzanne, can you drive? I can barely see the road." She took over and got us to the other side of Reno.

Day two, we left before daybreak. I drove first. Things went smoothly. By afternoon, Suzanne awakened after a long nap. "Where are we?"

"Cheyenne. I just filled up. We're getting back on the freeway."
"I missed it."
"Yep. You can see it two years from now when you return."

"Oh, no, Mom, I want to see it now. Imagine the fantastic garage sales here. Today is Saturday. Pull over. I'll drive."

An hour later, we drove down the ramp to the freeway with our found treasures crammed into her stuffed car. She revved the car up to eighty mph, just enough speed for a flashing red light and a loud siren to flag us over. We followed him back into the city to meet his honor, the judge. In his chambers, Suzanne gave an academy award winning performance but she still had to fork over $75. The irony was Bill's admonishment prior to our trip: "Watch out in Cheyenne; they thrive on out of state arrests."

Another day, I was at the wheel as we descended a wide, steep freeway into Denver. Nearing the bottom, I breathed an audible sigh of relief. "Mom, we have to visit the Molly Brown house. It's right here in our Triptik."

Minutes later we were squeezed into Molly's front parlor waiting for the docent's signal to follow her in single file through the smallest Victorian ever. After the second room, I said to the person behind me, "Excuse me please, I can't take this." Suzanne joined me. There were lots of angry looks but we escaped. At the reception area, she muttered, "This is not the ballroom we saw in the movie."

After more states, including a vicious thunderstorm-filled night in Kansas, a twilight in Kentucky, and a steep climb into the majestic beauty of the mountains in Asheville, North Carolina, we saw the long-awaited sign for Durham. By nightfall, we pulled into the parking area of a resort-looking, apartment complex surrounded by scores of pine trees and mounted the stairs to Suzanne's apartment. Sure enough, the key was under the doormat, as promised. I was reluctant to enter that brand-new apartment in the dark. Suzanne led the way. That night, we slept curled up on the floor. The next day we bought a mattress and other furnishings.

On the second evening, Suzanne's birthday, we ate Japanese. Three days later, I flew home. For the first time in our married life, Bill and I were alone with no children. It was a second honeymoon. Bill began searching for cruises. We were settling into our new life style, when Tee called. "I sold my house and I have a buyer for Mama's house, too. Last weekend was my yard sale. I sold so much it made my head swim. Now I'm packing up the stuff I'm shipping."

"Really? To where?"

"To California. "

"When did you decide all this?"

"Oh, Dot, I don't remember exactly, but I got to work right away. Tomorrow, I'll buy my bus ticket. I'm out of here next Monday. Ain't that something? Shucks, I don't see no reason to hang around here when I can be out there enjoying good weather."

"It took you all these years to make up your mind?"

She laughed, "So many people I know started dying."

"Are you sure this is really what you want to do?"

"Everybody keeps asking me that. Yeah, I'm sure. Now I'll be closer to you and everything."

"I'm really glad you're coming. It's just so unexpected."

"We can go play bingo, run up to Reno, do all those fun things we only got to do in the summer time."

"Tee, as soon as you find out, let me know your arrival date."

"Okay. With the grandkids gone, I'll be the baby now."

What did that mean?

After dinner that evening, I said, "Honey, guess what? My mother's moving to California."

"When? In the next year or so?"

How about next week?"

"You're kidding."

"Nope." I told him what she'd done.

"She'll have to live with us; she can't afford anything out here. Good thing Paul's room is available. She'll be a great help to you."

"That's true. But to be honest, I think she needs her own place. I'll check senior housing. That way she can develop new friends." I made a note to myself to start right away. I could forget about early retirement; I'd have to supplement her income. Even with the sale of two homes down South, San Jose's cost of living was astronomical. Oh, well that's what life was all about—surprises. Actually, I was glad to be able to do anything for Tee.

In two weeks, she was ensconced in our home. Her shipped items were still on their way. While awaiting her arrival, I learned just how scarce senior housing was. I had picked up a bus schedule and the senior center activities. Bill busied himself with important stuff: Spartan football and basketball game tickets for her. He said, "Having Tee participate adds to the athletics department scholarship drive."

The first few weeks we all were very polite and kind to each other. Tee surprised me, appeared to really be into basketball . . . cheering and carrying on but always chattering. After two games, I switched our seats putting her between Bill and me. At that particular game, she began her routine of sharing early; pulled goodies from her purse and said, "Peanuts. Peanuts. Want some peanuts, Bill? Gum?"

He was so into the game; he didn't hear her. Just at that moment, a spectacular play happened on the floor. He jumped up; she nudged him, "Peanuts? Gum?" I wanted to laugh when he realized he'd missed the play.

For Thanksgiving I made a Louisiana gumbo and washed my hands of cooking. Before noon the next day, Tee returned from shopping. "I'm preparing a proper Thanksgiving Day dinner."

Not long after those two incidents, Sweet William and I were alone in the house for a few hours. He said, "Christine might enjoy having friends of her own. Of course, I mean in addition to doing a few activities with us."

I said, "Oh, really?" She and I began our search. Everywhere we went, senior housing was still full; her name hadn't moved up on anybody's list. When we were leaving the last place of the day, I noticed an attractive mobile home park across the road. I drove over and meandered through lanes and drives searching for sale signs. Only two small units appeared.

Later I called the agent. He said, "I have just what you're looking for, a two-bedroom unit with space for gardening and proximity to a major bus route." He quoted the price and I arranged a visit for the next afternoon—fingers crossed. It was only twenty minutes away from me.

Tee loved it. As soon as the ink dried on her purchase papers, she set up housekeeping. Next thing we knew, she was employed, working with toddlers, earning a living. She learned her way around the neighborhoods near her, made new friends, and became the "mother of the church" which she attended but refused to join. That was her line in the sand.

Bill seized our renewed freedom and booked a Scandinavian cruise for the two of us aboard Princess Cruises. We lived big having a cabin with a terrace. One of our earlier stops was Copenhagen, Denmark where we witnessed nude sunbathers in the park from our bus. Back home, streakers were being arrested at ballgames for flashing their bodies. There was a changing of the guard in Stockholm while we were enroute to the amusement park.

On the eve of our Moscow trip, the Russians cancelled our visit. No reason was given. Instead of two cities, we had only St. Petersburg. We lined up to explore the Hermitage, the former winter palace of the tsar now turned museum. When we visited, there were marvelous art collections displayed, much of which were the spoils of war. Aside from the art, our group had the opportunity to climb the wide, golden staircase providing access to the upper floor. This lavish display of bygone days came at the expense of their starving peasants of the time. Later on the bus, we saw the long line of customers at a local bakery. Our guide said, "Often there is no bread left after standing for hours."

As we prepared to board the ship, a young Russian male offered a military uniform for sale. It caused me to doubt the validity of the Cold War being waged against the enemy, the Russians.

As a replacement for the failed Moscow excursion, the ship substituted Gottenberg, Sweden, noted for its jazz. We heard some samplings that day as we cruised the canal in one of its motorized boats. The next stop was Amsterdam. We boarded a small canal boat just in front of the Anne Frank house. Without the sign, I would never have suspected its past. It was a charming abode. Then it was on to Helsinki which reminded me of San Francisco or maybe it was just my longing to return to familiar surroundings. However, it was a pleasant visit with a craftsmen's market at the dock and interesting shops nearby.

At the end of two weeks, we disembarked in London for a five-day visit. By morning I had the flu. It consumed three days of my visit. We did get to see a play and eat in a carvery, a beef carving restaurant. By then, I was anxious to get to Paris, our final city. Tee had more than prepared me for the "city of lights" and she'd never set foot in it. It was divine. We stayed just steps away from the Pompadour Museum, shops of every kind, restaurants that welcomed dogs and their owners, free music at all hours, easy access to the Metro. One evening we walked over to the Latin Quarter to dine in a charming Greek restaurant before the cabaret. No matter where we ate in Paris, the food was exceptional. And we shopped to our heart's content just outside the hotel's side entrance.

The sights of Paris are phenomenal but nothing beats people watching. Tee would have loved every minute.

By now two years had passed. Paul and Karen, still employed at Kodak in Rochester, New York, were the proud parents of our first granddaughter, Amanda. Bill and I met Suzanne there for a family get-together that Thanksgiving,

Although Suzanne spent Christmas at home, her summer was spent in Germany on a Motorola internship. We were impressed with her achievements. At the end of it, she returned home for a short visit before returning to Duke for her final year.

In May of 1989, Bill, Tee, and I headed back to North Carolina. We by plane; Tee by bus. Once there, we marveled at the lavish graduation festivities. There were big and little parties and famous people like Debbie Allen, the movie star from FAME, her sister, Felicia Rashad from *The Cosby Show*, their husbands (both sports figures), and their mother. Their brother was in Suzanne's class. Meeting them was like a family get-together. Another graduate was millionaire Bill Gates' wife-to-be, Melinda. We never shook hands.

After graduation, we flew home; Suzanne and Tee drove back. Upon their arrival, Suzanne called, distraught and tired. "Why doesn't Gram know where she lives?"

"Well, her place is still new to her. Give her a break; she usually gets around town on the city bus."

Rather than look for an apartment, Suzanne moved back into her old room. Bill said, "Good, you can save money that way."

She began her career at Hewlett-Packard. By the end of the year, she purchased a condo in Milpitas and began toying with the idea of buying investment property. She bought a second condo in San Jose and leased it to a bachelor. An opportunity arose for her to work in Emeryville for Sybase which she accepted. I met her for lunch to see her new office high above the bay, though it didn't have a view of it. A half a dozen of my black and white photographs graced her walls. I was struck by the contrast between us: I had only a new wardrobe to show for my first year of work. But then I didn't have an MBA.

Paul and Karen left Kodak for Pizza Hut in Wichita. He was climbing the corporate ladder; she was raising their two children and teaching part-time in the junior college's business department.

Things had improved in the next generation for my people. We had higher-paying and more varied job opportunities.

Bill and me, Suzanne and Tee at Paul's and his bride-to-be Karen's FAMU graduations in Tallahassee, FL, May 1986

Tee at Suzanne's FAMU graduation, August, 1986

Suzanne, Paul and Karen at godmother's birthday party in Washington, D.C.

Checking in at my Booker T. Washington High School 30th reunion banquet

Firming up details before dinner

My topic as banquet speaker was "The Creative and Financial Rewards of Entrepreneurship"

*Me and Suzanne with
Paul and Karen's first child, Amanda*

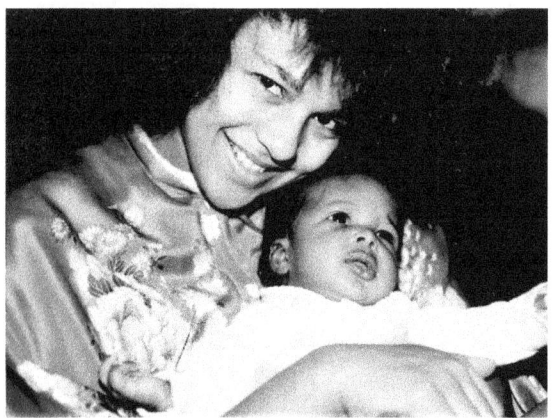

Amanda with her mom, Karen

Bill and me on one of our cruise ship trips

Aboard the Princess

Bill and me in San Diego on a dinner cruise

Adjustments

Bill arrived home one evening in 1994 to find me knee deep in painting our kitchen cabinets white. In no time, he engaged a kitchen planner. Pretty soon, we were visitors in our own home. The contractor and his crew of one had commandeered everything in the lower half of our split-level house. Dust was a half-inch deep and mounting. Meals were prepared on our narrow sun porch in a microwave, an electric fry pan, or a crock pot.

To escape it all, I enrolled in a metal sculpture class after work. I was curious about welding. I wanted to be able to wield that flaming torch even though I was more than respectful of it. I enrolled at Mission College in Santa Clara. When the class was difficult, I cheered myself up with my latest discovery: established artists would employ technicians/assistants to convert their 3D ideas into larger works. I strived for that day.

Meanwhile our redecorating, which had spread from the kitchen to the dining room, into the hallway gallery, and to the front door, was nearing completion. That good news was spoiled by my internal medicine doctor. She was concerned about an ongoing pain in my lower abdominal area. A gynecology appointment was scheduled. Next came ultrasound. I grew anxious. To relieve some of my stress, I focused on the people who would be most affected if I became incapacitated: my husband and my mother. Bill could manage. Tee, however, was having problems: one involved memory, another was with her next-door neighbor. "He's parking his big van in my carport."

Immediately, Bill, her hero, settled that matter.

Another day she said, "The park manager is bothering me."

Prior to this revelation, the two of them were friends. I spoke to him. He said, "Christine's starting to remind me of my grandmother when she developed dementia."

I ignored him; it was just old age. Even when she replaced her new living room furniture with someone's throw away stuff, I just figured she had been duped. She refused to discuss it. Guess it was none of my business. Finally, there was something I could handle: "My mailman messed up my mailbox. Now my key won't work."

I drove to her post office and learned she had verbally assaulted the carrier. Who was this person posing as my mother? I apologized on her behalf and picked up her mail. Glancing at her bank statements revealed bounced checks. I was furious. At the bank, I said, "You guys don't care about your senior customers; you're just enjoying the overdraft fees."

Back in the car, Tee said, "Dot, I'm waiting for my prize from that company. It's due this coming Sunday afternoon. I have to stay at home so I don't miss them."

Absolutely nobody—except Tee—believed that. I needed answers; answers which were probably hidden in her mobile home. While I frantically searched, she said, "Look, Dot, I bought these pretty gold things to help me win a prize."

They were gaudy junk. I was beside myself with anger. But held my tongue and continued my search. I was on to something. A creased, soiled police department receipt turned up. "Why did you call the police?"

"Somebody stole my pretty throw pillows."

Overwhelmed, I postponed dealing with my mother's increasing problems until after my upcoming ultrasound test.

In the imaging lab, my inner workings played on the screen. The technician excused himself but returned quickly with his supervisor in tow. They gestured, stared at the screen, and pointed to a round, orange-sized ball on my lower right side.

I said, "What is it?"

"Your gynecologist will consult with you in a few days."

"Tell me now."

They didn't; I knew it meant another surgery. The last one, twelve years earlier, had been a tubal pregnancy in my second marriage. It necessitated a second tubal ligation. The latest problem was in the same area. I fought to keep my chin up, anticipating the blow from the gynecologist.

A day later, swiftly and brutally, it came. "We have to remove it; it could be cancerous. We'll probably do a complete hysterectomy."

"What?"

"A hysterectomy."

There was no probably in it. Mama always said, "Suspicion is as good as the truth."

"When will you know?"

"In surgery, we'll slice away a piece. Send it to the lab. If the test is positive for cancer, we'll do a hysterectomy while we have you out."

"I don't know you. I just met you last week. I can't trust you to make a decision for me. You'll need to wake me up so we can talk about it."

The gynecologist laughed.

My surgery date, April 24, 1994, was less than three weeks away.

After surgery, my cancer had a name—ovarian. And a degree: Stage 1a. It was frightening. Gilda Radner, the comedienne, had died from it. Ovarian cancer played only one game—hide and seek. When found, it was too late. Stage 1a was promising. How absurd to say promising.

My gynecologist said, "We got it all."

During my hospitalization, Tee's manager and a neighbor brought her to see me. I watched her discomfort, her agitation. I needed to get her examined as soon as I could walk.

Once released, I was in such constant pain, I was incapable of doing anything. Our home was a remodeling wreck; I couldn't recuperate there. Bill had switched from defense contracts to GSA (General Service Administration) and was scheduled for a two-week assignment in southern California. He said, "You'll recuperate in a hotel down there."

Prior to departing, we met with my oncologist. As a Stage 1a, I had status to choose the option "to chemo or not to chemo." It was NOT.

Although the hotel was a good idea, the more I improved, the more confined and isolated I felt. In three days, I took the hotel van to the shopping center. The driver deposited me at the curb. Spying a nearby bench, I crept to it and nested there for at least fifteen minutes before entering the mall. Once inside, the parade of carefree shoppers posed a challenge. Just one bump would do me in. Spying another bench, I crept to it for safety.

From there, I pretended to be a shopper taking a break. My break lasted an hour until the van returned.

After that debacle, I confined myself to the hotel area or gingerly explored the wildlife area across the road with my Canon Eos. The camera, a gift from Bill three years earlier, was a catharsis. When I returned home, I enrolled in a photo journalism class in San Francisco with the intent of documenting the incidences and varieties of cancer cases where I worked. The rest of my summer was spent interviewing proposed subjects. At the conclusion of the project and the private exhibit in my home, some of my subjects expressed appreciation for the chance to speak candidly to me.

As I healed, Tee's condition worsened. Her doctor said, "Mrs. Burston has beginning Alzheimer's, a degenerative disease which attacks the brain." And scheduled a brain scan. Tee said, "Dot, what does all this mean?"

"It means you're losing your memory."

"Lordy, I declare. Ain't that something."

"Don't worry, I'll take care of you."

My brave front hid my fear. I hated my daddy for dying, for leaving me alone to face everything. I regretted being an only child. In the midst of feeling sorry for myself, I checked on things at Tee's mobile home. When I opened the heating unit cabinet, a stack of throw pillows landed on me.

"You found my pillows!" And she clutched them to her breast.

I stared at her—she was wasting away to nothing. Her size 14 shirt swallowed her; she was a size 5 at the most. Pretty soon Alzheimer's would have nothing to attack.

That evening, as I explained everything to Bill, he rolled his eyes. "Christine is just fooling around. She'll get back to her old self. You want to put her away for no reason."

He was not the helpmate I'd been led to believe. I was truly alone. When the phone rang later that evening, Suzanne said, "Mom, tomorrow I'm available to help look for a place for Gram."

The next day we searched within a two-hour radius of my house for adequate, loving care for Tee. My son, Paul, couldn't help, he lived on the East Coast with his family. Suzanne and I put up a strong front before each of us confessed. There was no facility which could serve Tee's needs.

When our fruitless, first day search ended, I was on the phone crying into the ear of an Alzheimer's volunteer.

In two weeks of searching, we witnessed the dreary conditions available to people in Tee's condition. We visited elaborate, costly facilities designed to please the families; the patients were unaware. While we searched, Alzheimer's continued to erode the vibrant, energetic, and happy person we loved and treasured.

One afternoon, after an especially grueling search, I returned home dejected. A message blinked on my answering machine. A facility less than thirty minutes away offered a solution. The next day we investigated the "inn." From the outside, it was attractive, landscaped, and in a nice neighborhood. The interior was pleasant, clean, and charming.

I whispered, "Suzanne, Tee's funds won't allow her access to this."

It was a surprise when the representative said, "It fits her budget."

At that point, we deemed it prudent to minimize Tee's symptoms so she would qualify. A visit was scheduled to include her.

On the next Sunday morning, Bill, though still adamant in his disdain for me, accompanied us. "Come on, Christine. Hold my arm. We're going to visit this place Dorothy wants you to see and then we'll be on our way."

Suzanne and I brought up the rear. We filed into a narrow, floral wall-papered room with a window facing a central, flower garden courtyard. I was last. Seats and sides had been chosen at the large oval table. Tee sat with her back to me at the head of it. I almost burst out laughing at the absurdity of her placement.

Instead, I looked away, to the far end of the table. There sat Bill, separated from Tee, the counselor, and Suzanne, both of whom sat at Tee's left hand side. Under my scrutiny, he raised the opened section of the newspaper blocking his face and upper body. I sat down to Tee's right, opposite the counselor, and crossed my fingers under the table. In my mind, I pleaded: *Please take this charming, engaging southern lady. She used to be my mother.*

Forms were slid across the table to me. I forced my hands to the table top. As I wrote, the counselor engaged my mother in conversation. Tee did well. With forms completed, the counselor said, "Would you like to tour the facility now?"

The two-story building was attractively furnished. All of the rooms were cheerful, sunny. We saw my mother's proposed room which would be shared with another newcomer. Along our tour, we met some of the residents. Suzanne and I exchanged glances—it was the right place.

Tee moved in two days later. My one remaining problem was Tasha, her dog. We couldn't afford to house her there, too. Suzanne's hands were full with a job, a baby girl, and two cats. My pet owning days were over; we traveled too much. Out of habit, I mentioned my dilemma to Tee.

"My friends will take care of Tasha. They love her to death."

I questioned that; her record was not sterling clean. With no other viable alternative, I agreed to meet her friends who lived in the mobile home park, too. Sure enough, they were delighted to become foster parents. On Tee's departure morning, she delivered Tasha before Bill and I arrived. Then we took her, her minimal furnishings, and personal belongings to the retirement inn. I was drained but much remained for me to do.

Her mobile home had to be prepared for the real estate market. A cleaning service and a garage sale were in order. One day as Suzanne and I went through Tee's papers and keepsakes, we came upon her junior college degree and grades, all A's and B's. Beneath it was her high school transcript.

"How dare they? Tee's high school grades were atrocious."

Suzanne took it. "Not exactly. She got A's in French and Latin."

"Those other teachers were biased. They didn't want her to go to college and made sure she wouldn't."

I had an ally in Suzanne; she always championed the underdog. Sure enough, she said, "Gram was probably just fooling around in high school."

I stared at her in disbelief. Then I recalled Tee's former classmate, saying, "Christine, you always made us laugh, almost got me into trouble."

Slowly a burden rose from my shoulders, "When a task is . . ."

My charming, engaging mother, Tee, later in life

Tee and me with my granddaughter, Sierra

Growing up no one ever said, "Stay away from the arts." But I felt a compulsion to not waste their hard-earned money; I chose speech therapy. Twenty years later on the verge of retiring, I boldly enrolled in a sculpture class at the San Jose Museum of Art. After a brief introduction on the first night, a chuck of clay plopped down in front of me. I stared at it, gave it a poke, and pulled off a lump. Some class time passed before a fellow "artist" exclaimed, "Dali!" She was pointing at me.

Filled with aspiration, stone carving, and everything else held my attention. When we got to *lost wax* though, I flourished. A dozen petite creations were ready for conversion to bronze. I turned my sights to welding and enrolled at Mission College in neighboring Santa Clara. My curiosity was rewarded. I explored metal scrap yards in search of material and ideas abounded. I even ventured into acrylic rods and created a quintet of gospel singers. Later, I studied wood carving with Ruth Waters, a noted wood sculptor. She examined my first bronze collection and some larger pieces, then offered me a show at the Peninsula Museum of Art in Burlingame, California. I wondered if I had wasted my early years or just saved the best for last.

Zyt Gallery is offering a voyage of discovery with three accomplished sculptors. Their separate and distinctive works contain themes ranging from humorous, political satire and spiritual enlightenment. Bronzes, metals and woods with interactive textures challenge the viewer and create exciting and in some cases controversial statements.

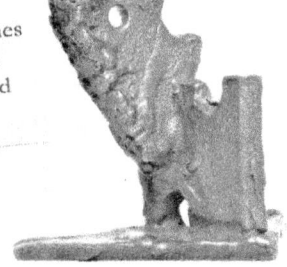

Dorothy Burston Brown "#348"

One of my metal sculture creations
Front   Back

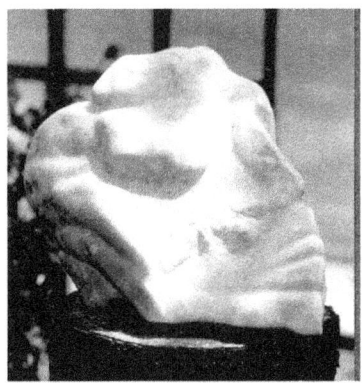

Early stone artwork

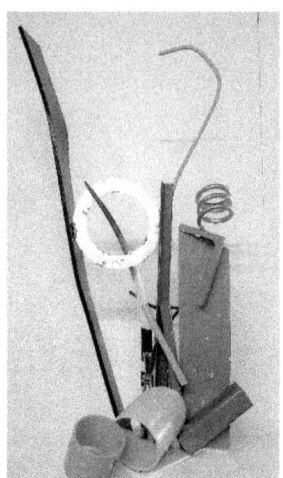

*Early metal
sculpture*

*Advanced metal
sculture class*

A Reckoning

It was 1997. Bill and I visited Mexico, Canada, Central America, and every American town Paul and his family set up housekeeping. Bill still worked but I had retired that June and Africa was calling us. He ignored the summons preferring creature comforts. Nowhere was that truer than on the beach in Oahu. "There's too much sand here," he said.

So, Africa called to only me. My eyes had been opened. African art was far more than child's play made crudely three dimensional. White people were collecting it like crazy; white artists were copying it. Until then, I had believed their words and ignored their actions. Not only was black beautiful, it was brilliant. We began an African art buying rampage in California, Nevada, and Louisiana. Bill studied and could name each tribe whose beautiful creation now graced our home.

My opportunity to see Africa came through Suzanne. She invited me to Central America. I agreed if we could spend the night and a day in New York city, the cruise departure point. "Good idea, Mom, we can rest a while. Be fresh for our trip. We'll take the girls to see The American Girl Store."

"Since we're going that far, why not fly on to Egypt? I really want to see it."

"Okay. Why not visit Petra in Jordan, too."

With no naysayers in the group, we made arrangements for this magnificent side trip prior to cruising to Central America.

In Cairo, Egypt, we were met by Hassan, our guide, and Ali, our driver who were pleased with Suzanne's attempts to speak their language. Our adventure began that night with an unusual point of interest. From our van, our guide said, "See the blue lights coming from the cemetery?"

We nodded.

"That's from televisions in vacated crypts which families no longer maintain, so homeless people have moved into them."

I said, "How clever."

Suzanne stared at me in disbelief.

Our hotel lay across the Nile River which thrilled me to no end; I was living in my grade school textbook. At the hotel, we fell asleep easily but were startled by the ringing of bells. Suzanne murmured, "It's the call to worship."

Early the next morning, while she dressed the children, I went to exchange money. The bank was next door but when I stepped outside, I could see the Nile at the end of the street which ran perpendicular to the hotel. I walked to its banks. Langston Hughes had spoken of it in his poem, "I've Known Rivers." Entranced, I stood there, marveling at how far I'd come until I felt the money in my pocket. Turning away, I resumed my mission, even skipped a bit.

After breakfast, an Egyptian specialist had been added to our tour. The seven of us crossed the Nile again. The tip of a pyramid appeared in the distance. Savannah, our four-year-old, pointed and said, "Triangle."

Soon the fertile gardens of the river gave way to the clamor of trucks, carts, camels, bicycles, and cars on the streets of Cairo. Our first stop was the great pyramid whose magnificence and the phenomenon of the stones transported to the site was a feat in itself. The specialist said, "Would you like to go into the great pyramid?"

"I'd love it."

Suzanne agreed, too. So, we followed him down the narrow passage once used to transport dead pharaohs. She turned back after only a few steps; I continued. Along the way, we met returning visitors which necessitated pressing against the stone walls to allow space to pass. Not too long afterwards, we arrived at the bottom of the passage and began our ascent. My specialist's upper body disappeared in no time. I followed his legs until they, too, vanished. Then I found myself in a large, quiet, spacious, high-ceilinged chamber. He beckoned me to the far end on my right where a large, rectangular, concrete container which once held a mummified body stood empty. In a few minutes, we went back outside.

Our next stop was the sphinx. The missing chunk of its nose was explained; French soldiers had shot it off. Some teenaged Egyptian girls joined us. "Why do you travel alone without men?"

"They had to work," I said. They nodded in understanding.

Among them were a few Nubians with dark brown skin and rounded faces. Their ancestors are often depicted battling Pharaoh's armies. Now their lands had been flooded by the construction of the Aswan Dam and a new town, New Nubia, was erected.

After a delicious lunch of fish, rice, and vegetables at a nearby restaurant, we explored the museum, a fantastic experience. From there we shopped in the medina where only weeks before it had been the scene of carnage. Tossing caution to the wind, I purchased some of the lovely wares. Later that night we boarded a train to make connections for our four-day river cruise. Unfortunately, we obtained no sleep in the upright seats and the constant ringing of telephones.

We were pleased to meet our new guide, Ali #2, and board the riverboat which was comfortable and spacious. Daily and once before sunrise, we visited different points of interest. Savannah was the darling of our guide not only due to her youth but because she looked Egyptian.

Once we were docked in Luxor, we walked among the enormous statues just steps from the river with chariots going past them all the time. Close at hand and to our delight was a two-story MacDonald's; we were more than ready for junk food. At one point, a group of Turkish tourists surrounded us and pointed to their cameras. After posing for pictures with them, we were paid in candy. My favorite bird, the ibis nestled in the trees along our docking spot.

On our last day aboard, one of the officers mentioned, "We call you Nefertiti."

Could it be—I was finally home?

When we arrived back in Cairo after a pleasant night in separate train cabins, Hassan and Ali grinned broadly and whisked us away to a lovely desert resort on the Red Sea. Our next adventure was Jordan. Suzanne guarded her children, Sierra and Savannah, and me all night from ferocious mosquitoes. In the morning, Hassan and Ali delivered us to the ferry. They unloaded our belongings and deposited them and us outside a chain link fence. Pointing to a non-descript building in the distance, Hassan said, "That is the ferry terminal. We aren't allowed to take you in there."

We walked through the gate alone surveying our new route which went through broken concrete pieces and sand. It did not bode well for the children, our rolling luggage or the Egyptian cloth bag containing my tall brass, long-spouted vessel for pouring tea. The absence of shade was blatant. With no alternative, we struck out for the terminal. Occasionally, we glanced back, Hassan urged us forward. I wondered if his fingers, like mine, were crossed.

We arrived safely and walked past "a seen better days, rusting, dusty bus" near the entrance. Inside, we cleared customs and were told to return outside. There a man waved us over to the "bus" where we relinquished all our luggage to him and boarded it. We had our pick of the empty seats; the girls chose the front row. We sat a few rows back in the stifling heat, carefully sipping from our precious water. Suzanne said, "Look. I think I see the ferry way over there."

Just then, Sierra yelled "Mom, Savannah asked me 'Don't you wish we had a bright, shiny, new bus?'"

Too soon, people stuffed the seats and the aisles. A thick haze of cigarette smoke engulfed us but we didn't complain. Soon our driver started up the bus. Although, it didn't purr, we crept in the direction of the ferry. In about 15 minutes, those passengers standing at the front bounded off the bus. To our surprise, the ones around us, permitted us to rise and move forward. We picked up the girls, our stuff from below, and followed the others to a low, open entrance in the side of the ferry. Up close we waited while Suzanne checked out our next step. She returned, "Mom, our luggage and everything is next to a car's tires parked on the ferry."

I was at a loss for words. She gathered up the remaining things. "We can kiss all this goodbye. No way will it be there when we reach Jordan."

Then we climbed the staircase to the passenger level whose few seats were already taken. We found a small clearing and stood with the girls. The ferry got under way. About 20 minutes passed and a kind soul gave us a table and three chairs. We thanked him, sat down, and munched sparingly on the meager food stuffs we'd brought on board. The call to prayer came; people assembled on the floor nearby.

Just before docking in Jordan, an employee came to our area and shouted, "United States of America, United States of America come." Embarrassed, we followed him downstairs to where the cars were parked. Suzanne guided us towards our stuff. It was all exactly as she had left it. We were ready to disembark.

Inside the terminal at customs, Suzanne and my granddaughters passed through after a cursory glance at their passports. I stepped up and was told to take a seat; they needed to examine mine. After a thirty-minute wait, they called me back to the counter, asked more questions, compared my picture to me, and allowed us to enter Jordan.

Unfortunately, the night was just beginning. On shore, we argued with our prearranged driver against his proposal: "Leave your luggage and take only what you need for one day. We'll leave the rest at a local hotel. When you return, you can pick it up."

Suzanne said, "It is not our fault you have a tiny car. You knew there would be four passengers."

I said, "Whenever you're picking up Americans, bring a big truck. We always have a lot of stuff."

"Call your company," Suzanne said, "I want to speak to your manager. We need a van now." She talked to his office. Soon a van arrived with an older driver who took us to a MacDonald's first. Not only was there food, there were toilets. Afterwards we made the two-hour drive to our hotel.

Our spacious bedroom held 3 queen sized beds and a marble bathroom. In the morning after a huge breakfast, our new driver for the desert crossing to Petra arrived. Along the way, we stopped for tea in a huge black tent and to climb the sand dunes of Jordan.

Upon our arrival in Petra, we were divided into horseback riders, Suzanne and Sierra, and chariot riders, Savannah and me. The mode of travel didn't much matter. Everybody had to wind through a rugged, narrow, loose-rock strewn, enclosed stone-walled path to arrive in Petra. The ride was truly rough but the wonderful library at the end was spectacular.

All facets of our detour vacation were memorable. Neither Suzanne nor I regretted our decision. As the finale, the ferry ride back was luxurious: plush seats, carpeted aisles, and more Turkish people paying in candy to pose with us.

Back in Egypt, Hassan and Ali waited outside the chain linked fence to whisk us back to Cairo. It was a relaxing drive back as we awaited the sunset over the desert. Suddenly, Ali pulled to the side of the road. Hassan hopped out and went to the rear of our van; so did my eyes.

There in full regalia on a pickup truck were police officers armed with weapons aimed in our direction. I almost regretted shopping in the medina days earlier and enjoying it. Things were settled shortly after. It was decided that the plain clothes officer from the trailing Turkish bus would join us in the van. The mounted, armed truck would follow for our protection. That's when we learned we should not have crossed the desert without an escort. They took us to a roadside house where we sat on the front porch devouring delicious fried chicken and fresh vegetables.

Once we flew back to New York, we checked into a hotel across the street from the United Nations and slept like logs. The next morning, we did laundry and prepared for our Central America cruise the following day.

One of Bill's final audits was in New Jersey. He invited me along; I was delighted. I still had a love affair with New York, a stone's throw away. It would be my second visit since leaving it back in 1962 as a bride. My first trip back in 1985 was a gift from Suzanne when she was interning at Arthur Anderson, an accounting firm. It had been a romp. We crammed everything possible into it—two Broadway shows: *A Chorus Line* and *The Tap Dance Kid,* shopping, a movie, and lunch in the World Trade Center. Even then I marveled at the city's continued ability to charm me, to render me young, stimulated, alive, ambitious.

This audit trip, Bill and I were staying in East Orange. Our fourth day had plans for dinner with his ex-roommate, Mike and his wife, Betty. Although I looked forward to the evening, I dreaded traveling to their Manhattan apartment on my own. Bill would join us after work. At my predetermined departure time, I bundled up in what passed for winter wear in California (an imitation fur coat with no substantial lining) and lumbered to the main road to catch the bus into the city. By car the day before, it appeared to be a short walk. However, sloshing through melted snow worn down by cars, made it tedious and long. I finally reached the "exposed to the elements" bus stop, a bus sign at the side of the road. By then, my feet were chilled in my unlined California boots. In an effort to ignore their growing numbness, I pulled out my subway directions and focused on memorizing them. A lost visitor was instant prey in the city.

When the bus arrived, I boarded it, moving like a mummy. As I rode, I fretted about my upcoming subway ride. I had never been gifted in getting around alone in the city. Would I get on the right train? Would I get off at the right stop? What would happen when I exited and climbed to the street level? My concern was not unwarranted; I traveled on the right train but in the wrong direction. With my usual aplomb, I relied on the kindness of others to guide me to my destination.

When Bill arrived at Mike and Betty's apartment, he found a relaxed me, cocktail in hand. Shortly, the four of us headed to a restaurant in Little Italy which came highly recommended by Bill's office mate back in San Francisco. A festive atmosphere greeted us upon entry into the storefronted café. Infected by it, we smiled and squeezed around and between crowded diners, skimmed the outer edge of the hectic galley kitchen, and ended up in a dead end, windowless, small, rear dining room. The scenario was so preposterous, I laughed all the way to our table.

When we dug into the robust Italian dinner, all the hassle had been worth it. About midway through the meal, a loud, roaring and banging of cymbals erupted. No visual warning alerted us. Magically, an obese drum blocked our only escape route. Shiny brass instruments cascaded from the top of it. Together they consumed the room. What passed for music bounced off the cinder block walls, hard ceilings, and concrete floors. I prayed no fire broke out in the kitchen because we would have been lost.

After more than enough music and food, we exited into a surprisingly warm night. I began dancing in the street. New York's magic made me do it. Nobody cared or stopped to stare. The city still touched me in ways California never could, but I'd lost that insatiable need to live here. In my years of maturation, life had taught me—people committed the prejudices, the atrocities. Often, it was more a matter of degree.

In early 2005, Bill retired. To celebrate, we flew to Buenos Aires, Argentina for a week. It was a lovely trip. When we returned, my sweet William turned into a lump on a log. Too much fun or movement upset him. Dancing, the way we had met, was out. Our brand-new bikes became spider magnets. His infrequent rounds of golf with friends ceased. Our house shriveled. To escape his sullen demeanor, I enrolled in more classes. I rose early, at the gym before 6 a.m. I explored jewelry making and painting classes, also hounded scrap metal places for pieces to create sculptures. I accompanied Suzanne on a study/travel tour of Costa Rica.

Later she divorced, then quit the corporate world to become a real estate broker. Her decision led to a new business for me—interior design and staging. I sparkled in my new profession and fizzled in my marriage.

Figures and Fragments is my second photography exhibit

Perceptive Decor

With a discerning eye, Dorothy deftly furnishes and accessorizes empty spaces, organizes and accents currently occupied homes for best showings, and handles all jobs large or small, tactfully and stylishly. Operating from a theatrical background and an active involvement in the visual arts, Dorothy molds staid environments into wonderful possibilities--the starting points for prospective buyers.

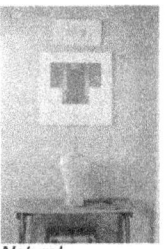

Natural

Classical

Serenity

Perceptive Decor provides such enhancement for your home that the prospective buyer feels "the search is over". Your home will be ready for showing and selling in a timely, attractive, and stress-free manner.

No More Discussion

On the last day of April 2007, Bill and I photographed my gorgeous, pink amaryllis, a surprise gift from him six years earlier. After the shooting session, he returned to his office/hideout to download the pictures. With such a warm and enjoyable experience for a change, I resolved to get to the root of his usual doom and gloom. His follow-up doctor's appointment for a case of shingles on the left side of his face was the next afternoon. We'd been there the Thursday before. On Tuesday, I'd go in with him. I had to; my upbeat, perky attitude was on its last leg. I even suspected my smile triggered his mood changes.

Tuesday morning, I dropped off my latest sculpture for a professional powder coating. I returned home to find Bill still in bed—at two in the afternoon. We snuggled for a few minutes. He said, "I feel tired."

I avoided comment for fear of riling him and made a mental note to tell his doctor later. I almost offered to make scrambled eggs for him but remained quiet. He made his own, showered, and dressed. We got in his car. Backing out, he said, "I've never been this exhausted in my life."

At the bottom of our hill, he said, "I'm almost on empty."

He referred to the car which he never kept gassed up.

"Make a U-turn. Go back home. I'll drive my Mercedes."

I waited two beats for his argument against that idea. Out it rumbled, "Dorothy, we don't have time to go back home to change cars. I have an appointment. I have to be on time."

I almost said better late registering than stuck on the freeway out of gas. But I didn't, trying to ensure a decent blood pressure reading for him. As his disgust built, I focused on my little red sports car which would have been beautiful on the road.

A few blocks from home, I whispered, "It has a full tank."

His beady eyes bored into my brain. "There will be no more discussion about gas."

I buried my head in my latest design magazine and awaited the last gulp of gas. At that moment, our thirty-six years of marriage seemed like a life sentence. He probably felt the same way. Sometimes to get us back on track, he surprised me with jewelry or flowers. The day before yesterday, he surprised me with, "I love you so much, it scares me."

I always said something sweet in return. At the moment, I truly meant it. Hell, I always meant it. I sneaked a peek at him. He was still handsome—especially in that blue-violet shirt. When we were dating, he resembled Muhammad Ali, without the poetics, but with the same fierce black pride.

Now in his early sixties, Bill, a handsome man, whom some thought resembled General Colin Powell, slowed our black 300M Chrysler into the entryway of the new hospital. It was approximately thirty minutes since we had left home. I closed my magazine, stuck it in the molded pocket of my door. Lately, being with him reminded me of living with my grandmother in the old Victorian house back when. His ups and downs often caught me off guard. I gazed at the new medical facility. Sprung from an old apricot orchard—an experiment gone awry, it resembled an artistic wonder. As a modern edifice of glass and concrete, it possessed no color and projected barren, cold, unyielding sharp angles. Its beauty lay in its minimalism.

Bill veered towards the parking garage as I hurried to put on my sandals. I skated my bare feet over the car's carpet in search of them. I had to dash from the car the minute he turned off the ignition. When I was slow, it annoyed him. Good. I found my popsicle-orange sandals. I slid my feet into them. I was ready.

Bill swung "black beauty" into the first space just inside the garage, a clear shot to the entry. My designer sandals weren't made for sprinting. He was out of the car fast which I found odd for an exhausted man but I kept my lips sealed and grabbed my purse.

"I'm not waiting for you," he said,

Before I reached the rear of the car, any connection between the two of us had dissolved. I wanted to scream, "We're early!" I didn't. Instead, I yelled, "Which floor?"

"The second," he shouted with neither a backwards glance nor a break in his stride.

He was in his punctuality mode. My good spirits wilted. I was there out of concern for him. Where was the lightness of yesterday? Only twenty-four hours earlier, he had said, "Take a picture of the amaryllis. It will never be more beautiful than it is today."

Regardless, I tried to catch him in my ridiculous sandals. Bill entered the hospital, way ahead of me. It was pleasant outside; a late afternoon breeze blew. It swayed me to a nearby bench to await his return; I resisted. Suddenly, it dawned on me—he had said he was tired, exhausted.

I told myself, "Hurry. Catch him. The stairs—"

Bill prided himself on climbing long flights of stairs. Rarely, if ever, did he take the elevator.

That afternoon, I covered the distance from the curb to the entry in no time. Inside, the modern, open space was empty. I asked myself where everybody was. Where were the usual long lines of people? Where was the congestion? I wanted all those things for Bill to slow down his trajectory. I said, "Calm down, Dorothy, take a deep breath. Relax, relax. He took the elevator. He was exhausted."

Yeah, he took it. How foolish of me to think otherwise.

I turned left to the elevator, just beyond the stairs and around the corner. I refused to check the stairs; he was probably on the second floor.

Still, my eyes gobbled up the first empty flight. No Bill.

To be sure, I drew closer, checked where the landing bent for the second flight.

I smiled.

As I turned away, I caught sight of a sleeve—a blue-violet sleeve—just above the half walled-in banister.

Spellbound. I watched Bill's right hand grip the banister.

It was too late to yell, "Take the elevator!"

He was in no man's land.

"Come back down, please. No. Stay where you are." There was nothing I could say. No argument made any sense. Exertion consumed us both.

I pushed my sandals towards the elevator. I wanted to beat him to the second level, greet him when he arrived, ignore his panting.

I arrived on the second floor in time. I squeezed through the first sliver of an opening and bounded for the atrium, medical two.

It was quiet, empty, save for an elderly couple seated on my right. At the staircase, I peeked down. Completely bare. He had to be registering.

I slowed down; didn't want to appear overly anxious. Just beyond the atrium was the registration counter. A lone registrar sat there. Odd. There was no line. I knew it; I told him we had plenty of time. That's when I saw him; the back of his blue-violet shirt. He stood at the atrium opening to the upper and lower floors. He leaned against the railing.

I breathed a sigh of relief. It was greater than the joy I derived from turning our street corner, climbing our hill, and finding his car in the driveway. He hadn't registered. Probably had to catch his breath.

Giving him a moment, I glanced to my right through a large expanse of glass which captured the southernmost vista of the valley. It glowed golden in the late afternoon sun. As an interior designer, I would have turned the seating to face the . . .

Bam!!!

One solid loud, smashing noise filled the space. It was as big as the dropping of some heavy object onto a solid surface.

No. Maybe it was the sound of a gun. Some fireworks sounded like that on the Fourth of July when I heard them from inside my house. No, it resembled a gun.

Stupidly, I remained erect, a target. Why weren't there screams? Where was the shooter?

The elderly couple remained seated, motionless. Were they hit? Was I in a nightmare?

I moved, shakily at first. I checked for Bill. His blue-violet shirt was gone. I lurched into action, charged for the point where he last stood. Fear gripped me.

Please don't let Bill be the victim. Don't let him be the innocent bystander. He'd escaped a mad man once before, years earlier in his 5th and Market Street high rise office in San Francisco.

I turned left just beyond a huge, square concrete post which bordered the atrium. There he was—lying on the floor.

I went to him. A few feet away, I dropped to my knees and crawled on all fours. I arrived at his feet, at his white sneakers. His hands were on either side of him. His long arms almost reached his knees.

I moved up his body, grasped his left hand in mine. My right hand gently touched his face. I called out his name.

No response.

I spewed forth each and all endearments, honeyed words, words of thirty-six years of togetherness. "Sweetie pie, Sweet William, Bill."

It was a clean hit. No blood. No evidence of body penetration on his blue-violet shirt. From somewhere outside me, I heard my own voice calling desperately, "Come! Please come and help my husband! Somebody. Somebody, please come."

I saw his face then. His eyes pointed up and back.

"Bill, honey. Bill, sweetheart. Please. Please wake up."

Muffled footsteps came close. Still, I stared at him, at his curled-up tongue. I studied his body. He never tried to protect himself. He never knew.

Gentle arms helped me rise; I couldn't get erect. I bent over. Soft voices questioned me. I answered. Medical personnel and equipment formed a curtain around Bill. Gentle hands drew me down to the drawn up padded bench which earlier had stood against the wall. The lady from the elderly couple came up, spoke to me. I smiled up at her.

I was upbeat, positive, without words. I was concentrating. I could make it happen. It only took hope. If Bill concentrated, too, he would hear me. He would look at me. Not focused at first, but he would hear me. Then focus on my voice, my face.

He'd have to stay in the hospital for a short while, to run tests. Then we'd get back in our shiny, black car. This time, I'd drive. But first, we'd stop for gas.

Medical personnel spoke, "Do you wish us to continue?"

Bill's doctor stood next to me. She said, "Why was he on this floor?"

"He said his appointment was here."

"This is the triage department." In a quiet manner, she enumerated his diseases: high blood pressure, sickle cell anemia, diabetes. Mr. Brown could have dropped dead any time."

The doctor's politeness saying "Mr. Brown" reminded me of another time in my life more than three decades earlier at Duke. That doctor had been polite, too, with my daddy, "Mr. Burston."

I traveled back even further in my memory, to the time when I was almost four years old. Papa, my grandfather, was sitting in one of the black rockers on our Victorian porch. No matter how hard I begged, he wouldn't move. No kisses made him smile. He just stared straight ahead. Never said a word . . ..

So, with Bill, I knew it wasn't a dream. It wasn't even a nightmare. There was no gunshot.

There was only the sound of him hitting concrete.

"There would be no more discussion."

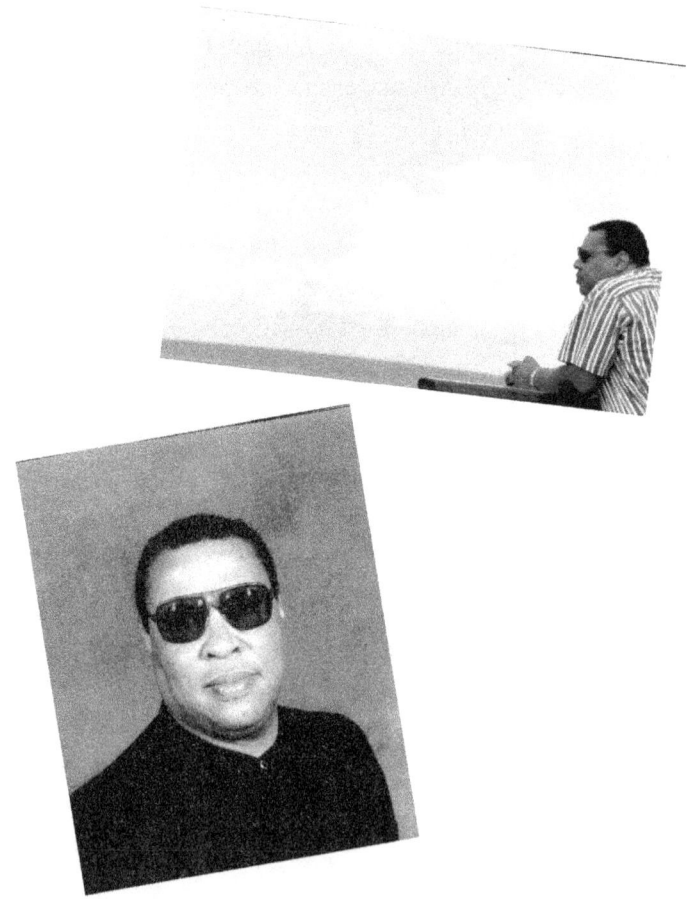

Me in front of cruise ship in Bahamas

Suzanne on a cruise in the late eighties

Paul and Bill after a cruise golf expedition

*Trying to find
a new balance
after Bill—
out with Suzanne
at a dance in
Oakland, CA*

Art in Oakland | An Evening to Celebrate with Don Cheadle

Marcel Diallo and Don Cheadle

Dorothy Brown and Adimu Madyun

*I wanted to meet Don Cheadle, the movie star —
attended this Oakland, CA affair alone*

The Denouement

The last Sunday afternoon in June 2007 was a hot one here in my North Carolina home town. Back for my fiftieth high school reunion just as Bill had planned it six months ago. I never expected this to be his last gift for me.

I drove around aimlessly with nothing to do. The Happy Hill picnic didn't start for another hour. Even then black people wouldn't arrive on time; that was our habit. Hunger gnawed at me. I should have grabbed some fast food near the freeway. I started to but the words of my high school sweetheart, Billy, echoed in my head, "Dorothy, there'll be more food at the picnic than you can shake a stick at."

I headed for the picnic. In no time, I was across the street from the park, rolled down my window and parked the car close to the curb. No barbeque scents wafted in. In fact, the would-be chefs and their entourages were missing. Although it was my first time, the turnout looked small. If things didn't pick up in a hurry, I'd have to find something to nibble on. Maybe the picnic goers were waiting for the temperature to cool down. I opened my door and climbed out. The humidity draped me like a cape. How long could I endure the stickiness?

Locking the car, I sauntered onto the impoverished grounds. Here and there a struggling shoot of grass fought to survive. No pine trees but a few unknown saplings strained to remain upright. The park, a tribute to a late black kindergarten teacher, was shabby compared to what I'd seen of Dr. King's Park across town. There, attractive pavilions and rolling grassy plains were enviable by comparison. Maybe only national movement leaders warranted stately parks. In a way, she, Miss Bea, was lucky to have a park at all. Not that there's anything wrong with being a kindergarten teacher. Her park was more of a neighborhood affair sponsored by the city.

Small old houses and duplexes bordered it on three sides. On the fourth stood a large, outsized metal warehouse of a sort.

Its juxtaposition made me feel right at home. They always gave black people the worst things even when pretending to honor them. Any better location would have been pretentious. If I recalled correctly, she had lived nearby. Actually, my opinion didn't matter; any tribute was better than nothing. I never recalled a tribute to a kindergarten teacher before in my whole life. There. My home town distinguished itself by honoring an often forgotten individual. With that conclusion, I examined my surroundings.

In my musing, I had ambled into the middle of the grounds. From that perspective, I pivoted to get a panoramic view. Everything around me was blatant, blunt. There was no softness. I craved beauty even though my southern history had enured me to not expect it. To keep up my spirit, I plastered a broad smile across my face. One that could withstand anything my hometown delivered. I was ready. I reconsidered the smile; it might turn people off.

Wearing a weakened version, I began strolling the inner perimeter of the park, tried to assume a more carefree guise. Still, I crossed my fingers in hopes of seeing a familiar face or of being recognized. A third of the way from my starting point, I sensed the presence of another body in rhythm with me. It paused when I paused and moved forward as I advanced. It couldn't have been tailing me for long; I'd only just begun my venture. I continued to stroll, even pretended to search for my group, my family.

Sure enough, my shadow copied me. Preparing myself, I whirled around like a high fashion model on the runway. My shadow almost tripped but recovered and jerked her head to the side away from me. She appeared to be my mother's age or slightly younger, in a simple print dress. I stared, willed her to turn back to me. When she did, I grinned like a Cheshire cat.

She dismissed all pretenses and headed straight for me. I didn't meet her halfway. She started it; let her close the gap. When she was within arm's reach, she said, "Ain't you Dorothy Burston?"

"Yes."

"Lord, honey." And she sighed. "Girl, there was somebody dying to see you. She was a very, very, very good friend—of your father's. Talked about you a lot. How is your mother doing?"

"She's fine. In excellent health." *If you don't count Alzheimer's.* "Thank you," I said.

"I'm so glad to hear that. Well, this friend of mine who knew your father so well, really wanted to see you before she died. Yes, she did."

I turned and walked away. Then I caught myself. Wasn't this the type of thing I came back for? Didn't I crave that callousness? Wasn't I seeking that intent to hurt? I turned back.

She was gone. In her stead, three beautiful dark horses ridden by three black people appeared at the large building across the street. I was so surprised, my mouth hung open. Growing up, I never saw black people on horseback. Oh, we may have steered a mule or two but ride a horse? For fun?

Gaping made me thirsty. I remembered an unfinished bottle of water in my car and went to get it. As I gulped the tepid water, a familiar face on a porch across the street caught my attention. Although quite aged, it was him—Bunny's half-brother. I screwed the cap on the bottle and ambled over to talk to him.

After an awkward greeting, I asked, "How's Bunny?"

"He's dead."

How dare he be so curt. I wanted to slap his face. I couldn't; he looked down at me from the porch. From somewhere, words flew from my mouth. "How did he die? How long was he ill?"

"Our daddy shot him."

His lack of tact was shocking. In a stupor, I mumbled my regrets, stumbled back across the street to the picnic. Still slightly dazed, I heard "testing, testing, 1, 2, 3 . . . testing."

Considering it a personal invitation, I hurried to the sound's direction. An elderly lady in a soft, pale-blue summer dress waylaid me. "Pardon me, but aren't you Sam and Christine Burston's daughter?"

Not missing a beat, I was nine years old again, "Yes, ma'am."

Her friend, slightly behind her said, "How is your mother?"

"In excellent health. Thank you." Lie number two.

The first lady said, "I'm relieved to hear that. We tried to dissuade Christine from going so far away. Leaving her family, friends, surroundings. Selling all her property, everything like that."

I guessed daughters didn't count.

Her friend took over. "You couldn't tell Christine Burston a thing. She was bound and determined to get out there to California."

"Yes, I recall you cautioning her, 'Bad things can happen when you take chances like that. Move all that way.'" She turned to me. "Baby Whitfield, she and her husband used to own the café, picked up and moved out there to California. Couldn't stand it. Moved back here to a nursing home. When will Christine be coming back?"

"I doubt she'll ever return. She's real happy. Just moved into a new place. Doesn't have to lift her finger to do a thing."

I left them before they could say more. A few months before Bill's death, I moved Tee to a gated facility to prevent her from wandering away. The sheriff had returned her three times to the old place.

I resumed my search for the mic testing area. A female voice filled the air, "Welcome to our annual picnic. I'd like you to welcome Reverend Burston who will deliver the prayer for the occasion."

I barely made it to the area when my cousin Warren took the mic. I couldn't stop grinning. I was so happy to see him. I wanted to hug him but he must have prayed for at least eight minutes, I bet. As soon as he said, "Amen," I was on him, hugging and clinging like I'd been rescued from drowning. After a while, Warren held me away, "Let me look at you... always was the prettiest little thing. You're still your grandpapa's grand baby."

"What do you know about my father's father, Willie Burston?"

"I know he always made us kids keep quiet on his corner. Told us, 'My baby's taking her nap.'"

We laughed.

"Baby, I got to run off and leave you. Another affair in less than an hour. How long you gonna be in town?"

"Four more days. Go on 'bout your business. Before I leave, we'll get together."

Alone again, my eyes surveyed the area for some less obvious place to view the activities. I spied what appeared to be a food concession of a sort and headed for it. Seeing Warren had not erased my hunger pangs. Sure enough, there it was—tons of prepared foil and saran wrapped food on a table. Nearby, Tupperware and large commercial cooking vessels waited.

I also noticed an elderly couple manning the tent. Relieved, I entered. "Good afternoon, I'm Dorothy Burston."

"How do you do."

Cordial—not a good sign. Close up I saw the food was not for sale. But I didn't know how to extricate myself gracefully.

The man said, "So you kin to the good reverend, I reckon."

"Yes, sir." I stood awkwardly counting the number of beats before I could escape my faux pas.

The lady left her table and drew nearer to me. "We wondered who you were, hanging all over him like that. Knowed you weren't the wife; she bright skinned."

"My grandfather on my daddy's side and Warren's father were brothers."

Fussing with the lid on a casserole, she said, "I see." She looked pointedly at me. "Y'all kissing cousins."

I didn't respond. My count was up; I started to leave.

The old man stopped me, "What cha daddy's name?"

"Sam. Sam Burston."

"I 'member him. Old devil cancer got him back in '72."

I resumed my leaving.

He interrupted me. "Your mother, Christine, was that Best girl."

Looking over my shoulder, I smiled.

He laughed. "Alva Best's daughter. 'Member my folks talking 'bout Mr. Alva, the man of integrity. Deacon in the church. Took advantage of his wife's pretty young sister who came to live with them. Yeah. Christine Best—their love child."

I couldn't move. Alva Best was Papa, my adopted grandfather, my great uncle.

"Alva's wife, Miss Smithie, raised that child, like she was her own."

I thought to myself, now that's where he's wrong. To outsiders, Mama may have painted that picture. But I knew who she loved—Rhone, their son. And if this old buzzard was wrong about that; he was wrong about everything.

His mockery grew stronger. "None of it changed who your grandfather was. Sad part was his wife. Helpless. Caught in the middle between her husband and her sister."

I floundered. Such a vile tale he wove. Who were these evil people? I opened my mouth to protest but words wouldn't come. Instead, I heard Aunt Burrell's voice in my head, "Where there's smoke, there's fire."

"Yeah, old Alva, upstanding."

His laughter chased me to my car. I called Olivia, my cousin, up in Baltimore. Interrupted her hello with, "Who was my real grandfather?"

"Why, Uncle Alva, your Papa."

"No, Olivia. I mean who was Tee's real father? My real grandfather?"

"Are you listening to me, Dot? Uncle Alva, your Papa, was Tee's real father."

"No. He just treated her like that. He loved her so much. Besides, Laney, Mama's younger sister . . ."

"Uncle Alva, your Papa, loved you to death. And we were all crazy about him."

"How come you never said anything about him and Laney?"

"I thought you knew. The way I heard it, Laney was something else. Your mother, Tee, was not her first baby either. That baby died before she was three years old."

"How could Papa do something like that? How could Mama stand for it?"

"She had no choice, Dot. Women were powerless. Look at her sister, my grandmother."

"Mama wasn't like her; Aunt Sister Hattie always acted so old, so religious. Not Mama, she spoke her mind."

"Remember the arguments they used to have?"

"Mama just got sick of her always bragging about being the mother of her church."

"Wrong. Aunt Smithie teased my grandmother about marrying their stepfather when their mother died. She tried to make light of both of their situations. My grandmother had no choice, if their younger sisters and brothers were to survive."

"I gotta go."

"No. You listen. It's time you knew the truth. Marrying their stepfather kept the family together. Then she had my daddy, Marie, and Aunt Willie Mae. As for your grandmother, Aunt Smithie, she tried to help raise their teenager siblings. Took in two others before Laney. It was the sisterly thing to do back then. But Laney was something else. Except for having Tee."

I ended the call without saying goodbye. From somewhere I heard a voice, my voice cry, "Oh, Mama . . .."

> Succinctly, the South had triumphed,
> had deluged me with tacit implications,
> had cut me to the quick with facts, and
> had forced me to live again.

Dancing with
Maasai tribe members in Kenya

Acknowledgements

I wish to thank my parents, Sam and Christine "Tee" Burston, for their enduring love, caring, and dedication to providing the best education possible for me within their means.

My thanks to my two children, Paul and Suzanne who trusted in me to guide them to adulthood. I knew they believed the day they proudly brought their playmates in to see my mural on our dining room wall.

Although my grandmother has been long gone, I fondly recall her great humor, her spirit, her playfulness, her floral skills, and her pride in our family. Beside her stood my grandfather, Papa, who loved us all fervently.

Later in life, my children and I had the everlasting love of Bill Brown, my second husband. He was the dearest man and father in the whole world. The universe smiled on us when he entered our lives.

My sincere appreciation goes to two teachers who greatly influenced the person I became: Mrs. Juanita Exum Burnett, my seventh-grade teacher, and Mrs. Marguerite Carson Armstrong, my high school theater arts teacher. Each in her own way not only educated me but provided life models for me to emulate.

One of the great pleasures in my life was the opportunity to create, direct and manage the company of players known as The Young Blacks of San Jose. The original actors were Lisa Brown (no relation), Delores Sample, Andrea Batiste, Larry Washington, and my own two children, Paul and Suzanne Brown. They stimulated my creativity and inspired me to be the best that I could be.

I am eternally grateful to both Jaap Bongers, past instructor at the San Jose Museum of Art, and David W. Ogle, past sculpture and ceramics instructor at West Valley College in Saratoga, California, for introducing me to the visual arts and encouraging me to explore the medium.

In all that we do as individuals, if we are extremely lucky, we add more friends who inspire us, who lend a helping hand. I was fortunate to have Audrey Walton Thompson, my first year college roommate (from New York) who was with me for all the monumental moments in my life until she passed; Lynn Rogers, creative writing instructor with Metropolitan Adult Education through San Jose Unified School District and her writing class students who listened to my stories and provided invaluable feedback; Kimberlie Ingalls, my editor; Felece Wilson, my proof editor; and most of all to Paula Hoelker-williams, my dear friend and technical editor. To each of them, I am eternally grateful.

Lastly, my loving thank you to Bill for his final gift to me: travel arrangements for my 45th Booker T. Washington High School reunion. It served me well to surround myself with longtime friends during those early transitioning days without my sweet William.

From left to right:
1–me,
2–my graduation night revealer,
3–she and I were going to work together in Washington, D.C., live with her sister, &
4–my fellow baritone horn player from band

Left most: my fellow baritone band member

Right most: my graduation night revealer

www.ingramcontent.com/pod-product-compliance
Lightning Source LLC
Chambersburg PA
CBHW031132160426
43193CB00008B/119